The Workplace before the Factory

The Workplace
before the Factory

ARTISANS AND PROLETARIANS, 1500–1800

EDITED BY

Thomas Max Safley *and*
Leonard N. Rosenband

Cornell University Press

ITHACA AND LONDON

To Amy, Michael, and Rebecca

CONTENTS

PREFACE

Over the past several decades, the study of work processes has become one of the most dynamic fields of historical research. Seen as economic behavior, work organizes human relations and material resources for the purposes of production and profit. Yet the interest in work exceeds the simple creation of goods and services. Scholars have long recognized work as one of the most important contact points between social groups, and specifically between elites and commoners, merchants and artisans, and manufacturers and laborers. Work was a context for the exercise of power within any community. As such, it constituted an economic relationship with social, political, and cultural ramifications.

The period roughly from 1500 to 1800 was a time of economic transition; entrepreneurs pursued markets, gathered or fashioned products, accumulated capital, and invested it in new production processes. Because technological progress was limited until the end of this period, however, work organization is the key to any understanding of the economic and social changes in work itself and in the lives of working men and women.

Though dynamic, the history of work is also a dispersed field. Few publications or associations dedicate themselves to the dissemination of new information and ideas on the topic. This collection grew from the recognition of that fact and the desire to bring together a number of younger scholars, some of whom are less well known in North America than they should be, to examine work processes and their social and economic consequences in various contexts over time.

What follows are the proceedings of a colloquium held at the University of Pennyslvania on October 11 and 12, 1990. Its success depended to a large extent on the assistance and cooperation of numerous colleagues and friends.

Many experts offered recommendations for possible contributors, a choice made more difficult by the editors' express intention to span time and geography as well as work processes. Those deserving particular thanks are Domenico Sella of the University of Wisconsin–Madison, Merry Wiesner-Hanks of the University of Wisconsin–Milwaukee, Hermann van der Wee of the Catholic University of Leuven, Gwynne Lewis of the University of Warwick, Joan Thirsk of Oxford University, and James Amelang of the University of Florida. The essayists represent new directions in the study of work; some of their scholarship appears here in English for the first time.

Providing a forum for discourse requires more than willing participants; financial resources are necessary as well. The heads of several institutions were more than generous in their support of this project. Special acknowledgment must go to Stephen Nichols, former Associate Dean for the Humanities of the University of Pennsylvania; Richard Beeman and James Davis, Chair and Acting Chair of the Department of History of the University of Pennsylvania; Thomas Childers, Director of the Center for European Studies of the University of Pennsylvania; Lynn Hollen Lees, Director of the Seminar on Work and Population of the University of Pennsylvania; Robert Hoover, former Dean of the College of Humanities and Social Sciences of Utah State University; and R. Edward Glatfelter, Head of the Department of History of Utah State University. These colleagues provided more than essential funds; they provided equally necessary and much-appreciated counsel and encouragement.

Shaping conference papers into essays can be a frustrating exercise for editor and author alike. The contributors to this volume responded to the various rigors of publication in a gratifyingly professional manner. Though it may seem gratuitous to acknowledge those who profit from an endeavor of this sort, their efforts are undeniably the key to success.

Rosalind J. Beiler collated, typed, and retyped many versions of each essay. Moreover, she was a shrewd reader and astute critic, whose comments surely improved the entire volume.

Finally, Reva Rosenband and Michele Rothenberg supported the entire project from beginning to end, advising in all matters of organization, reading drafts of many of the essays, and listening critically to even more of the ideas. They were partners in the enterprise.

THOMAS MAX SAFLEY and LEONARD N. ROSENBAND

Philadelphia, Pennsylvania, and Logan, Utah

The Workplace before the Factory

INTRODUCTION

In 1582 a merchant named Jacob Seyfrid approached the linen weavers of the German city of Memmingen with the request to produce a large consignment of *Golsch*, a blended linen cloth. To overcome any distrust, he offered to advance the weavers the credit necessary to alter their production processes. The weavers refused, providing their own assessment of the market for Golsch: no demand existed for such cloth; thus, they rarely wove it. Seyfrid took his proposal to the neighboring city of Mindelheim, where local producers annually delivered eight thousand pieces of the specified cloth.[1]

Illustrating the self-defeating conservatism of urban, artisanal corporations, this merchant's tale teaches us even more about early

---

1. Stadtarchiv (hereafter StA) Memmingen 476/5. *Aus dem Verhör der Kaufleute am 27. August 1584.* "Er hett gern mehr golschen gehabtt auch die zunfftige darumb zugesprochen welt gern daruff gelihen haben und hett ain grosse suma khaufft aber nit bekhomen khoenden, hab khain anlehen uff golschen abgeschlagen, wie sy im dann noch schuldigt, so hab er jn khain neher zallen, denn sy an der schaw gangen. Item er muest zu Mindelhaim khauffen wiewol jm dieselben nitt gefallen und jn geduenckh die selbig schaw fallen werd, derhalb wer es jetzt die recht zeyt dar man golschen alhie wuerckhte und er jn boesserung wider trete wurden die hiegigen golschen wider zu verschleyss khomen wa alhie die wolle zubekhomen were, den sy heur zu Mindelheim bis jn 8000 Golschen einblaycht dess jne ain toschult gegen hieiger statt sey."

1

modern capitalism. Above all, it testifies to the web of transactions that bound capital and labor. Despite their control of supplies and their access to markets, capitalists were not always able to dictate terms to the men and women who labored with their hands. Rather, they engaged in delicate negotiation, balancing the opportunities provided by capital against the mastery of artisans. At the heart of these negotiations was work in a bewildering array of settings: individual shops, integrated networks, and concentrated mills. Each system of production consisted of a daunting variety of economic and noneconomic considerations and entitlements.[2]

The interplay of workers, materials, skill, scale, and technique created new possibilities for control and dependency. Some of these opportunities forged capitalism; some emerged from it; some hindered it.

Capitalism is usually understood as a system in which those who control capital determine the allocation of resources and the production of goods by workers who must sell their skill and energy.[3] The emphasis rests on concentrated capital and wage labor and, therefore, distorts the reality of manufacture in the Old Regime. Accordingly, we must first explore the nature of capital itself, which is simply money or value invested in a productive process. In the hands of the Memmingen entrepreneur, it was probably fluid and tangible. But it took other forms in early modern industry. Capital might be fixed in complex facilities such as large-scale workshops, the proto-factories of a Plantin or a Montgolfier, or even larger enterprises, such as mines, shipyards, or bleaching fields. More often it took the form of circulating capital, that is, raw materials waiting to be worked. But it might as easily be intangible in an age that placed particular emphasis on status and estate. Nothing else so clearly ex-

2. Richard Price, *Labour in British Society: An Interpretative History* (London, 1986); Sidney Pollard, *The Genesis of Modern Management: A Study of the Industrial Revolution in Great Britain* (Cambridge, Mass., 1965); John Rule, *The Experience of Labour in Eighteenth-Century English Industry* (New York, 1981); E. P. Thompson, *The Making of the English Working Class* (New York, 1963); W. H. Sewell, Jr., *Work and Revolution in France: The Language of Labor from the Old Regime to 1848* (Cambridge, Eng., 1980); William Reddy, *The Rise of Market Culture: The Textile Trade and French Society, 1750–1900* (Cambridge, Eng., 1984); Michael Sonenscher, *Work and Wages: Natural Law, Politics, and the Eighteenth-Century French Trades* (Cambridge, Eng., 1989); Keith Thomas, "Work and Leisure in Pre-Industrial Societies," *Past and Present* 29 (1964), 50–66; E. P. Thompson, "Time, Work-Discipline, and Industrial Capitalism," *Past and Present* 38 (1967), 58–97; and idem, "The Moral Economy of the English Crowd in the Eighteenth Century," *Past and Present* 50 (1971), 76–136.

3. See Charles Tilly, *The Contentious French* (Cambridge, Mass., 1986), p. 5.

plains the value added by patronage in ambitious enterprises or by skill in modest ones.

Capital assumed many guises in early modern production; so did the capitalist. Most definitions imply that he was a single person, an individual in untrammeled pursuit of opportunity. The lone entrepreneur, however, shared pride of place with an array of persons and groups. Any improving master, who owned his tools and materials and employed several journeymen to create goods for sale in local or regional markets, may be considered a petty capitalist. (Ironically, if he turned his hand to the task, he remained an artisan, too.) Groups also used capital to control resources and production. Well known are family consortia and early common-stock enterprises. In the same category are an array of associations, from guild masters to government functionaries, who used their collective powers to develop certain forms of enterprise. The state itself frequently invested in strategic production, providing capital-intensive facilities and dictating the organization of work within them.[4]

The early modern capitalist functioned within a system characterized by extraordinary complexity and diversity. Fragmented markets for goods and services forced entrepreneurs to confront a dizzying range of local regulations and customs. These might pose barriers to otherwise simple transactions or, as the Memmingen entrepreneur discovered, create alternative opportunities for profit. In either case, the negotiations involved in the organization of production were seldom straightforward. Quite apart from structural or regulatory barriers to production, the synchronization of skill in trades little-touched by the rhythms of mechanization or the expec-

4. On the role and identity of people and states in the organization and management of production, see Clive Behagg, *Politics and Production in the Early Nineteenth Century* (London, 1990); Carlo Cipolla, *Before the Industrial Revolution, European Society and Economy, 1000–1700*, 2d ed. (New York, 1980); Richard Goldthwaite, *The Building of Renaissance Florence: An Economic and Social History* (Baltimore, 1980); David Landes, *The Unbound Prometheus: Technological Change and Industrial Development in Western Europe from 1750 to the Present* (London, 1969); idem, *Revolution in Time: Clocks and the Making of the Modern World* (Cambridge, Mass., 1983); Jan De Vries, *The Economy of Europe in an Age of Crisis, 1600–1750* (Cambridge, Eng., 1976); Domenico Sella, "European Industries, 1500–1700," in *The Fontana Economic History of Europe*, vol. 2, ed. Carlo Cipolla (New York, 1977), pp. 354–426; Peter Payne, "Industrial Entrepreneurship and Management in Great Britain," in *The Cambridge Economic History of Europe*, vol. 7, part I, ed. Peter Mathias and M. M. Postan (Cambridge, Eng., 1978), pp. 180–230; F. F. Mendels, "Proto-Industrialization: The First Phase of the Industrialization Process," *Journal of Economic History* 32 (1972), 241–61; and Neil McKendrick, "Josiah Wedgwood and Factory Discipline," in *The Rise of Capitalism*, ed. David Landes (New York, 1969), pp. 65–81.

tation of uniformity challenged the managerial skills of most early capitalists.[5]

Central to these concerns were the producers themselves. These artisans retained mastery over their own skills, their own tools, their own products, and their own sense of the craft. On the local level, corporations of craftsmen often minutely regulated the work process. By monopolizing admission to a craft and entrance to the market, they legitimized skill as a social and economic boundary; by setting wage, quality, and price standards, they defined the essential dimensions of production. The artisans' power existed in the mysteries of skill, their control over technique and technology, as well as participation in a culture and community defined by work. Power in the workshop resided in the application of this skill, the practice of which could not be separated from the organization of work. Yet skill was much more than technology and technique in the age of manufacturing. It exceeded the strategies by which a given technology was employed. Artisans acquired a craft-consciousness from the manipulations intrinsic to their work and from the power to organize their skills.[6] Hence, in the early modern period they enjoyed not only a degree of collective economic self-determination, but also a unique culture based on the techniques of work. This was a circumstance with which entrepreneurs, sensitive to market demand, had to contend.[7]

Putting capital to work frequently meant challenging the preten-

5. T. S. Ashton, *An Eighteenth-Century Industrialist: Peter Stubs of Warrington, 1756–1806* (Manchester, Eng., 1939); Robert Darnton, *The Business of Enlightenment: A Publishing History of the "Encyclopédie," 1775–1800* (Cambridge, Mass., 1979); E. J. Hobsbawm, "Custom, Wages and Work-Load in Nineteenth-Century Industry," in *Essays in Labour History*, ed. Asa Briggs and John Saville (New York, 1967), pp. 113–39; D. F. McKenzie, "Printers of the Mind: Some Notes on Bibliographical Theories and Printing-House Practices," in *Studies in Bibliography*, vol. 22 (Charlottesville, Va., 1969), pp. 1–75; Leonard N. Rosenband, "Productivity and Labor Discipline in the Montgolfier Paper Mill, 1780–1805," *Journal of Economic History* 45 (1985), 435–43; Eric Hopkins, "Working Hours and Conditions during the Industrial Revolution: A Re-Appraisal," *Economic History Review* 2d ser., 35 (1982), 52–66.

6. Rule, *The Experience of Labour*, passim.

7. Steven Epstein, *Wage Labor and Guilds in Medieval Europe* (Chapel Hill, N.C., 1991); Sean Wilentz, *Chants Democratic: New York City and the Rise of the American Working Class* (New York, 1984); James F. Farr, *Hands of Honor: Artisans and Their Work in Dijon, 1550–1650* (Ithaca, N.Y., 1988); J.-L. Ménétra, *Journal of My Life*, with an introduction and commentary by Daniel Roche, trans. Arthur Goldhammer (New York, 1986); Natalie Z. Davis, "A Trade-Union in Sixteenth Century France," *Economic History Review* 2d ser., 19 (1966), 48–69; Cynthia M. Truant, "Solidarity and Symbolism among Journeymen Artisans: The Case of Compagnonnage," *Comparative Studies in Society and History* 21 (1979), 214–26; Douglas A. Reid, "The Decline of St. Monday, 1776–1876," *Past and Present* 71 (1976), 76–101.

sions and powers of those who toiled with their hands. Individual workshops experienced a degree of autonomy determined by the existence and accessibility of markets for supplies and products. Artisans could not easily abandon their work; so those who turned to the market depended on merchants or middlemen when local supply and demand were inadequate. The merchant's power was embedded in the knowledge and control of markets.

Of course, workers had their own powers and their own means of expressing them. The sheer variety of work stoppages—from riots and demonstrations to strikes and rebellions—has long fascinated historians. Though tactics varied over time and place, workers have always struggled to retain control of their labor. Unwilling to submit to the vagaries of artisanal production and artisanal entitlements, entrepreneurs resorted to a range of expedients to deprive skilled hands of this control. They used debt peonage and wage dependency to subjugate workers. Moreover, they exploited their own better access to materials and markets and their presence in local politics to create conditions that lessened opportunities for artisanal independence. Far more commonly, however, capitalists and workers determined production by voluntary, or at least nonviolent, agreements and contracts. When Seyfrid found no artisans willing to produce his cloth in Memmingen, he sought other labor markets. Markets function necessarily on the basis of such unspectacular accords.

Workers and capitalists bargained and battled over the cost and quality of raw materials, the organization and pace of work, and the accessibility of local and foreign markets. Linking these issues was the work culture of the artisans, their unique right and ability to employ traditional materials and methods and enjoy monopoly access to markets. This culture formed the principal bulwark against accelerated production, innovative techniques, and new goods. It was a barricade against capitalism.

The storming of the barricade and the consequences for workers is the theme of this book. Though workers lost historically, they often mounted effective rearguard actions. The outcome was by no means predestined. The process is no less complex than the burgeoning system from which it arose; it can neither be envisioned solely in terms of innovation and resistance nor be reduced to a simple conflict between modern and traditional.[8] The interplay between

8. Landes, *The Unbound Prometheus*, passim.

master and worker must be understood as an extended negotiation, shaped by the peculiar circumstances of specific industries and markets, in which every attempt at control and every change in conditions elicited a response from below. The shops of the early modern world give evidence of an ongoing exchange between the ambitions of the masters and the traditions of their subordinates. Transformations in work process and organization wrought clear changes in the culture of miners, the politics of artisans, and the consciousness of shophands. And these changes below simultaneously shaped the direction of industrial development, transforming the transition.

By definition, the proletariat neither owns the machines with which it produces goods for market nor participates in the whole production process nor sells the goods that it fashions. Yet, mechanization alone did not create mobile, wage-dependent workers. Convincing arguments for the consequences of work organization have been made for urban and rural, preindustrial, textile producers, working on contract for merchant entrepreneurs. In these studies the relationship of worker to capital defined the proletariat. Freed of its connection to modern industry, the proletariat emerged wherever artisans depended upon external sources of capital to provide access to supplies of raw materials and markets for finished goods. Proletarianization, then, is the process that moves workers from a position of control over the organization of their work to one in which that organization is imposed from the outside. At its most fundamental, the rise of a modern working class is the saga of power in the workshops, and proletarianization is the process that deprives workers of their power.[9]

What emerges from the essays in this book is a vision of proletarianization as the manifold ways in which external control and command of skill influenced the vulnerability or dependence of workers. It weakened the intimate connection between the worker, the process, and the product, gradually stripping artisans of their tradi-

---

9. Karl Marx, *Capital: A Critique of Political Economy*, trans. B. Fowkes (New York, 1976); Rule, *Experience of Labour*; Price, *Labour in British Society*; Thompson, *Making of the English Working Class*; Raphael Samuel, "The Workshop of the World: Steam Power and Hand Technology in Mid-Victorian Britain," *History Workshop Journal* 3 (1977), 6–72; Christopher H. Johnson, "Patterns of Proletarianization: Parisian Tailors and Lodève Woolens Workers," in *Consciousness and Class Experience in Nineteenth-Century Europe*, ed. John Merriman (New York, 1979), pp. 65–84.

tional power. Briefly put, process and product began to pass out of the workers' control and slowly became the property of agents outside the workshop. This often occurred with the support of the state or in the name of the state. Structural or circumstantial factors might render workers vulnerable to external control, but these factors alone could not make workers dependent. The external control itself placed the worker in a set of new and complex relationships to superiors, peers, and subordinates.

These essays examine the relations of power in the shops from a variety of perspectives and yield an array of suggestions regarding opportunities or means for shaping workers and their work. The ways in which capitalists exercised power influenced the culture of workers and determined their vulnerability and dependence. What ultimately emerges is the end of a monolithic vision of proletarianization and capitalism.

External circumstances and their regulation affected the course of proletarianization. Christopher Clark, Haim Burstin, and Thomas Safley examine the organization of work among the artisanal craftsmen of rural New England in the eighteenth century, the unskilled laborers of the Faubourg Saint-Marcel in eighteenth-century Paris, and the linen producers of the imperial cities of Upper Swabia in the sixteenth and seventeenth centuries, respectively. In each instance, matters not directly related to the organization of work played a key role in determining the dependence or vulnerability of workers. Clark demonstrates that diffused, rural manufacturing, which was both labor- and capital-poor, adopted structures that assured its independence. Domestic production, following the seasonality of rural life and using the labor of family members, was ubiquitous in New England and resistant to external domination. By the same token, unskilled Parisian laborers, active in an unregulated market, adapted personal and familial connections to assure regular work opportunities and to prevent outside competition. As Burstin suggests, these informal networks assumed almost guildlike proportions, assuring the workers near-monopoly control over certain sectors of the market for unskilled labor, especially transport. Failure rather than success characterized the experience of linen producers in urban Swabia. Controlled access to raw materials and finishing processes, especially bleaching, were a source of constant concern to early modern textile workers. Through accounts of a series of weaver rebellions, Safley offers evidence that the long-term failure to regulate critical transaction costs left linen weavers vulnerable to domination by individual entrepreneurs or groups of merchants in the guise of city councils. The relations of power within the shops cannot be separated from conditions outside.

Yet power was exercised at the point of production. Accordingly, other essays enter the workplace. The results reveal varied visions of private and state capitalism.

Susan Karant-Nunn, Roberta Morelli, and Christina Vanja assess proletarianization in early modern European mining, an industry that evolved from private ownership to state sponsorship in each case with fateful consequences for the miners. Using evidence from Saxon silver mines in the fifteenth and sixteenth centuries, Karant-Nunn follows the evolution of mining enterprise from its small-scale entrepreneurial base to the development of concentrated production under the aegis of the Saxon ruling house. As a result of changing organization and control, the miners gradually lost their status as skilled artisans and became wage laborers, tied to the mines by regulation and obligation. Morelli finds much the same development in Tuscan iron mining during the sixteenth century. Investment in new technology forced a shift from diffused to concentrated production, and regulation of materials and trade by the Medici dukes created a situation of simultaneous monopsony and monopoly. The outcome was a stratified labor force, reflected in extreme wage variations. Masters became petty merchants; skilled laborers enjoyed artisanal status; unskilled workers degenerated into a protoproletariat. On the basis of visual sources, especially the illustrations from Agricola's *De Re Metallica,* Vanja concentrates on women miners and finds that their fate paralleled that of their unskilled male comrades. Long relegated to peripheral occupations outside the pits, such as breaking, sorting, firing, and rinsing the ore-bearing rock, women were excluded from mining altogether as a result of industrial development. Thereafter they found work only as colporteurs or as housekeepers in the communities of miners. In the mines of early modern Europe, state capitalism caused the miners to lose control of the work process, which passed into the hands of the representatives of external investors.

Christopher Johnson and Robert Davis discover similar shifts in the relations of power in other state enterprises. In the woolen industry of Lodève, which produced cloth for the uniforms of eighteenth-century French armies, Johnson shows how merchants and the state made common cause to suppress the independence of weavers. State regulation made illegal all weavers' associations; merchant innovation moved the industry toward concentrated, capital-intensive production. Workers found some compensation for their new dependence in regular employment. Davis's study of the Arsenal of the Republic of Venice, which supplied the navies of that great maritime power, exposes it as a protofactory. Work was subcontracted and organized in line production; the *arsenalotti* lived in the vicinity of the compound in conditions resembling a mill town. The *Patroni* restricted the movements of workers through and within the walls of the Arsenal in such a way that the artisans' traditional access to tools and materials—a form of control over the application of their skills—was disrupted. Resistance to these innovations proved futile, with the result that the workers lost a degree of self-sufficiency in the workplace. Yet attempts at control likewise failed to coalesce completely, and a forced consensus emerged in the guise of patrimony.

The authority of the state was not a prerequisite for the sort of managerial innovation that changed the relations of power and the organization of work. Jaume Torras, Leonard Rosenband, and Jan Materné explore the means available to merchants and managers to shape and control their workers. As Torras demonstrates, the clothiers of Igualada, a town in Catalonia, favored selective employment tactics. They avoided giving work to the master weavers, whose control of production was fortified by their guild. Instead, the entrepreneurs sought contracts with journeymen, whose exclusion from the guild left them vulnerable to external domination. Rosenband examines the Enlightened management techniques of one of Old Regime France's foremost families of papermakers, the Montgolfiers. By using incentives and penalties to shape workers' behavior and by replacing experienced, tradition-bound hands with carefully selected, relatively pliant ones, the Montgolfiers liberated themselves from many of the constraints faced by their *confrères* and shifted the balance of labor relations in their own favor. Materné tracks attempts by printing masters at the Plantin printing house in Antwerp to introduce a new method of production: the concurrent, asynchronous printing of books. By dividing a book into segments to be printed simultaneously, masters increased the speed with which books were produced and reduced periods of idleness among journeymen. They also forced pressmen to coordinate their activity. As a result, pressmen lost a degree of independence acquired through individual production schedules. In all cases, managerial techniques aimed at a reorganization of production deprived individual craftsmen of their traditional control over the application of their skills.

As a collection, these essays reveal the extraordinary variety of means by which power in the shops might be taken out of the hands of the workers. Masters and managers altered the application of skills in the workshops in many ways: through the new production patterns of the Plantin press, the selective employment of workers in Igualada, the advanced management techniques of the Montgolfiers, the new patterns of capital investment and work organization in the mines of central and southern Europe, and the space restrictions in the Venetian arsenal. But less direct methods were also available. Competition for or regulation of access to raw materials in the Swabian textile industry reduced the viability of independent artisanal production. The suppression of workers' associations in Lodève weakened the collective sensibility and power of weavers. In sum the possible ways of proletarianization were many.

There was no single route to advanced capitalist production. Its maturation followed highways and byways; it had neither a fixed locus nor a fixed chronology; it required no necessary connection to certain technologies or preconditions. Rather, the one unifying characteristic of capitalism was that the capitalists, those who made capital available, assumed increasing control of the application of skill for the purpose of private gain.

Capitalism and proletarianization are two perspectives on the same historical phenomenon. Viewed from above, capitalism is the disposition of capital in the economy; viewed from below, it turns on the assumption of power in the workshop. Whereas practitioners and historians of business understand capitalism as an economic system with noneconomic ramifications, laborers and labor historians also recognize it as a change in the politics of production.

Christopher Clark

1 Social Structure and Manufacturing before the Factory: Rural New England, 1750–1830

The most striking thing about North America in the eighteenth and nineteenth centuries was that its role in the Atlantic economy changed radically within the space of three generations.[1] In 1760 the white settler societies of the eastern seaboard were colonial dependencies of Britain, theoretically subject to mercantilist economic regulation and to metropolitan demands for staple commodities. By 1850 the northeastern United States was becoming a metropolitan region in its own right, the locus of a rapidly expanding commercial and industrial capitalism whose influence was starting to reach across a continent and around the world. In the "world-system" terms developed by Immanuel Wallerstein and others, the American Northeast was part of the "periphery" or "semi-periphery" in the mid-eighteenth century, but a "core region" a century later.[2] Historians are increasingly taking up the challenge of explaining how this change occurred.

1. Research for this essay was supported in part by a Kate I. and Hall B. Peterson Visiting Fellowship of the American Antiquarian Society.
2. Immanuel Wallerstein, *The Modern World-System III: The Second Era of Great Expansion of the Capitalist World Economy, 1730–1840s* (San Diego, 1988); for an example of the application of the world-system model to New England, see Robert Paynter, *Models of Spatial Inequality: Settlement Patterns in the Historical Connecticut River Valley* (New York, 1982).

Central to the change was the emergence of patterns of capital investment and technological application in manufacturing sufficiently advanced to rival those of the leading western European industrial powers. Most American scholars of this Industrial Revolution, just like many of their European counterparts, once focused on the dramatic outcomes of this transformation: the factory system, machine technology, and the origins of mass production.[3] Historians widely assumed that these powerful forces of industrial capitalism imposed themselves on a comparatively backward economy, sweeping small-scale industries, including craft and household-based manufactures, into oblivion. Whether from a "world-system" perspective or not, rural regions in particular seemed largely to be victims of outside forces beyond their control.

Recent work in several fields and disciplines has suggested the need for a new approach to studying the process of economic change and the role of small-scale manufactures in it. For instance, just as Europeanists no longer equate industry with the factory system, stressing instead the long-term origins of industrialization—rural manufactures, cottage industry, hand technology, the variety of forms of manufacturing activities, and the persistence of these characteristics well into the machine age—Americanists are gaining a new appreciation of the complex and varied sources and locations of early American manufacturing growth. First, we can now recognize a distinct nonfactory, precapitalist manufacturing economy that began in the American Northeast during the eighteenth century and reached its peak in the first quarter of the nineteenth century. These early manufactures had similarities, but also striking contrasts, with prefactory industries in Europe; the American case throws valuable light on the broader relationships between early industry and the emergence of industrial capitalism, factory production, and a working class.[4] Second, the work of Robert Brenner and his critics on early modern Europe has not only stressed the influence of class

3. For a critique of this emphasis see Philip Scranton, "The Workplace, Technology and Theory in American Labor History," *International Labor and Working-Class History* (hereafter *ILWCH*) 35 (1989), 3–22.

4. James A. Henretta, "The War for Independence and American Economic Development," in *The Economy of Early America: The Revolutionary Period, 1763–1790*, ed. Ronald Hoffman, et al. (Charlottesville, Va., 1988), pp. 45–87; Christopher Clark, *The Roots of Rural Capitalism: Western Massachusetts, 1780–1860* (Ithaca, N.Y., 1990), chaps. 3 and 7.

structure on economic change, but also revealed important national and regional variations in social structures and the patterns of change to which they gave rise. Again, these insights are beginning to shape analyses of American regions; social structure and other internal factors played an active role in the process of economic change.[5] Finally, Marshall Sahlins has argued that local cultures have played a crucial part in shaping capitalist development from region to region: "the specific effects of . . . global-material forces depend on the various ways they are mediated in local cultural schemes." Though Sahlins was writing about the Pacific, and by implication about other parts of the world subject to European expansion, his point can readily be extended to emerging "core" regions, such as New England in the late eighteenth and early nineteenth centuries. There, as elsewhere, regional social structures and cultural values imprinted themselves on capitalist development and gave it distinctive characteristics.[6]

By the end of the colonial period, the contribution of American labor to the Atlantic economy was considerable. Slaves in the Chesapeake region and the Lower South were producing large quantities of staple commodities—tobacco, rice, indigo, and naval stores—for export to Europe. Independent farmers in Pennsylvania, often with the help of immigrant indentured servants, were opening up a substantial export trade in wheat. Manufactures were also increasingly important. American iron, most of it produced in the Middle Colonies, competed with Britain's own production. American ships—many of them built in New England—formed a significant part of the British merchant fleet. Manufactured goods of many kinds from Britain and elsewhere were shipped to America to cater to an expanding American population and rising consumer demand.[7]

As transatlantic trade was expanding, American manufactures

5. The relevant essays are collected in *The Brenner Debate: Agrarian Class Structure and Economic Development in Pre-Industrial Europe*, ed. T. H. Aston and C. H. E. Philpin (Cambridge, Eng., 1985).
6. Marshall Sahlins, "Cosmologies of Capitalism: The Trans-Pacific Sector of 'the World System'," *Proceedings of the British Academy* 74 (1988), 5.
7. Among numerous studies of the early American economy and its transatlantic connections, see J. M. Price, "The Transatlantic Economy," in *Colonial British America: Essays in the New History of the Early Modern Era*, ed. J. P. Greene and J. R. Pole (Baltimore, 1984), pp. 18–42; on imports of consumer goods to late colonial America, see T. H. Breen, "'Baubles of Britain': The American and Consumer Revolutions of the Eighteenth Century," *Past and Present* 119 (1988), 73–104.

themselves were, from small beginnings, starting to grow rapidly. It is helpful to think of prefactory American industry as divided into two zones: urban production in the port towns of the Atlantic seaboard; rural production scattered throughout the interior. Each took a different path and presents a distinct set of conceptual problems.

Artisanal production in the port towns was particularly closely connected with the patterns and rhythms of the Atlantic economy. By the mid-eighteenth century Philadelphia was one of the great urban centers of the English-speaking world, and its artisanal workshops and culture drew migrants from many parts of the Atlantic rim. New York was already catching up; Baltimore was starting to expand on the basis of its wheat exports. All these towns, along with Boston, Charleston, and smaller ports, developed craft manufactures based on processing imported goods and fulfilling the myriad consumer demands of growing urban and rural populations.[8] When Atlantic trade was depressed—as, for instance, at the end of the Seven Years' War—many coastal craftsmen suffered. For instance, the accounts of Joseph Titcomb, a blacksmith and ship chandler in Newbury, Massachusetts, show that while demand was strong in 1760 and 1761, he had considerable work; the slump left him with little but routine repairs until trade started to revive again in 1764.[9] The ports' dependence on overseas trade left their manufacturers vulnerable to trade fluctuations.

Nevertheless, many port towns were nuclei for further rapid manufacturing expansion after the American Revolution. Often in fierce competition with British and other foreign manufacturers, urban American workers turned out an increasing range of goods to supply national and international markets in the late eighteenth and early nineteenth centuries. But market competition, trade fluctuations, political instabilities (especially between 1793 and 1815), and population growth all led to greater urban impoverishment and proletarianization. Trades that had once preserved craft status and a

8. See J. M. Price, "Economic Function and the Growth of American Port Towns in the Eighteenth Century," *Perspectives in American History* 8 (1974), 123–86; Gary B. Nash, *The Urban Crucible: Social Change, Political Consciousness and the Origins of the American Revolution* (Cambridge, Mass., 1979).

9. Joseph Titcomb, Account Book, Manuscript Collection, American Antiquarian Society, Worcester, Mass.; on the depression at the end of the Seven Years' War, see Nash, *Urban Crucible*, chap. 9.

progression from apprentice to journeyman to master became increasingly capitalist in character: apprentices became cheap labor; journeymen became proletarians; the masters who survived the rigors of competition became bourgeois manufacturers.[10] Labor politics reflected these conditions. In 1799 the Federal Society of Journeymen Cordwainers of Philadelphia organized what is traditionally regarded as the first strike by a permanent union in the United States. Six years later the cordwainers' union was successfully prosecuted for conspiracy, an early legal landmark in the protracted struggle between American labor and capital. Urban conditions rapidly generated the bases for industrial capitalism. In New York and other cities, domestic putting-out in the clothing trades brought thousands of women into the meshes of what would become the sweatshop system. In Philadelphia, the largest U.S. urban center of textile production, capitalist control of domestic spinning and weaving advanced sufficiently during the first quarter of the nineteenth century to pave the way for a transition to factory production. As in Britain, this transition would throw hand-producers into deepening poverty. In short, the ports of the eastern seaboard displayed classic patterns of industrialization and proletarianization, patterns that evolved in conjunction with the rhythms of the Atlantic economy.[11]

The second, more unusual zone of manufacturing activity developed in the countryside, where more than nine-tenths of the population lived in 1790. Manufactures of one kind or another existed throughout America. But rural New England between 1750 and 1830 presents a distinctive example, partly because it was relatively disconnected from the rhythms of the Atlantic economy, and also

10. Billy G. Smith, The "Lower Sort": Philadelphia's Laboring People, 1750–1800 (Ithaca, N.Y., 1990) presents striking evidence of hardships and lack of opportunity in the city. Changes in work patterns and class relations are discussed in W. J. Rohrabaugh, The Craft Apprentice: From Franklin to the Machine Age in America (New York, 1986); a good contemporary account is Moneygripe's Apprentice: The Personal Narrative of Samuel Seabury III, ed. R. B. Mullin (New Haven, 1989); H. B. Rock, Artisans of the New Republic: Tradesmen of New York City in the Age of Jefferson (New York, 1979); Sean Wilentz, Chants Democratic: New York City and the Rise of the American Working Class, 1788–1850 (New York, 1984), chap. 1.

11. On early unions, see, for example, P. S. Foner, History of the Labor Movement in the United States: From Colonial Times to the Founding of the American Federation of Labor (New York, 1947), chap. 5; on urban women's work, see Christine Stansell, City of Women: Sex and Class in New York, 1789–1860 (New York, 1986), esp. chaps. 1 and 2; on Philadelphia, see Philip Scranton, Proprietary Capitalism: The Textile Manufacture at Philadelphia, 1800–1885 (Cambridge, Mass., 1984).

because it evolved a highly decentralized, diffused, and varied manufacturing system that only gradually came under the effective control of capitalist entrepreneurs. The relationship between rural manufacturing in this period and the emergence of industrial capitalism seems more complex and problematic than in the urban zone. To some extent New England replicated conditions in Europe that have been identified by scholars such as Hans Medick, Maxine Berg, Jean Quataert, Louise Tilly and Joan Scott, Charles Sabel and Jonathan Zeitlin, William Reddy, Gay Gullickson, K. D. M. Snell, and others.[12] But clear contrasts with European experience are also evident, and it is in the balance between similarities and contrasts that the New England case reveals much about the broader issues surrounding early manufacturing and proletarianization.

Social structure and demographic change played a stronger role than transatlantic markets in shaping rural manufacturing, and the study of work routines reveals the character of their effects on manufacturing development. New England between 1750 and 1830 provides an example of the kind of "alternatives to mass production," discussed by Sabel and Zeitlin. But we must consider what sources of instability in the system ensured that its patterns did not, in the long run, actually survive. Equally, in light of Jean Quataert's emphasis on the continuities and complexities in rural manufacturers' experiences, we need to ask whether rural manufacturing in fact contributed much to the transition to capitalism and to proletarianization.[13] Answers to both these questions lie in understanding the ways in which rural producers organized their work.

12. Peter Kriedte, Hans Medick, and Jürgen Schlumbohm, *Industrialization before Industrialization: Rural Industry in the Genesis of Capitalism*, trans. B. Schempp (Cambridge, Eng., 1981); Maxine Berg, *The Age of Manufactures: Industry, Innovation, and Work in Britain, 1700–1820* (London, 1985); Jean Quataert, "A New View of Industrialization: 'Protoindustry' or the Role of Small-Scale, Labor-Intensive Manufacture in the Capitalist Environment," *ILWCH* 33 (1988), 3–22; Louise Tilly and Joan W. Scott, *Women, Work and Family* (New York, 1978); Charles Sabel and Jonathan Zeitlin, "Historical Alternatives to Mass Production: Politics, Markets, and Technology in 19th-Century Industrialization," *Past and Present* 108 (1985), 133–76; W. M. Reddy, *The Rise of Market Culture: The Textile Trade and French Society, 1750–1900* (Cambridge, Eng., 1984); G. L. Gullickson, *The Spinners and Weavers of Auffay: Rural Industry and the Sexual Division of Labour in a French Village, 1750–1850* (Cambridge, Eng., 1986); K. D. M. Snell, *Annals of the Labouring Poor: Social Change and Agrarian England, 1660–1900* (Cambridge, Eng.,'1985).

13. Sabel and Zeitlin, "Historical Alternatives"; M. J. Piore and C. F. Sabel, *The Great Industrial Divide: Possibilities for Prosperity* (New York, 1984); Quataert, "A New View of Industrialization."

Rural New England in the mid-eighteenth century had, like other North American regions, a relative abundance of land, widely distributed throughout the population, and a shortage of labor. New England had evolved a dependent labor system to deal with this shortage. But whereas the southern colonies relied on slavery and the middle colonies heavily on indentured servants, New England households made most use of family labor. Slaves, and even servants, were comparatively rare, and low rates of transatlantic migration reflected an absence of employment opportunities in an economy where most work was done by family, kin, or neighbors.[14]

Production patterns also differed from those in colonies farther south. Most of New England's chief colonial exports, such as fish and ships, were products of the coast. Although some farming regions furnished crops and other goods for export, much of the interior had only weak links with the Atlantic market. There were no staple export crops, and most rural output was used locally. Consequently, the intention to sell in distant markets played only a small role in decisions about production, either of farm goods or manufactures. Farm households practiced mixed farming. Most were far from being literally self-sufficient, and local exchanges of goods and labor—usually without cash—supplied many of their needs. Land ownership was a realizable ambition for most families, and many combined farming with small amounts of seasonal and household work at manufacturing tasks to provide themselves or their neighbors with basic clothing, tools, and furnishings.[15]

Rural manufacturing began to grow in scope and importance after 1750 for two reasons. First, though ownership of property was widespread, it was neither universal nor egalitarian. New England's natural rate of population increase was high. Although migration to new regions relieved some of the pressure, earlier-settled areas in Connecticut, eastern Massachusetts, and the Connecticut Valley in western Massachusetts faced a potential population crisis as available land became scarcer. Fewer and fewer families had enough land on

14. See Daniel Vickers, "Working the Fields in a Developing Economy: Essex County, Massachusetts, 1630–1675," in *Work and Labor in Early America*, ed. Stephen Innes (Chapel Hill, N.C., 1988), pp. 49–69; P. G. E. Clemens and Lucy Simler, "Rural Labor and the Farm Household in Chester County, Pennsylvania, 1750–1820," in ibid., pp. 106–43; L. G. Carr and L. S. Walsh, "Economic Diversification and Labor Organization in the Chesapeake, 1650–1820," in ibid., pp. 144–88.

15. Clark, *Roots of Rural Capitalism*, chap. 2.

which to settle all their sons as farmers; as each generation succeeded the next, more and more people had to find other activities with which either to supplement or to replace farming as a means of livelihood. The growth of rural manufacturing was primarily a result of this need for a structural adjustment in the economy.

Second, political events aided the growth of rural manufacturing. Protests against Britain in the 1760s brought temporary nonimportation agreements and pressure to refrain from using British goods. When protest turned to war in 1775, military needs and the cessation of British imports further stimulated rural manufactures, both in craft workshops and in households. Although rural producers were clearly unable to meet the demands placed on them, during the 1770s and 1780s manufacturing became firmly and widely established on a new footing in large parts of the countryside. Foreign visitors noted the ubiquity of craft and household production in the New England interior. Even when British imports flowed again after the end of the Revolutionary War in 1783, rural manufactures survived and even flourished. Roger Newberry of Suffield, Connecticut, would write in 1791 that manufactures "have been rapidly improving since the commencement of the late war, but more especially since the conclusion of it." This was in part because, rather than simply adjusting to market demands, producers continued to function in response to the locally generated, structurally induced requirements of the rural economy.[16]

Production of all kinds expanded, both in households and in specialized workshops, and manufacturing appeared throughout the landscape, even in small settlements. By 1810 the federal census recorded a profusion of furnituremaking, leather manufacture, tool- and implement-making, woodenware production, metalworking, hatmaking, clockmaking, brewing, distilling, boot- and shoemaking, and a variety of other occupations in rural areas from northern Vermont to Long Island Sound. Above all, there was textile production, most of it in households. In Massachusetts alone, the census recorded 4.1 million yards of cloth produced outside "manufacturing establishments," compared with only thirty-six thousand yards from cotton mills, and fewer than seven thousand yards from woolen mills. Of household-made cloth, more than two million yards were recorded in the counties of Berkshire, Hampshire, and Worcester,

16. Ibid.; Henretta, "War for Independence," pp. 66–81.

the rural western and central parts of the state.[17] The 1820 census, which attempted to classify individual men by occupational group (farming, commerce, or manufactures) found that even in Maine, the least industrialized New England state, more than 11 percent of working men were in manufacturing; in Massachusetts and Rhode Island the proportion was more than 30 percent.[18] For reasons that will soon be apparent, these figures certainly understated rural peoples' involvement in manufacturing.

Four different patterns of rural manufacturing organization can be identified, all common throughout the late eighteenth and early nineteenth centuries: (1) independent household production involved men and women in home-based manufacture on their own account; (2) itinerant producers moved from house to house, practicing the crafts of weaving, tailoring, or dressmaking, often using materials provided by their employers and eking out an existence on board, lodging, and minimal wage payments; (3) exchange production involved the labor of other households, usually local, procured by the swapping of work or goods; and (4) craft production proper took place in separate workshops, often in the central villages or towns, and was often arranged on formal hierarchical distinctions between masters, journeymen, and apprentices. Businesses were usually small. Rarely was formal capitalist control or employment of wage labor predominant or permanent; as James A. Henretta has pointed out, this was primarily a *Kaufsystem*, controlled by households, not a *Verlagssystem*, run by merchants. Even the most heavily capitalized rural manufactures—gristmills, sawmills, and the carding and fulling mills that sprang up throughout the countryside from the 1790s on—were small employers of labor and engaged largely in custom work, in the latter case for the benefit of household textile producers.[19]

These four kinds of productive organization are, however, ideal types; in practice they were frequently mixed. Individuals might be engaged part of the year in one activity and another part in a differ-

17. *A Series of Tables of the Several Branches of American Manufactures exhibiting them in every County of the Union . . . 1810 . . .* (Philadelphia, 1813); other rural manufactures included stockings, wire-cards, nails, guns, soap, linseed oil, paper, combs, bricks, carriages, and wagons.

18. *Census for 1820* (Washington, D.C., 1821).

19. Henretta, "War for Independence," passim; Clark, *Roots of Rural Capitalism,* pp. 95–100.

ent one, and in a different kind of organization. Because the structural characteristics of the New England countryside preserved widespread access to land but made living exclusively from the land increasingly difficult, manufacturing became a by-employment, a supplemental source of livelihood for households whose members also did farm work and other tasks. Rural manufacturing took its essential character from this search for livelihoods as people adapted it to their particular needs. New England amply illustrated Jean Quataert's observation that rural people often did not have "occupations" into which they could be classified.[20] Instead they occupied themselves by fitting together a constantly shifting assortment of tasks.

This was so for both men and women. Much manufacturing was done seasonally; the rhythms of the farming year helped dictate when labor was freed from other tasks and when raw materials such as flax, wool, leather, and lumber were available to be worked. Many farmers made shoes or woodenware for short periods in the winter. Craft producers, too, varied their activities from season to season. Production was often part-time, and the hiring of labor intermittent. Both Connecticut and New Hampshire provide examples of early nineteenth-century furnituremakers who worked at house-carpentry in the summer months. In western Massachusetts some clothiers ran their own businesses part of the year and worked as hired weavers or laborers at other times.[21] Such patterns were common well into the nineteenth century. David Burt, a blacksmith in Barre, Massachusetts, between 1796 and 1842, worked at topping and heeling shoes, making and heading tacks, woodworking, and growing crops on his own land, in addition to routine tasks at his forge. In "most towns" in Barnstable County, Massachusetts, according to the *McLane Report* of 1832, house carpenters also worked part-time as wheelwrights, cabinetmakers, coopers, or painters.[22] Women who organized textile production in their homes had to accommodate a

20. Quataert, "A New View of Industrialization," p. 5; idem, "The End of Certainty: A Reply to Critics," *ILWCH* 35 (1989), 35–36.

21. Edward Strong Cooke, Jr., "Rural Artisanal Culture: The Preindustrial Joiners of Newtown and Woodbury, Connecticut, 1760–1820" (Ph.D. diss., Boston University, 1984), p. 18; Clark, *Roots of Rural Capitalism*, p. 110.

22. David Burt, Account Book, Barre, Mass., 1796–1842, Manuscript Collection, MS 1984.12 BV pc, Old Sturbridge Village Research Library, Sturbridge, Mass.; *Documents Relative to Manufactures in the United States*, 22d Cong. 1st Sess., House Executive Document no. 308 (Washington, D.C., 1833): vol. 1, 117 (hereafter cited as *McLane Report*).

range of other household duties; as Laurel Thatcher Ulrich has shown, having unmarried daughters or other relatives who could be assigned substantial manufacturing tasks was an advantage. Even those young women combined spinning or weaving with other jobs around the house and yard.[23]

Household textile production not only rose, but intensified for many women, who assumed increasing responsibility for weaving cloth as well as for spinning yarn. In York County, Maine, in the 1730s, 40 percent of estate inventories listed spinning wheels; only 3 percent had looms. By the end of the century, 60 percent of estates had spinning wheels and 25 percent had looms. By the early 1820s in parts of western Connecticut up to nine out of ten inventories listed spinning wheels. This accompanied a deepening sexual division of labor in late eighteenth- and early nineteenth-century households. As men's and women's responsibilities and activities became more differentiated, women handled textiles and clothing; men made tools or woodenware. Spatial separation became more common, too. Many men took their work out of the house itself into workshops in ells or sheds or on separate land altogether. A recent survey of four hundred nineteenth-century farm sites in southern Maine, New Hampshire, and Massachusetts found that more than two-thirds had at one time included a workshop for manufacturing.[24]

Work routines were closely tied to individual circumstances and to intermittent demand for goods and labor. Rates of work rested to some degree on individual needs for income or goods in exchange for their labor. Apart from farm labor, household service, and some general manufacturing, where payment was for the day or part-day, most wage payments were by the piece or by the task. Certainly poorer workers faced the discipline of producing goods at the low rates acceptable to more prosperous households that worked only part-time. Women workers in particular, in shoemaking or the

23. L. T. Ulrich, "Martha Ballard and Her Girls: Women's Work in Eighteenth-Century Maine," in *Work and Labor in Early America*, ed. S. Innes, p. 94.

24. Ulrich, "Martha Ballard and Her Girls," p. 90; Cooke, "Rural Artisanal Culture," p. 43, table 1. On gender differentiation, see Jeanne Boydston, "Home and Work: The Industrialization of Housework in the Northeastern United States from the Colonial Period to the Civil War" (Ph.D. diss., Yale University, 1984), pp. 102–3. See also idem, *Home and Work: Wages and Ideology of Labor in the Early Republic* (New York, 1990). The survey of farm sites is reported in T. C. Hubka, *Big House, Little House, Back House, Barn: The Connected Farm Buildings of New England* (Hanover, N.H., 1984), p. 66.

clothing trades, worked long hours for pittances; manufactures, for them, were rarely a lucrative source of earnings. Much men's work varied in intensity and rhythm. Specific trades and even localities established customary expectations of a normal day's work, but piecework, outwork, and contracting left it largely to individuals to maintain this rate. Employers were often faced with the choice between keeping a slack hired hand or having no help at all. As W. J. Rohrabaugh has shown, the period up to the 1820s was also one in which U.S. alcohol consumption rose to record levels. Workers had time for drinking and sociability. Although some urban crafts had disputes over working hours and conditions during this period, few such issues in the countryside spread beyond individual workplaces.[25]

Yet men's and women's work also followed patterns dictated by the family life cycle and the easier availability of family compared with hired labor. In Hallowell, Maine, between 1788 and 1798, Martha Ballard had spinning and weaving done for her in her own home by other women. But up to the early 1790s these women were usually her own daughters or nieces, who stayed for an average of twelve months at a time working in her household. As they married or moved away, Ballard had to rely increasingly on young women hired from other families, who invariably stayed for much shorter periods. Eventually Ballard gave up searching for help and gave her loom to one of her daughters. In 1817 Tobias Walker, who grew up on his father's farm in Kennebunk, Maine, became a shoemaker at the age of twenty, but he worked at his trade only until his father's death, seven years later, left him in charge of the farm itself. In South Amherst, Massachusetts, from 1810 onward, a maker of wooden faucets employed his three sons when they were neither in school nor required for urgent farm tasks such as haying. In each case, family circumstances helped determine when and by whom manufacturing work was conducted.[26] Whether female or male, household- or workshop-based, rural manufactures perpetuated and

25. W. J. Rohrabaugh, *The Alcoholic Republic: An American Tradition* (New York, 1979), pp. 7–10; on drinking and sociability, see H. G. Gutman, "Work Culture and Society in Industrializing America, 1815–1919," *American Historical Review* 78 (1973), 531–88, examples on 543–46; J. A. McGaw, *Most Wonderful Machine: Mechanization and Social Change in Berkshire Paper Making, 1801–1885* (Princeton, 1987), p. 54, cites examples of breaks for drinks; an account of labor disputes is in Bruce Laurie, *Artisans into Workers: Labor in 19th Century America* (New York, 1989), pp. 63–66, 73–91.

26. Ulrich, "Martha Ballard and Her Girls," p. 94; Tobias Walker is discussed in Hubka, *Big House, Little House, Back House, Barn*, p. 165; the Amherst faucetmaker is mentioned in Clark, *The Roots of Rural Capitalism*, p. 97.

intensified the economy's existing characteristics: reliance on family and local labor and embeddedness in networks of local exchange. In Ballard's case, and in many other middling farm households, manufacturing patterns were closely tied to family needs and abilities; as her family got smaller, both its demand for cloth and its ability to obtain labor declined.[27]

The distribution of manufacturing across the landscape was not, however, random. Wherever output exceeded local demand, areas became associated with the production of particular types of goods. Southwestern Connecticut became a center of metalworking and clockmaking; different towns in western and central Massachusetts became noted for the manufacture of tools and of wooden goods such as chairs, ax handles, pumps, and bobbins. Farmers in the Connecticut Valley of Massachusetts came to specialize in broommaking on a seasonal basis, using locally grown broom corn; others in nearby hilltowns began to make broomhandles for them. Even clockmaking in Connecticut, increasingly organized for large-scale, standardized output with the injection of merchant capital from around 1810 onward, long relied on farmers who made parts on a seasonal basis. As one manufacturer wrote as late as 1847, "I used to get my plates a good share of them, of A. B. C. & the rest of the Alphabet in the Town about to the North of here. Farmers and others used a leisure day in winter to get out a few plates." He indicated that this practice had only recently died out.[28]

The clustering of groups of workers in a trade in a particular locality reflected the structural conditions in which manufacturing grew up and, in many cases, helped perpetuate household independence and the intermittent character of rural production. A good example was carriage- and wagonmaking, which were widely diffused across rural New England but, nonetheless, grouped around centers in which makers combined satisfying local needs with producing batches for urban markets. There were some specialists, especially makers of high-priced carriages for the wealthy, but most combined wagonmaking with other tasks. Charles Glover, of Newtown, Connecticut, was a wheelwright and furnituremaker, who produced wagons part-time. Ira C. Goodale of Belchertown, Massachusetts, was a young man who alternated between summer farm

27. Ulrich, "Martha Ballard and Her Girls," pp. 94–98.
28. J. A. Wells to Daniel Pratt, June 22, 1847, quoted by D. R. Hoke, *Ingenious Yankees: The Rise of the American System of Manufactures in the Private Sector* (New York, 1990), p. 95.

work and making wagons, in the hope of raising cash to take him to college. Few men, however, made complete wagons. Emerson Bixby, a blacksmith of Barre, Massachusetts, obtained work from time to time making the iron parts for wagons. John Miller, a painter in Worcester, Massachusetts, divided his time between house decorating and painting carriages and wagons for individual customers and about four different local wagonmakers. His income from carriage-painting fluctuated from month to month: in April 1816 it was his only source of earnings; that October it accounted for only 5 percent. Like so many other participants in rural manufacturing, Miller worked intermittently, putting together tasks to make his living. By about 1830 thirty men in Belchertown, Massachusetts, were turning out about six hundred small wagons each year. According to one report, "the various parts of the wagon are made in all parts of the town, some employed on the wheels, some on the bodies, seats, etc.," and wagonmakers maintained a complex web of interacting contracts with one another to sustain this division of labor.[29]

Local conditions and social structures imprinted themselves on manufacturing, producing variations from one area to another even in the same trade. A striking example is provided by Edward S. Cook, Jr.'s, comparative study of late eighteenth- and early nineteenth-century furnituremakers in the towns of Newtown and Woodbury, located in the Housatonic Valley of western Connecticut. The two towns had comparable access to transport and markets. "One- or two-bench" shops, each manned by one or two craftsmen and apprentices, were common to both. Cooke found, however, that patterns of manufacturing organization and the type of furniture produced differed markedly from one town to the other. He attributed this to differences in the makeup of the furnituremaking population. In Newtown, Connecticut, most makers were born locally and retained strong family and kin connections, including some access to land. The furniture they made tended to be of uniform, traditional style and of high quality. It met local demand, the character of which the furnituremakers well understood. In Woodbury, by contrast, most makers were migrants from a variety of other Connecticut towns where they had been unable to remain. Sharing no

29. Glover is referred to in Cooke, "Rural Artisanal Culture," p. 17; Goodale in Clark, *Roots of Rural Capitalism*, pp. 101, 115, 127–28; Emerson Bixby, Account Book, 1824–55, Manuscript Collection, Old Sturbridge Village Research Library; John Miller, Account Book, 1816–17, Manuscript Collection, American Antiquarian Society; Belchertown is listed in *McLane Report*, vol. 1, pp. 294–95.

tradition they tended to produce more sloppily made, but highly decorated, articles that they sold in markets with which they had few personal connections. Such structural influences on supply affected a wide range of rural production and help explain some of the variations in manufacturing patterns to be found throughout the countryside in this period.[30]

Several factors promoted the expansion of this rural manufacturing system. Population growth and the resultant pressure on scarce land constantly increased the impulse to use manufacturing as a source of livelihood. Creaky and uneven as the system was, therefore, it was always being renewed. As many craft producers found that their output exceeded local demand, those with time and resources began to make batches of goods for sale beyond their localities. Blacksmiths started to spend part of the year making tools or scythes by the dozen, to supplement their regular custom-work, shoeing horses and repairing farmers' equipment. Chairmakers turned out wooden parts in large quantities and either assembled them for sale or contracted to supply them to other makers who arranged the assembly. The peculiar character of New England labor-scarcity, which made help available but rarely on a full-time basis, promoted such a division of tasks; men engaged in by-employments were rarely able to obtain the range of skills they needed to become craftsmen in their own right. Sharing out simpler tasks through local exchange solved the scarcity of skills and led, in turn, to the development of simple gauges, templates, and hand-powered machinery to promote uniformity where parts had to be assembled together. Such circumstances inspired the "Yankee ingenuity" of which New England craft producers were so proud. Moreover, instabilities of credit and fluctuating demand for batches of goods long discouraged specialization in the production of expensive items.[31]

Because much production was closely tied to patterns of local exchange, especially the noncash exchange of goods and labor, house-

30. Cooke, "Rural Artisanal Culture," chaps. 2 and 5; on sociostructural influences on manufacturing, see Clark, *Roots of Rural Capitalism*, chap. 3. An important English example of the influence of social structures is provided by Pat Hudson, who traces the contrasts between the woolen and worsted regions of eighteenth-century West Riding, Yorkshire, to differences in agriculture, land-holding, and property distribution; see Hudson, *The Genesis of Industrial Capital: A Study of the West Riding Wool Textile Industry, 1750–1850* (Cambridge, Eng., 1986).

31. On templates, gauges, and simple machinery, see Hoke, *Ingenious Yankees*, p. 10; on instabilities of credit, see Clark, *Roots of Rural Capitalism*, pp. 127–28, 236–39.

holds with little land needed to make goods to exchange for food-stuffs from neighbors with produce to spare. Equally, purchasing domestically made manufactures was a means of disposing of sur-plus farm produce. As a commentator noted in the early 1830s, preference was often given to locally made goods because of "the greater certainty of obtaining substantial articles, and the facility of payment, in the barter of agricultural products, and other articles that could not be turned to account for foreign remittance."[32] Just as manufacturers made goods to assist their broader family and house-hold strategies, households in turn often cushioned manufacturing activity when times got hard. Aaron Marble, a blacksmith of Charl-ton, Massachusetts, was sending scythes by the dozen to Boston mer-chants from 1816 onward, but found that demand fell sharply after the financial panic of 1819. Only in the mid-1820s did he resume shipments in large quantities. In the meantime, he had kept going with other sources of household income, including his wife's earn-ings from weaving cloth. Without the context of this household support, Marble might have been forced to give up manufactures altogether.[33] Local exchange and family support, therefore, had something of a tariff effect, protecting rural producers from both the competition of goods imported from outside the region and the effects of fluctuations in the wider markets they were beginning to supply.

The expansion of manufacturing and contacts with markets nev-ertheless drew rural producers more closely into relationships with merchants and others whose economic power could command some control of household labor or its products. Before 1820 an increas-ing amount of household textile production was placed on an out-work basis, either for wealthier families or for merchants who would accept cloth and clothing items in exchange for store goods. Ele-ments of a Verlagssystem were becoming more apparent. But socio-structural influences still checked its development. The intermittent availability of labor, the complex and conflicting demands of farms and households in the rural economy, and the close ties between manufacturing and individuals' searches for livelihoods all meant that even between 1810 and 1830, as diffused rural manufacturing

32. *McLane Report*, vol. 1, p. 82.
33. Aaron Marble, Account Book, Manuscript Collection, Old Sturbridge Village Research Library.

reached and passed its peak, effective entrepreneurial control over the system was possible only under certain circumstances. Rural women who took outwork from neighbors or merchants were rarely entirely dependent on it. Merchants and early mill owners had to seek far and wide for outworkers when they needed them and, even when they had arranged for work to be done, had constantly to use threats and blandishments to get it finished. Even worse, they found it hard to control the quality of the products themselves.[34]

The relatively few wealthy families in rural New England who could readily afford to hire labor faced comparable difficulties. Levi Lincoln of Worcester owned several farms there and in nearby towns; he was constantly seeking farm laborers to run them and constantly complaining about their shoddy work. His wife, Martha Lincoln, who organized linen and woollen production in their own household, also put out combing, spinning, and weaving to women in neighboring families between 1790 and 1820. As large producers of crops and meat, the Lincolns had goods to trade with poorer families in exchange for this work, and their account books reflect a multitude of reciprocal connections that enabled Martha Lincoln to organize textile production on a fairly extensive scale. But just as her husband had problems keeping farm labor, Martha Lincoln was constantly having to adjust to the circumstances of the rural economy. Few of her spinners or weavers worked exclusively for her. Some also took wool or flax to work up on their own account. Whereas in the 1790s Martha Lincoln had about twelve regular workers, by 1815 or so she needed about twenty-three to maintain a comparable level of output. To compensate for having to find a larger pool of women to call on, she came to rely most heavily on a few young or unmarried women, who presumably had fewer conflicting demands on their time and attention.[35]

34. G. H. Nobles, "Merchant Middlemen in the Outwork Network of Rural New England," in *Merchant Credit and Labour Strategies in Historical Perspective*, ed. R. E. Ommer (Fredericton, N.B., 1990), pp. 333–47, provides a valuable overview of the spread of putting-out; Clark, *Roots of Rural Capitalism*, pp. 176–79, discusses the constraints on it.

35. The foregoing discussion is based on Martha and Levi Lincoln, Account Book, 1794–1802, Lincoln Family Papers, octavo vol. no. 18, and Martha Lincoln, Account Book, Lincoln Family Papers, octavo vol. no. 15, Manuscript Collection, American Antiquarian Society; I am grateful to Andrew H. Baker for drawing my attention to these accounts. A general discussion of the Lincoln family's farming operations, in-

Rural social structure and economic organization largely preserved the Kaufsystem, at least until the 1820s. Only in shoemaking,
and then principally in one region—eastern Massachusetts—did the
Verlagssystem successfully take root before then, precisely because
sociostructural conditions there differed from those of most other
areas. Eastern Massachusetts—the immediate hinterland of Boston
and smaller ports such as Salem and Lynn—had been the first part
of New England to face land shortages. During the late eighteenth
century, artisan shoemakers began to produce shoes and boots in
batches for coastal merchants, for resale particularly in southern
markets. As Mary H. Blewett has shown, these same men began employing women in their households to stitch, or bind, shoe uppers,
while they concentrated on the soles and assembling the two parts of
the shoe. From about 1810 onward, shoe merchants began to exercise more direct control of household labor. Instead of taking complete shoes from families, they put work out separately to female
binders, organizing bottoming and assembly among male cordwainers in their own towns. But until the third decade of the nineteenth century, this pattern was fairly exceptional; it did not even
apply widely to shoemaking elsewhere in New England before the
1830s.[36]

Early manufacturing growth in rural New England was, therefore,
largely outside the scope of capitalist control. Exceptions to this,
such as shoemaking, were the result of particular circumstances. On
the whole, sociostructural conditions allowed individual households
and craftsmen to retain considerable autonomy, not least because
few of them were solely reliant on a single source of work. As James
Henretta has emphasized, this was attributable to the absence of the
mass poverty and risk of starvation that formed the context for
much early modern European rural manufacturing. Consequently,
relationships between manufacturing and demographic change also
differed from the patterns many European scholars have identified.
New England's late eighteenth- and early nineteenth-century manufacturing system absorbed surplus labor at the peak of a population
boom; it was not the means by which population levels revived after

cluding the difficulty of finding and controlling labor, is in R. B. Lyman, Jr., "'What
is done in my absence?': Levi Lincoln's Oakham, Massachusetts Farm Workers, 1807–
1820," *Proceedings of the American Antiquarian Society* 99 (1989), 151–87.

36. M. H. Blewett, *Men, Women, and Work: Class, Gender, and Protest in the New England Shoe Industry, 1780–1910* (Urbana, Ill., 1988), chap. 1.

demographic disaster. Nonetheless, it did permit a generation of New England farm families to maintain high fertility rates even after land had begun to be too scarce for them to place all their sons in farming. Moreover, the widespread diffusion of manufactures in the early nineteenth century helped temporarily to sustain populations in upland regions of western Massachusetts, Vermont, and New Hampshire where soil and climatic conditions made farming precarious. When structural changes began to undermine this far-flung system, the whole economies of some of these places went into long-term decline.[37]

For the rural manufacturing system was not stable. From 1810 onward it faced increasing pressures for change, both from external and internal sources. This instability suggests that New England was not able to sustain the conditions in which, to use Sabel and Zeitlin's term, its particular form of "flexible specialization" could be maintained. But it did mean—and this reiterates a point also made by Henretta—that unlike in much of Europe, where capitalist relationships were established before widespread mechanization or factory production, in New England the growth of capitalism and industrial concentration coincided. For another generation or more, at least up to the Civil War, this would mean that rural manufactures would survive in a new role, as auxiliaries to the needs of a rapidly growing factory-based industrial capitalist system.

External pressures on rural manufacturing derived directly and indirectly from the increasing integration of regional, national, and transatlantic markets. Above all, this integration of markets gave increasing power to merchants, who could exercise control over the distribution and sale of goods. Accumulated profits from trade were also redirected into manufacturing, most dramatically in the large and increasingly widespread investments that merchants were making in factory textile production. By the 1820s household textile producers were being squeezed by factory competition or, as in many parts of southeastern Massachusetts and Rhode Island, employed as outworkers by textile mills. Some mill owners even encouraged farm families to settle near them by providing land, so that women's and

37. Henretta, "War for Independence," pp. 51, 58; on manufacturing and population, see Clark, *Roots of Rural Capitalism*, pp. 179–80, 190; H. S. Barron, *Those Who Stayed Behind: Rural Society in New England in the 19th Century* (Cambridge, Eng., 1984) surveys the literature on rural depopulation while emphasizing the danger of exaggerating its extent.

children's labor would be available to them. Also by the 1820s the highly capitalized, integrated mills of the Waltham-Lowell system were beginning to draw young rural women, particularly from northern New England, into direct employment by offering cash wages and supervised boarding houses as inducements.[38]

These changes were, in turn, only possible because of the internal pressures on the rural manufacturing system. Intensive demands, particularly on the labor of women in rural households, were leading to shifts in household production and reproduction strategies. Fertility rates began to fall; family members were less readily available for household labor; an increasing number of families abandoned textile manufacturing and sought new forms of income that would allow them to purchase factory-made textiles instead. This, in turn, led to the creation of new forms of rural outwork controlled by local merchants, who distributed to rural families straw and palm leaf for braiding into hats or materials for making buttons. By the 1830s eighteen thousand women in Massachusetts were engaged in straw hatmaking alone; many thousands of others, there and in neighboring states, were engaged in making other goods for merchants. The rise of the Verlagssystem in New England accompanied, rather than preceded, the growth of the factory system. The shift away from textiles to other goods helped merchants control the process. Raw materials for hat- and buttonmaking were usually imported and, hence, unavailable other than in stores. The amounts produced exceeded families' demands for the goods, so merchants had a reasonable expectation that finished work would be returned to them.[39]

Craft manufacture and outwork were to a large extent becoming

38. On family-system mills and farming land, see B. M. Tucker, "The Family and Industrial Discipline in Antebellum New England," *Labor History* 21 (1979–80), 55–74; on the Waltham-Lowell system, see Thomas Dublin, *Women and Work: The Transformation of Work and Community in Lowell, Massachusetts, 1826–1860* (New York, 1979); and R. F. Dalzell Jr., *Enterprising Elite: The Boston Associates and the World They Made* (Cambridge, Mass., 1987).

39. For a fuller discussion, see Clark, *Roots of Rural Capitalism*, pp. 180–84. See also Thomas Dublin, "Women and Outwork in a Nineteenth-Century New England Town: Fitzwilliam, New Hampshire, 1830–1850," in *The Countryside in the Age of Capitalist Transformation: Essays in the Social History of Rural America*, ed. Steven Hahn and Jonathan Prude (Chapel Hill, N.C., 1985), chap. 2. An English example of the parallel expansion of outwork and factory production is discussed by S. O. Rose, "Proto-Industry, Women's Work and the Household Economy in the Transition to Industrial Capitalism," *Journal of Family History* 13 (1988), 181–93.

subject to the disciplinary logic of capitalist competition. Merchants sought larger and larger batches of goods to meet demand. This meant finding more labor to do the work, which required improved standards of uniformity and, hence, even tighter production controls. Connecticut clock manufacturers pushed forward the mechanization of parts production, leaving only certain types of work to rural subcontractors. Shoe merchants organized larger central shops for assembling shoes and boots, leaving only basic binding and bottoming tasks to outworkers. Toolmakers began to standardize products and techniques. Even button manufacturers and palm leaf hatmakers ultimately began to concentrate their activities in factories and to reduce the role of outworkers in the production process. Makers using older techniques and routines survived, but they were often forced into self-exploitation to keep up with the pressure for cost-cutting and improved output. Rural crafts such as cabinetmaking were moved into factories or, where they continued on a workshop basis, began to follow the same techniques of routinization that urban artisans had faced at the beginning of the century. Bosses demanded more regular attendance at and attention to work, and they altered piece-rates or issued special incentives to increase output.[40]

To exaggerate the speed or completeness of this capitalist transformation of rural industry would be wrong. For one thing, financial instability and heavy reliance on credit and noncash exchanges made new ventures extremely vulnerable to bankruptcy and dissolution. An attempt in the 1830s to concentrate and routinize carriage manufacture, for instance, in a large works employing more than one hundred men in Amherst, Massachusetts, was ruined in the 1837 panic. Carriage production, where it continued, returned to small shops and interdependent producers. Particularly in regions where farming remained prosperous, such as in the Connecticut Valley of Massachusetts, small-scale production of goods such as brooms continued on a seasonal basis well into the middle of the nineteenth century. Larger broom workshops set up in the 1820s and 1830s

---

40. On clock- and toolmakers, see Hoke, *Ingenious Yankees*; on shoemaking, see Blewett, *Men, Women, and Work*; on cabinetmaking, see Christopher Clark, "The Diary of an Apprentice Cabinetmaker: Edward Jenner Carpenter's 'Journal,' 1844–1845," *Proceedings of the American Antiquarian Society* 98 (1988), 303–94.

proved more vulnerable than farmer-broommakers to financial instability and, ultimately, competition from the Midwest.[41]

It was precisely in more prosperous farming regions, however,
that crucial distinctions began to be made among rural producers,
distinctions that would lay part of the foundation for the emergence
of a New England working class. Shifts in household strategies did
not lead exclusively to the substitution of capitalist outwork for
household textile production. Some evidence suggests an initial, general rush into the new forms of outwork established in the 1820s and
early 1830s, but rate-cutting by merchants, the disruptions of the
boom and slump of the mid- to late 1830s, and the prospects of
alternative earnings from butter- or cheesemaking led many women
in families with adequate farmland to withdraw from outwork or
limit their involvement to small stints of it. Women in poorer families, however, continued to take in outwork because they needed
store goods and had fewer resources with which to obtain them.

By the 1840s, in both Massachusetts and New Hampshire, the
bulk of rural outwork was being done by poor women. They formed
the core of workers upon whom merchants relied to get work done,
whereas more prosperous families took in work more irregularly.[42]
Increasingly, this marked a class distinction in rural society between
middle-class and proletarian families, the latter more likely to rely
on wage-work and outwork for their livelihoods. It is also possible
that whereas frequent outworkers often took work from merchants
in their own names and were credited with payments directly, occasional workers were more likely to have work credited to their husbands' names in merchants' books. Of 236 women who braided palm
leaf for an Amherst, Massachusetts, merchant in 1850, 37 percent
were listed under a man's name, 63 percent in their own name. This
may correspond with the distinction Tilly, Scott, and others have
made between the family labor economy (in which women's and children's work is regarded as a contribution without specific compensation) and the family wage economy (in which women's earnings are
measured separately). That, in turn, may also have been one of the

41. See Clark, *Roots of Rural Capitalism*, pp. 235–36, 243 on carriagemaking; see
ibid., pp. 100–103, 236–37, 248 on broommaking; see also G. H. Nobles, "Commerce
and Community: A Case Study of the Rural Broommaking Business in Antebellum
Massachusetts," *Journal of the Early Republic* 4 (1984), 287–308.
42. Dublin, "Women and Outwork," pp. 51–69; Clark, *Roots of Rural Capitalism*, pp.
185–89.

marks of proletarianization. Farmers with means maintained their sense of independence from capitalist control by handling family business on their own authority.[43]

The precapitalist rural manufacturing system dissolved more rapidly in southern New England, where the internal and external structural pressures on it were greatest, than in Vermont, New Hampshire, and Maine, where many aspects of it were still untouched in the 1830s. Manufacturing returns from Connecticut and Massachusetts, published in 1832 in the *McLane Report*, recorded little surviving household cloth manufacture, but substantial evidence of the production of other goods. In northern New England, by contrast, homespun, although in decline, was still widespread. The different rates of change and the many ways in which older facets of household and workshop production, hand-techniques, and by-employments long continued to play a role in rural New England all pose the question whether we should emphasize the changes that occurred in the middle decades of the nineteenth century or stress the continuities that were maintained with later patterns of life and production. This question has been addressed specifically in recent exchanges between Jean Quataert, who has stressed continuity, and Jonathan Prude, who has pointed to the transformative elements in New England rural manufactures. Because they point to different facets of the new social structures that were emerging in mid-nineteenth century New England each throws valuable light on the region's complex transition to capitalism.[44]

Evidence of continuity is to be found in the continued close connections between rural manufacturing and the land. Well into the middle of the nineteenth century, male workers in rural craft workshops took time off to go haying in the summertime. Some manufacturers returned to farming after accumulating capital to buy land or being squeezed out by competition. For example, John Birge, a Connecticut cabinetmaker, switched to clock manufacturing in the 1830s, and then retired to farming, possibly after failing in the 1837

43. Sweetser, Cutler and Co., Account Books, Boltwood Collection, Jones Library, Amherst, Mass.; Tilly and Scott, *Women, Work and Family*, chap. 6; see also Blewett, *Men, Women and Work*, p. 48.
44. Quataert, "The End of Certainty"; Jonathan Prude, "Protoindustrialization in the American Context: Response to Jean H. Quataert," *ILWCH* 33 (1988), 23–29.

depression.[45] A factory agent in Amesbury, Massachusetts, when asked what would be the effects of a decline in manufacturing said that "recourse must be had to the land. A great many must be satisfied with what they produce therefrom. . . . Instead of the operatives being consumers as they now are, they would be growers of breadstuffs."[46] But this opportunity was in actuality only available to those with access to sufficient land to avoid using manufactures as a means of livelihood. These families maintained the family labor economy; men often influenced decisions as to whether women or children would take in outwork. In the same way that Quataert and other scholars have noted in parts of Germany, France, and northern Italy, many ultimately withdrew from manufacturing and contributed to a reruralization of the countryside. Farming and manufacturing, which had developed side by side for several generations, were increasingly split off from each other.[47]

Yet poorer families increasingly found themselves entirely dependent on wage-work, lending support to Prude's view that change and proletarianization were as important an inheritance of noncapitalist manufacturing as continuity and family stability. Admittedly, social distinctions long remained blurred. Outwork from rural merchants helped many marginal families maintain their household economy and cling to the land through the middle of the nineteenth century. But evidence from two Massachusetts state reports of the late 1860s suggests that, in prosperous farming areas, families with land had largely given up such by-employments altogether.[48] As in eastern-Massachusetts shoemaking from the beginning of the century, outwork became disconnected from any prospect of family advancement up the agricultural ladder. And as several historians have noted, early optimism that opportunities for young rural women to take factory work would contribute to family stability rapidly faded

45. G. Pixley and O. B. Pixley, *David Birge Marries Abigail Howland: Their Ancestors and Descendants* (Baltimore, 1974), no page.

46. *McLane Report*, vol. 1, pp. 78–79.

47. Quataert, "A New View of Industrialization," p. 12; D. R. Holmes and J. H. Quataert, "An Approach to Modern Labor: Worker Peasantries in Historic Saxony and the Friuli Region over Three Centuries," *Comparative Studies in Society and History* 28 (1986), 191–216.

48. *Report of the Special Commission on the Hours of Labor, and the Condition and Prospects of the Industrial Classes, February 1866*, Mass. House, doc. no. 98 (Boston, 1866); *Report of . . . Henry K. Oliver . . . Specially Appointed to Enforce the Laws of Regulating the Employment of Children in Manufacturing and Mechanical Establishments . . . for the Year 1868*, Mass. Senate, doc. no. 44 (Boston, 1869).

in the 1830s and 1840s. Increasing numbers of rural migrants to the Lowell, Massachusetts, mills never found their way back to the countryside, becoming, instead, urban dwellers. By the 1840s fewer rural women were prepared to follow them to the mills.[49] Even before the onset of mass immigration in the 1840s and 1850s permanently solved New England capitalists' labor shortage, the roots of the New England working class had been laid in the structural shifts of the manufacturing economy.

These structural shifts—now largely determined not by rural conditions but by markets and the demands of capital—led to further transformations in rural manufacturing. Clockmaking in western Connecticut had exemplified circumstances in which the conditions of rural manufacturing stimulated technical change in order to secure sufficient regularity and uniformity of production. By the 1840s, however, clocks with wooden movements were driven from the market by cheap, brass-movement clocks made in new, larger factories. As a result, parts of rural Connecticut lost their role in clock production. Where rural manufacturing survived after 1830, key products such as textiles, furniture, and tools were increasingly concentrated in factories, leaving small producers and outworkers to handle more marginal, accessory goods at cheap rates. Even where households preserved a degree of formal independence, they were subject to influences beyond their own or their neighbors' control.

The distinction between the earlier, precapitalist phase of rural manufacturing and the system that emerged by the mid-nineteenth century consisted in the social relationships that each entailed, both within rural localities and in their connections with the wider economy. Because work routines evolved at the intersections of these structural changes with individuals' and families' searches for livelihoods, they came under pressure as broader economic changes swept the countryside. As propertied rural families withdrew from manufacturing, it became proletarianized, by-employments declined, and a more dependent workforce became more subject to industrial work-discipline or the need to exploit themselves to make ends meet. This is not to say that individuals lost all power of agency; skilled male workers in particular retained significant bargaining power in an expanding economy where skill was scarce. But the labor process was profoundly shaped by broader social structures. Studies of labor

49. Dublin, *Women at Work*, esp. chap. 10; *Farm to Factory: Women's Letters, 1830–1860*, ed. T. L. Dublin (New York, 1981), pp. 24–36.

protest and union organization suggest that there was a spectrum of
levels of militancy inversely related to workers' connections to the
rural family economy. Capitalist work routines inspired a range of
responses, from rural textile workers who rarely took strike action
but used absenteeism and other forms of silent protest, to the mili-
tant British immigrants in the textile mills of Manayunk, Pennsylvania, studied by Cynthia J. Shelton. Proof of this relationship lies in
the shoe industry, where, as Blewett has shown, women outworkers
tied to the family labor economy were much more reluctant supporters of the great strike of 1860 than their sisters working in shoe
factories.[50]

New England shared much with other American and European
regions in which manufacturing took root and flourished in rural
societies. But because its eighteenth-century background was that of
an area with low levels of staple exports and poor connections with
the Atlantic economy, New England's early manufacturing history
was also unusual. Substantial investments of commercial capital came
at a later point in most of New England's industrial evolution than
they did in many parts of Europe, or in the mid-Atlantic region.
When they did come, the simultaneous expansion of the putting-out
and factory systems made New England industrialization particularly
rapid. New England's distinctiveness, however, resulted from its unusual endowments of those factors—demography and property distribution—that helped shape rural manufacturing everywhere. It il-
lustrates the general rule that local circumstances profoundly
influenced the terms on which industrial capitalism took shape. And,
as elsewhere, New England's rural manufactures also helped shape
capitalism's mythologies. How many of the late nineteenth- and
twentieth-century celebrants of "Yankee ingenuity" remembered
that its roots lay, not in capitalist enterprise, but in the myriad demands of making livelihoods in a complex, household-based rural
economy?

50. Jonathan Prude, *The Coming of Industrial Order: Town and Factory Life in Rural
Massachusetts, 1813–1860* (Cambridge, Eng., 1983), chap. 5; C. J. Shelton, *The Mills of
Manayunk: Industrialization and Social Conflict in the Philadelphia Region, 1737–1837*
(Baltimore, 1986); on women shoemakers' protests, and divisions between shop and
family workers, see Blewett, *Men, Women, and Work*, pp. 34–41, 94–95, and 115–40;
on wage and hours campaigns by Lowell mill women, see also Dublin, *Women at Work*,
chaps. 6 and 7.

Christopher H. Johnson

2   Capitalism and the State: Capital
Accumulation and Proletarianization in the
Languedocian Woolens Industry,
1700–1789

The problem of the relationship of the state to the development of capitalism has become quite complex. For the generation of
John Clapham and T. S. Ashton, of course, the foundation of capitalist economic growth was unquestionably laissez-faire. Their historical work bolstered the neoclassical economics movement best
represented in the Chicago School and realized politically in Thatch-
erism and Reaganomics. Even for many economic historians who endorsed Keynesian economics in contemporary societies, the very nature of capitalism was wedded to the notions of liberty propounded
by Adam Smith, the Physiocrats, and the architects of the French
Constitution of 1791. And old-fashioned Marxists added to the
chorus, wary as they were of assigning autonomous powers to the
superstructure. But a new generation of non-Marxist economic historians, led by people like Barry Supple, Ralph Davis, Robert Lively,
and Douglass North, and of Marxists such as William Appleman
Williams, Eric Hobsbawm, and Immanuel Wallerstein developed
perspectives, popularized most persuasively by Robert Heilbroner,
arguing that the modern state and modern capitalism evolved hand-
in-glove, with the neocorporatism, welfare state, or social democracy
(whichever term one prefers) of the twentieth century, a culmination

37

rather than a deviation from the capitalist road.[1] Western Marxist social theory has also come to terms with the role of the state in shaping essential parameters of historical change, first through the Frankfurt School's recognition of the capacity of the authoritarian state to redirect basic economic relationships, then through the full-scale integration of Max Weber in the historical work of people like Theda Skocpol. Today the mature theory of Jürgen Habermas simply takes for granted the equal status of the state and its mechanisms with capitalism; these twin systemic forces have, over the past three or four centuries, effectuated what he calls the "colonization" of people's lifeworlds, the cultural, social, and personal networks of their communicative interaction.[2]

One of the central historical problems in the debate over the state has been mercantilism's role in capitalist development. The laissez-faire school naturally did everything possible to demonstrate, in good Smithian fashion, that the use of the power of the state, whether it be military punishment of commercial rivals, colonization, the support for coerced labor systems and trade in slaves, tariff and export subsidy manipulations, state-sponsored trading companies, diplomatic leverage to open up markets, a reinforced guild system, state promotion and regulation of manufactures, the hoarding of bullion, or any other aspect of the mercantilist package, was in the long run inimical to real economic progress. But as our understanding of the seventeenth-century economy has deepened, the role of

1. Barry Supple, "The State and the Industrial Revolution," in *The Fontana Economic History of Europe*, vol. 3, ed. Carlo Cipolla (Glasgow, 1973), pp. 301–57; Ralph Davis, *The Rise of the Atlantic Economies* (London, 1975); Robert Lively, "The American System," *Business History Review* (March 1955), esp. 80–81; Douglass North and R. P. Thomas, *The Rise of the Western World* (Cambridge, Mass., 1973); W. A. Williams, *The Contours of American History* (Cleveland, 1961); Eric Hobsbawm, "The Crisis of the Seventeenth Century," in *Crisis in Europe, 1560–1660*, ed. Trevor Aston (Garden City, N.Y., 1967), esp. pp. 46–62; Immanuel Wallerstein, *The Modern World System II: Mercantilism and the Consolidation of the European World-Economy, 1600–1750* (New York, 1980); Robert Heilbroner and Aaron Singer, *The Economic Transformation of America; 1600 to the Present* (San Diego, 1984); Charles Maier, *Recasting Bourgeois Europe* (Princeton, 1975); David Gordon, Michael Reich, Richard Edwards, *Segmented Work, Divided Workers* (Cambridge, Mass., 1982).

2. Perry Anderson, *Considerations on Western Marxism* (London, 1976); Max Horkheimer, "The Authoritarian State," in *The Essential Frankfurt School Reader*, ed. Andrew Arato and Elke Gebhardt (New York, 1978), pp. 95–117; *Marxist Inquiries: Studies of Labor, Class, and States*, ed. Michael Burawoy and Theda Skocpol (Chicago, 1982); Jürgen Habermas, *Legitimation Crisis* (New York, 1975) and esp. Jürgen Habermas, *The Theory of Communicative Action*, vol. 2 (Boston, 1987).

such policies in overcoming crisis conditions, especially for England and France, has become increasingly apparent. Josiah Child's dictum that "power and profit ought jointly to be considered" seemed to trace the pathway to success in the age of Locke and Louis XIV.[3]

But did it do so as the eighteenth century wore on? Obviously by the 1770s Smith, Turgot, and their circles thought not. Just as clearly, parliamentary enclosers and slave-trade profiteers in England, Royal Manufacturers and legions of guildsmen in France vehemently disagreed. What had happened in England, of course, was that the architects of economic progress on the land, in commerce, and to a lesser degree in manufacturing had *become* the government. Parliament was their club (in both senses of the word), the Bank of England their staff, and the Justice of the Peace courts their net. They willingly abandoned the older elements of state support, such as chartered companies, monopolies, and the guilds, for these newer, less direct, but even more powerful buttresses of their economic interests. In France, however, the older forms were linked in myriad ways to the very capacity of the state, and the society of privilege that supported it, to survive. By and large, the progenitors of economic progress—or so it appeared—wished to break away from the shackles of the guild system and the tyranny of the inspectors of manufactures. As Michael Sonenscher has shown, thousands of Jacques Ménétra thumbed their noses at guild requirements, hired unapprenticed workers in large shops or under sweated conditions, and, like Ménétra, made contributions to technological progress.[4] The French *corporations* were in turmoil before and after Turgot's ill-fated attempt to abolish them in 1776.[5] Hungry *nouveaux arrivés* in

3. See esp. Wallerstein, "Struggle in the Core—Phase I: 1651–1689," *Mercantilism*, pp. 74–127; Charles H. Wilson, *Profit and Power: A Study of England and the Dutch Wars* (London, 1957) and "The Other Face of Mercantilism," in *Revisions in Mercantilism*, ed. D. C. Coleman (London, 1969), pp. 118–39. The French pathway was clearly a bumpier one, and Wallerstein, keying to differences between the two in colonial productivity and France's commitment to continental hegemony, provides an interesting discussion of the problem. Still a consensus seems to be growing that Colbertisme, although less successful than England's more multifaceted mercantilism, provided a potent antidote to the economic crisis of the mid-seventeenth century.

4. Michael Sonenscher, *Work and Wages: Natural Law, Politics, and the Eighteenth-Century Trades* (Cambridge, Eng., 1989) and Jacques-Louis Ménétra, *Journal of My Life*, with an introduction and commentary by Daniel Roche, trans. Arthur Goldhammer (New York, 1986).

5. S. L. Kaplan, "Social Classification and Representation in the Corporate World

the woolens industries of Reims, Sedan, Bédarieux, even Louviers, railed against the inspectors while their seemingly mossbacked rivals in the royal manufactories rued the collapse of standards and quality among the lesser traditionalists who cheated to survive.[6]

Thus for eighteenth-century France, the problem of the state and economic development would seem to break down something like this: the Colbertian system and the military/diplomatic support that helped sustain it in areas of both supply (the Antilles, Canada, Spain) and demand (the Mediterranean and the Levant) succeeded in revitalizing the French economy, especially as Fleury & Company put the system fully into practice in the twenties and thirties. But the renewed internal and international instability of the midcentury placed the system in jeopardy. The support system became a prison and, like any prison, bred corruption and desperate acts. By the 1770s state intervention in the economy appeared a proven disaster: *Colbertisme* had outlived its temporary usefulness. The economy needed to give way to laissez-faire, a fact demonstrated by the innovativeness and profitability of those who managed to operate beyond the law.

This is essentially the argument of James Thomson, whose outstanding book on Clermont l'Hérault (then called Clermont de Lodève) and the Levant woolens trade appeared several years ago.[7] In his elaborately detailed examination of Clermont, along with considerable work on the other two mainstays of the trade with the "Echelles" of the eastern Mediterranean, Saint-Chinian and Carcassonne, Thomson demonstrates that although Colbertian regulation and encouragement served to stimulate the French advantage (helped by industrial sclerosis in the English West Country), by the

of Eighteenth-Century France: Turgot's 'Carnival'," in *Work in France: Representations, Meanings, Organizations, and Practice*, ed. Kaplan and Cynthia Koepp (Ithaca, N.Y., 1986), pp. 176–228.

6. See esp. the dossier of petitions to the National Assembly in 1789 in the Archives Nationales (herafter AN), F12 678.

7. James Thomson, *Clermont-de-Lodève, 1633–1789: Fluctuations in the Prosperity of a Languedocian Cloth-making Town* (Cambridge, Eng., 1982); see also P. Boissonnade, "Colbert, son système et les entreprises industrielles d'état en Languedoc (1661–1683)," *Annales du Midi* 14 (1902), 5–49; idem, *Colbert: Le triomphe de l'étatisme* (Paris, 1932). In the mid-eighteenth century, the producers of the stiff woolens of the English West Country moaned about their inability to compete in the Levant trade because of the high quality of the lighter, more supple, and more lustrous fabric from Languedoc. See J. D. Mann, *The Cloth Industry in the West of England from 1640 to 1880* (Oxford, 1971), pp. 40–42.

1750s the inspection system and the variety of shady practices in Marseille (the sole port of export to the Levant for Languedocian woolens) and among the manufacturers themselves to circumvent it began an irreversible decline. Manufacturers who had benefited from the old system did not innovate to increase productivity, but either devised ways to try to fool the inspectors and the customers (short bolts, overstretching, poor dyes, reduction of weft thread, poor finishing on the hidden half of bolts, use of higher proportions of cheap wool in the thread, etc.) or simply quit the business while they were ahead and bought land. This naturally further undermined the industry, and by the 1780s, all was lost. Another "pre-industrial cycle" of the rise and fall of regulated manufacturing reached completion (Thomson compares it with the earlier cycle in Italian manufacturing outlined by Domenico Sella); the routine, the blinders of a *Verlagssystem* of manufacturing, sanctioned and over-seen in detail by the state—including the precise designation of what villages might work for which town and time-consuming visits to each cottage by inspectors—ultimately condemned an entire region to the dustbin of history. To cinch his point, Thomson points to the one exception in the Levant-trade story, Bédarieux. This town came late to the trade, only receiving open authorization to participate in 1758, and operated largely on the basis of a *Kaufsystem* in which in-dependent producers bought and sold at each of the various levels of production, and corporate restrictions did not exist. This open-market environment, though in many respects more primitive than the putting-out system, created the natural economies consequent of competition *and* a cloth of consistently high quality. On the eve of the French Revolution, the cheaters of Clermont had even begun to put the seal of Bédarieux on some of their ill-made cloth.[8] On the broadest scale, Thomson makes the rather spectacular argument that protoindustry run by protoindustrial capitalists fell on its face, whereas what many would regard as an earlier stage, the Kauf-system, succeeded in providing the basis for modern industry not only in Bédarieux but also in nearby Mazamet, which had been left out of the Levant trade completely. Thus the stage theories of proto-

8. This complaint came from Bédarieux. See report of March 1788, AN, F12 1387. On the various aspects of decline and fraud in the later eighteenth century, see Thomson, *Clermont*, p. 174; C. Carrière, *Négociants marseillais au XVIIIe siècle* (Institut historique de Provence, 1973), vol. 1, pp. 401–12; N.-G. Svranos, *Le commerce de Sa-lonique au XVIIIe siècle* (Paris, 1956); and AN F12 1378–82, 1387.

industrialization, as developed by Franklin Mendels and the Göttingen school, seem inapplicable to the Languedocian experience.[9]

I have no intention of rehashing the debate that protoindustrialization has already engendered, but I will make a couple of points beyond the main argument I wish to pursue in this essay. First, side by side with the Bédarieux and Mazamet success stories, another, equally vital Languedocian–Rouergat Kaufsystem of the Old Regime *collapsed* in the nineteenth century. This was the production of *cadis*, *pinchinats*, and other narrow-loom unfulled woolens largely destined for the Americas to clothe slaves and the poor. Its epicenter was at Marvéjols, but its work force consisted of independent cottage spinners and weavers spread across the southern Massif Central and the *causses*. Its decline owed much to the upheavals in trade caused by the Revolution and Empire, but it was destroyed entirely by competition from cotton goods and cheap woolens made in England, Germany, and the New World.[10]

Second, there is the experience of Bédarieux itself. Many smaller clothiers in the late-eighteenth century Levant trade (particularly Protestants whose legal and social disabilities condemned them to marginal status) operated mainly as merchants trading in cloths produced by a Kaufsystem chain of exchanges. They were often dyers, who traditionally contributed their skills along that chain, but who increasingly found it possible to combine dyeing and finishing, thus often taking over the functions of the Clermontois or Carcassonnais clothiers for whom they had worked. But in fact the key actors in the history of *draps de Levant* production—a point not grasped by Thomson—were merchant-manufacturers, who bought, washed, and sorted wool; put it out for production without relinquishing ownership; and then oversaw the finishing processes in their own establishments. These were the people who received the initial rights from the government to participate in the Levant trade. The Seymondy family was the first and, for many years after its original designation

9. James Thomson, "Variations in the Industrial Structure of Pre-Industrial Languedoc," in *Manufacture in Town and Country before the Factory*, ed. Maxine Berg, Pat Hudson, and Michael Sonenscher (Cambridge, Eng., 1983), pp. 61–91; Franklin Mendels, "Protoindustrialization: The First Phase of the Industrializing Process," *Journal of Economic History* 32 (1972), 241–61; Peter Kriedte, Hans Medick, Jürgen Schlumbohm, *Industrialisierung vor der Industrialisierung* (Göttingen, 1977).

10. Paul Marres, *Les Grandes Causses*, vol. 2 (Tours, 1935), pp. 73–80, 157–63. S. Chassagne, "L'industrie lainière en France à l'époque révolutionnaire et impériale (1790–1810)," in *Voies nouvelles pour l'histoire de la Révolution française* (Paris, 1978).

in 1713, the only Bédarieux firm sending cloth to Marseille for export. After the right was generalized in 1758, Bédarieux merchants were still screened individually by the government. The two pioneers of the fifties and sixties were the Vernazobres, a branch of a prominent Saint-Chinian family who relocated in Bédarieux, and, above all, the Martels. By the mid-1770s the brothers Martel had created a putting-out empire, employing spinners and weavers in a dozen villages roundabout, while building in Bédarieux a huge concentrated operation that included washing, sorting, and carding activities on one hand and all the finishing operations from fulling to packing on the other. There was no question as to why they undertook such capital improvements: to demonstrate the highest degree of quality control combined with the highest level of productivity possible. Demonstrate to whom? Obviously, in the long run, to their Levantine customers now increasingly skeptical of the Martels' rivals in Clermont, Saint-Chinian, and Carcassonne, but above all to the French government. On three separate occasions the Martels applied for the designation *Manufacture Royale*; their last application was pending when the Revolution broke out. The point is simple enough: Although the open Kaufsystem may have contributed to a free-wheeling, entrepreneurial outlook among many Bédarician businessmen and labor market advantages accrued to them because of the absence of official guild status among carders, weavers, and finishers (though these men did have their *confréries* and consistently sought incorporation), the stimulus of the state was what pushed the leaders of the draps de Levant business in Bédarieux to abandon the Kaufsystem for the more capital-intensive, labor-disciplining, and productivity-enhancing Verlagssystem. In short, even in Bédarieux, the apparent regional capital of free enterprise, state pressure and capital-intensive modes of productive organization coincided to produce economic progress.[11] None of this gainsays the fact that Clermontois and many others, caught up in what they conceived to be the labyrinth of state regulation, opted to cease being capitalists.

The most interesting contexts in which to examine the relationship of the state to economic development, particularly in terms of the technologies of industrial organization, the control of the labor

11. For details, see C. H. Johnson, *The Life and Death of Industrial Languedoc, 1700–1920* (Oxford, forthcoming), chap. 1. The essential source materials—petitions, reports, etc.—are in AN, F12 1382, 1387.

market, and workshop discipline—that is, to the proletarianization/ productivity problematic—are those that in fact produce for the state, whether as public enterprises or, the more normal case, as contractors with the government. The question of the impact of defense contracts and military spending on contemporary scientific and technological development is enormously complex (with competent economists supporting various views), but there is little doubt that they stimulate growth. The U.S. Pacific Northwest is the classic example; other positive historical examples also exist. Without John Wilkinson's cannon-boring skills, perfected over long years of government solicitude and protected for many more by patents, the use of the steam engine as an effective power source would have been long delayed. The technology of interchangeable parts, the secret of mass production, owes much to the American small-arms industry where government subsidies and patience brought long-term success. Private initiative alone would not have been able to survive the years of operation in the red necessary to perfect the product. And even so, as Merritt Roe Smith has shown for Harpers Ferry, worker and community resistance could still undermine the new system's potential, despite the government's input.[12]

In the eighteenth century, textiles were the arena where innovation contributed most profoundly to emergent industrial capitalism. Moreover, it was the technology of industrial organization, particularly the ability of capitalists to command labor, rather than the technology of labor-saving machines, that was initially central to development. This was particularly the case in woolens production where only carding had been efficiently mechanized before the turn of the century, at least on the continent. It is, therefore, instructive to look at the evolution of the organization of production among France's most important defense contractors in the area of textile manufacturing, the firms of the Languedocian city of Lodève, located just to the north of Clermont. At every turn, in fact, these companies pioneered in the development of efficient production techniques, a process rooted above all in the proletarianization of their work force. By the time of the French Revolution, Lodève, a city of eight thousand, had created a factory system without ma-

12. See T. S. Ashton, *Iron and Steel in the Industrial Revolution*, 2d ed. (Manchester, 1951), pp. 63–68; F. Deyrup, *Arms Makers of the Connecticut Valley, 1798–1870* (Northampton, Mass., 1948); M. R. Smith, *Harpers Ferry Armory and the New Technology: The Challenge of Change* (Ithaca, N.Y., 1977), esp. chap. 9.

chines, but would soon take the lead in that development as well. As I argue at length in my book, it was Lodève's *leadership* that carried Languedoc textiles generally into the machine-industrial age. Its firms continued to serve as models not only for their competitors in army cloth elsewhere, but for the private sector as well. At virtually every crucial step in the process, the hand of the state was present, either directly as the demanding customer of the city's *fabricants*, or as their legal ally in their efforts to subordinate labor and thus lower their costs. The government's ultimate threat, of course, like that of any other customer, was to take its business elsewhere. It made the threat regularly, but at the same time provided the aid necessary to enhance productivity. Those who paid the price were not, in fact, the taxpayers, but Lodève's artisans-become-workers, who came to comprise one of Europe's earliest and most volatile working classes. James Thomson, incidentally, simply ignores Lodève, apparently on the mistaken assumption that government contract work is an inherently "artificial" element in economic life.[13] It is precisely this sort of laissez-faire mythology that this essay seeks to dispel.

Lodève, a diocesan capital and a fortress of the Counter-Reformation, had a textile history dating back to the thirteenth century. Typical of the piedmont region of lower Languedoc, it owed its existence to industry, for the surrounding terrain was barren; only the valleys of the Lergue and Soulandres rivers provided good arable land. But these rivers also provided something much more important: abundant, sparkling-clean, and soft water, perfect for harnessing power, washing wool, and fulling cloth. The site's proximity to the great open plateaus known as the causses and to the mountain regions to their east and west meant easy access to the wool of the justifiably renowned *mouton de Languedoc*. Add olive oil, produced in abundance locally for the production of soap and for bathing weft thread, and we have a perfect environment for a woolens *fabrique*.[14]

In the seventeenth century, Lodève was typical of many small wool centers across France, operating on the basis of independent *corps de métier* with little outworking and producing a sturdy, well-made broadcloth suitable for both military and civilian male clothing. The

13. Thomson, *Clermont* and "Variations," passim.
14. Marres, *Les Grandes Causses*, vol. 2, pp. 45–51; Marres, "Le lodévois," *Bulletin de la Société languedocian de la Géographie* 47 (1924), 53–166, 194–236; E. Appolis, *Un pays languedocian au milieu du XVIIIe siècle: Le diocese civil de Lodève, étude administrative et économique* (Albi, 1951), pp. 440–94.

incorporated *marchants-drapiers* (there were only thirty-four of them in 1634) were barely more influential than the chief guilds, the weavers and the *pareurs* (finishers who directed the operation of the nappers and croppers and sometimes the fullers as well), with which they had to cooperate in the productive process. The clothiers' confrérie in fact was called "la confrérie des marchants drapiers et des cardeurs de laine." Although the carders were subordinate to the clothiers, in the same way that nappers and croppers were to pareurs, the gulf between them was not great, at least if one is to judge from the payments each made annually on St. Anthony's Day—5 sous from the clothiers, 2s. 6d. from the carders.[15] Cloth production involved a series of negotiations among relative equals. Incredible variations in size, shape, and quality, despite efforts at regulation, were the result.[16]

But with the Colbertian reforms, things changed rapidly. Every clothier was forced to register and swear to abide by a list of standards enforced by a state inspector of manufacturers. Only the more substantial clothiers were registered; the ne'er-do-wells were weeded out.[17] Moreover, the law increased restrictions on outsiders dealing with weavers or even pareurs in Lodève. By 1700 an elite of merchant-manufacturers was in formation.[18]

The Colbertian system thus served the interests of the more substantial merchant-manufacturers of the town. In the 1680s they shed all pretense of any association with the carders, whose attempts to form their own guild got nowhere. This coincided with the first important moves into the countryside in search of carding and spinning labor. Government officials gave their support. For example, in 1702 the Conseil de Ville de Lodève, in an action sanctioned by Intendant Basville, ordered the reduction of the day-wage of male agricultural workers in its rural jurisdiction from more than ten sous per day (plus bread) to nine, and women from seven to five. Those who asked for more, as well as those who paid, were subject to a five-

15. E. Martin, *Cartulaire de la ville de Lodève* (Montpellier, 1900) (hereafter *CVL*), p. 335.

16. *CVL*, pp. 312–60.

17. *CVL*, pp. 375–86.

18. An interesting indicator of this was the provision of militia numbers demanded by the government in 1705. The marchands-drapiers had to provide and outfit four soldiers while each of the other corps de métiers, including the much larger weavers' guild, had to furnish only one. E. Martin, *Histoire de la ville de Lodève* (Montpellier, 1900), vol. 2, p. 201.

sou fine. The effect, certainly, would be a goad toward accepting outwork in carding and spinning.[19] To encourage this decision, Lodève clothiers publicly promised to "furnish the tools: cards, spinning wheels, spools, warping frames, looms appropriate to each job." At new wage rates established in 1703, a hard-working rural family could scribble, card, and spin enough to bring in 30 sous a day, much more than they could make at the back-breaking work in the fields, even with bread provided—especially in the winter months. And to warp and weave, especially when the tools were provided! In recognition of their growing control over the productive system, Lodève's clothiers were awarded the official designation "fabricant" in 1708.[20]

Beyond the confines of the Lodévois itself, where agricultural wage-labor was significant, the city's outworking network stretched into the causses de Larzac to the north and east, where independent but poor sheep raisers jumped at the opportunity actually to earn specie by carding and spinning, and to the valley of the Sorgue in the diocese of Vabre, which had long produced cheap grades of woolens such as cadis. This entire "pays sans pain" was officially assigned by a DeBernage ordinance in 1722 "to work only for Lodève."[21]

The repercussions of out-working for relations of production in Lodève itself were profound. Long standing mistrust and conflict, between the merchant-manufacturers and the weavers and pareurs centered on three major issues: the extent to which the latter could work for outsiders and what *marque* the cloth would bear if they did; the limits of weavers' and pareurs' rights in changing Lodévois fabricants; and, above all, the multiple questions relating to procedures and tools utilized by the weavers and pareurs—in other words, the extent of the rights of the owners of the raw materials of production to regulate the work of the actual producers. Fabricants were already attempting to set up looms in their own premises and to supervise directly the work of the pareurs. A final conflict focused on access to master status within each of the three guilds, both sides seeking to open up access to the other, while tightening up entrance into their own. Weavers and pareurs not only sought to become fab-

19. Martin, *Histoire de Lodève*, 236.
20. *CVL*, pp. 339–40.
21. *CVL*, p. 342.

ricants but knew that heavy competition among the latter would put
their guilds in a better bargaining position; fabricants, of course,
wanted more weavers and pareurs to choose from.[22]

Such questions were at the heart of a major suit brought by the
weavers' and pareurs' guilds against the fabricants before the Parlement of Toulouse in 1719. In summary, the decision said that (1) all
three guilds must receive "legitimate aspirants who present themselves," a process subject to review by a judicially appointed panel of
masters; (2) weavers and pareurs were allowed to work for outsiders,
but only "if the merchants of the said Lodève do not furnish work
for them"; (3) "the Court permits, nonetheless, the said marchant-
fabricants to have work *chez eux* as many master weavers as they
wish," but no more than one for every two working in their own
workshops; and (4) master weavers were permitted no more than
two looms in their shops.[23] Although by no means wholly favorable
to the fabricant (it also affirmed the prohibition against them "not to
trouble the supplicants in the function of their trade"), this decision
was the opening wedge in a struggle for dominion by the emerging
capitalist class of Lodève. Weavers' work on the premises of the fabricant and the limitation of freedom of choice for whom one might
work were critical steps toward the proletarianization of Lodève artisans. Beneath it all lurked the more profound fact that less and less
carding and spinning was being done in Lodève itself.

Since carding and spinning were traditionally in the province of
the fabricants, little could be legally done about it. But according to
the statutes of the weavers' guild, carrying weaving work outside the
city was to be carefully regulated, and giving work—at least for any
of the specialties of the Lodève guild—to non-guildsmen elsewhere
was expressly forbidden. Apparently, rural weaving was, at first,
done largely in small towns or villages, such as those of the Sorgue
valley, where recognized guild structures existed.[24] Production was
also limited to narrow-loom *petites Lodèves*, sold mostly on the re-

22. Marres, *Les Grandes Causses*, vol. 2, pp. 44–51, 66–80; L. Dutil, *L'état économique
du Languedoc à la fin de l'ancien régime (1750–1789)* (Paris, 1911), pp. 243–53, 289–92.
23. Martin, *Histoire de Lodève*, vol. 2, pp. 483–84. A final, smaller point forced
weaver and pareur masters to carry the product of their work to the central Bureau
de Contrôle in Lodève for inspection by the jurés-gardes of the fabricants and receive
no pay for it. *CVL*, pp. 389–93.
24. This is a hypothesis based on Paul Marres's discussion of this area; work for
Lodève may also have been done in Saint-Affrique, *Les Grandes Causses*, vol. 2, pp. 68–
69.

gional commercial market.[25] Although the volume was small, a crucial change had occurred.

Government stimulus to these developments that steadily enhanced the power of the clothiers at the expense of the weavers and finishers produced the desired result: a better quality cloth at lower prices. A state inquiry in 1728 made this assessment: "Lodève has one of the finest manufacturing establishments in the kingdom, whether measured by the excellence of its cloth or by the colors one gives to it; these broadcloths are long-lasting and sell at comparatively low prices."[26] Lodève's volume of production was 5,510 pieces in 1725, about half of which went to the army.[27] No doubt enthused by this report and anxious to reward his *pays natal*, Cardinal Fleury, the son of a Lodève draper, convinced the Council of State in 1729 to make the city the "principal" supplier of woolen cloth to the French military.[28]

The ongoing achievement of high volume, good quality, and further productivity gains that assured low prices, so pleasing to the state, would not have been possible without the state's full cooperation in the creation of capitalist relations of production. The decision of 1719 was just the beginning.

The year 1740 turned out to be the annus mirabilis for the city's capitalists. The commencement of the War of Austrian Succession—and the enormous increases in military demand it occasioned—brought about a visit from the inspector-general of manufacturers for all Languedoc, Le Mazurier. In a remarkable report,[29] he de-

25. Martin, *Histoire de Lodève*, vol. 2, p. 469. Petites lodèves, unlike draps de troupe, required only one person at the loom.
26. "Enquête sur les manufactures du Languedoc" (1727–28), mémoire by Jean Méjeanelle, in *CVL*, p. 403.
27. At this date a "piece" was approximately 20 meters (16 aunes) long and 1,400 warp threads across; before fulling, it was about 2 meters wide, after, 1.2 meters. Weavers needed about ten days to produce one piece. The figures are from the Archives Départmentales de l'Hérault (hereafter ADH), C 2501.
28. Jacques Fleury registered in the year 1687. *CVL*, p. 377. The continuity in quality thereafter is noted by many observers. See, for example, J. B. Tricou, "Mémoire instructif sur l'état actuel de la fabrique de Lodève," October 5, 1755, ADH, C 2500 and Balainvilliers, "Mémoire sur le Languedoc," 1788, MS 48, Bibliothèque de la ville de Montpellier, pp. 172ff.
29. "Memoire contenant les éclarcimens résultans des opérations que Le Mazurier a eu ordre de faire, dans le fabrique de Lodève pour parvenir à y établir le bon ordre par un reglement," November 7, 1740. ADH, C 2389. Le Mazurier also issued a *fixation* for the Levant trade the following year; Thomson (*Clermont*, chap. 9) argues

tailed the progress made in restructuring production to that point and laid out a new set of regulations designed to carry the process further. Inspector-general Le Mazurier described precisely how the industry was run.

"Nearly all the fabricants have working on their premises most of the workers who prepare the wools . . . for . . . the carders. There are even some who have enough room in their buildings to set up weaving looms, presumably without the privileges of mastership extended [to those who work them]." This point turned out to be moot, for on October 18, 1740, in response to Le Mazurier's preliminary report, a *billet de congé* was issued by the central government abolishing the weavers' *maîtrise* altogether.

The inspector-general continued: "There are about 130 carders in town, none of whom have master status, who have spun in their dwellings about a third of the warp thread of all cloths as well as the weft for the [best quality cloths]. . . . Part of the wool is turned over to them already scribbled and ready to card, part picked, sorted, and oiled only and ready to scribble. The other carders for the warp are dispersed in the villages of the dioceses of Lodève, Vabre, Alais, and Béziers." Similarly, weft thread, to be spun on French wheels, was partly done in town and partly in the country. The warp thread then went to twenty-one warpers for twisting in their mills and mounting on their warp-frames. All were located in Lodève. "The weavers of Lodève number some 210 masters who have more than 300 looms, which suffice the manufacture of broadcloth even in the years of the greatest work." Coming off the loom, "the cloth is then picked over and repaired (*épotoyer*) by the women workers paid by the day who also pick and sort the raw wool in the first stage of operations."

As of 1740 Lodève fabricants put out a majority of their carding and spinning to a far-flung network of rural artisans, most of whom were women working part-time. Fabricants, supported by the law, had subordinated Lodève carders to the status of unincorporated subcontractors whose wives, sisters, and daughters spun at home, a condition now precisely the same as their rural competitors. Weavers now faced the same fate, for with the loss of the maîtrise protections,

---

this undermined competitiveness without improving quality, although it certainly gave the upper hand to larger manufacturers over their workers and over smaller clothiers. My argument is that such governmental action must be viewed as (at least) a two-way street.

the way was open to broadcloth production in the countryside. Equally ominous, larger firms had already been hiring non-guildsmen to weave in locations and on looms provided by the fabricant.

Le Mazurier went on to describe the finishing process with the same precision. "The fulling mills, numbering 47, are either owned outright or leased by the fabricants, with the exception of nine that still belong to master fullers. The fabricants have workers [in the mills] called *planquets* [master pareurs] who label the broadcloths with names, qualities, and numbers, oversee fulling, napping, and shearing, and give them their final dressing themselves. The fabricants furnish them with soap that they procure from five soap-manufacturers in Lodève as well as teasels that they import largely from Provence, shears that they buy from Sedan but mostly from Nyon in Switzerland, and presses, which they have in their own warehouses and number 45 to 50; all this is done in such manner that the planquets have only to worry about their labors and that of their journeymen [*garçons*], whom they pay themselves."

Le Mazurier then pinpointed a problem troubling productivity that would be the focus of protracted struggle (as it was also in Sedan and Louviers): "However, according to the privileges of mastership of these workers (*ouvriers*) (who number 27) . . . the fabricants do not have the option of giving the oversight of the finishing processes to the most skilled worker if he has not been received as a master of Lodève; moreover, a master planquet currently in the service of a fabricant may leave him [in the middle of a set of orders] and take all his journeymen with him to the service of another." This is the kind of problem that the decision of 1719 settled to the detriment of the weavers. The master finishers had been able to withstand the control over fixed capital effectuated by the fabricants because of their own control over the labor market—there were only twenty-seven of them to serve forty-seven fulling mills and slightly fewer presses—and their monopoly over training and hiring skilled men. And no journeyman, whatever his skill level, could contract work directly with a fabricant. All this was guaranteed by the planquets' guild privileges, their intangible, legally recognized property in their skill. In the following paragraph the inspector-general gives us a good idea of the value of that property in the mid-eighteenth century. About a fourth of the fabricants did not own fulling mills and "make use of those of others as well as their planquets, in consideration for which a division of the payments by these outsiders is made—to wit, a third to the profit of the fabricant for his mill and the tools that belong to him and two-thirds for the payment of the master planquet and his journeymen," in other words, a two-to-one ratio of the value of labor to that capital. Clearly those skills were critical to the success of the entire operation: Harnessing their possessors to the will of the clothmaker and his chief customer would not be an easy task.

Control of the dyeing process lay in the hands of ten prominent fabricants who had progressively bought out independent dyers. Many fabricant families originated as dye-masters, a process of mobility that would continue.[30] The lucrative monopoly established by the ten not only paid them twenty-five livres per day in use-rights when the other fabricants dyed their cloth in their works, but assured them priority in times of heavy demand. It was no accident that they and their relatives did the largest volume of business in more expensive colored cloth, a profitable advantage that stimulated their leadership in the standard *gris-blanc* used for infantry uniforms.[31] There can be no doubt that the government approved of this concentration of productive power. Le Mazurier praised their work to the skies: "They succeed in making the varieties of their colors as well as any manufactory in the Realm."

All of this said, however, the inspector-general's main point was yet to be made: "One can see from these details that the fabrique of Lodève is built on solid footing and, finding itself in a favorable situation with regard to wools and good waters, . . . can become quite flourishing; but, having been covered by no carefully conceived regulation, there are prevalent abuses and poor procedures that I will note in outlining the articles for a projected set of regulations that will be aimed at establishing corrective measures." He then laid out a forty-five-article *règlement en forme* that was adopted with minor changes by the central Conseil du Commerce and imposed on Lodève the following year.

The goal, of course, was to improve quality while cutting costs. Although army cloth occupied center stage, the document clearly shows an interest in improving the city's "commercial cloth" as well. The pathway to improvement involved a dual thrust: greater direct control over the work process by the fabricant and the reduction of

30. I have done a careful study of fabricant families, their origins, and their continuity in the business. Johnson, *Industrial Languedoc*, chaps. 2 and 5.

31. Le Mazurier, "Mémoire" (not paginated—section on dyeing early in the report).

the competitive potential of smaller fabricants. These classic elements in the history of capital accumulation, we must remind ourselves, are found not in nature (that is, through the analysis of business practice and its results), but in a "fixation," as it was then called, a government document telling businessmen what to do in order to stay in business. And businessmen followed it, prospered as a consequence, and become models of success for others who followed in their wake.

Several examples will have to suffice, for the règlement and its justifications occupy well over one hundred pages. The very first article set the tone: In view of the facts that (1) width was often lost on rapidly worked basic gris-blanc cloth because of careless control of the shuttle and (2) fewer warp threads than required were strung, often due to defective reeds, the fabricants were authorized to inspect the cloth "on the loom" and take whatever disciplinary measures were necessary to correct problems, including ordering weavers to purchase new reeds. Spot checks by local government inspectors were also authorized. This right to invade the weavers' homes in effect made them an extension of the fabricants' premises, a veritable dispersed factory. As if to underline this point, fines (twenty livres per occurrence per weaver) for failing to live up to these rules fell upon the fabricant for whom a weaver worked. The smaller fabricant, whose irregularity of orders meant irregularity in payment to workers, normally attracted less skilled and less well-equipped weavers. He would therefore be all the more likely to face injurious fines, thus making his precarious position in the market all the more so.

The same result—but with a vengeance—would arise from the various articles dealing with the wools employed. For fabricants the largest element in their cost-price, despite the significant increases in fixed capital in the previous thirty years, was raw materials, above all wool. The less fortunate among them were the most likely to overload with less expensive local wools, to slip wool shorn from skins (*pelade*) into their mixtures, and to do the poorest job in preparing the wool. To counter these abuses, the règlement levied a prohibitive fine of one hundred livres for using pelade and ordained the use of hot water in the first wash of raw wool as well as the beating of washed wool on wattle mats. Although Le Mazurier was probably correct that such measures to remove impurities early on would save money in the long run, the capital outlays for charcoal, kettles, and mats would be virtually impossible for more marginal fabricants. If they failed to comply, confiscation of their wool and a twenty-livre fine would result. The weeding-out process continued.

Among many examples found in the later inspectors' reports, the fate of fabricant Louis Roudéry is instructive. He sold only twenty-four bolts to the army in 1744. Although he had made the transition to the new regime of wool preparation, he found it necessary to search beyond Lodève for weavers whose prices were lower. Unfortunately, so also was their attention to the regulations. On June 3, 1744, Roudéry was brought before a panel consisting of the mayor of Lodève, Master Fulcran Belliol, a member of one of the main clothmaking families of the city though not currently manufacturing himself; the *Procureur du Roy*, Fulcrand Martin, the diocese's chief judicial official as well as its seventh largest fabricant; and Henri Sauclières, the inspector of manufactures of Lodève. The charge was fraud. Sauclières had made a visit to a weaver in Cornus, a developing outworking center, and found his loom was understrung by sixty-eight warp threads. Roudéry protested that he had given his warper sufficient thread to fulfill the requirements. Unfortunately the hard-pressed fabricant had not been able to travel to Cornus to check this piece and another already finished. The sentence was not in doubt: the two pieces were confiscated "to the profit of the poor in the hospital of the present city" and Roudéry was slapped with a fifty-livre fine. The blow appears to have been mortal, for Roudéry had disappeared from the fabricants' list three years later.[32]

As for the growth of labor discipline, besides the whip of a vastly expanded pool of available labor with the breaking of their guild, Lodève weavers also faced costly new procedures and a battery of fines for poor workmanship. Le Mazurier estimated that the principal problem with even the best-made Lodève cloth lay in the fact that weavers used dry weft thread, thereby creating an inherent looseness of weave and unevenness of the finished cloth that harmed appearance, warmth, texture, and durability. The solution, already pioneered at the urging of the army by fabricants Salze and Luchaire, was to bathe the warp in a light coating of glue and dampen the weft with olive oil and water. Besides the loss of time and damage to the loom entailed by this new procedure,[33] it contributed to the home weavers' entrapment by his fabricant. To be properly paid,

---

32. ADH, C 2500.
33. On damage, see later petition by home-weavers of 1771, "Tisserands de Lodeve à . . . le Prince de Beauveau," ADH, C 6766 (Plaintes et Placets).

weavers had to deliver their cloth in the same condition they received their thread—dry—in order to assure that they had not stolen thread. It could take as long as a week for a thirty-foot *demi-pièce* to dry out. Le Mazurier wondered why this should be a problem. Since most weavers now worked for one fabricant anyway, he reasoned, they should not have to lose time waiting for the next order because they had an ongoing current account with a specific fabricant and both could wait for the cloth to dry before totaling up. Besides, the fabricant would provide the drying space.

Le Mazurier's logic here is obviously inexact—or perverse—for what this did was to lock in the weaver's relationship with a single fabricant, always waiting for a week to be paid for his previous work and unable to shift—at least without fear of retribution for this or that error—to another before being paid by his current employer. Strategies to forestall exit, the worker's most elementary right and primordial source of power, are foremost in the minds of right-thinking capitalists.[34] It is quite remarkable, however, to see such a sophisticated strategy proposed by a bureaucrat in the age of Louis XV. And to leave no doubt about the matter, article 19 of the document, all in the name of ending abuses to the weaver, ordained that weavers would be paid per "pound of weft," dry weft, as calculated before and after weaving.

Should a weaver consider quitting, the fabricant had an armory of fines for weavers' errors, which he might signal the inspector to examine. Normally, he would protect his workers by repairing or covering up weaving errors at later stages in the process. Obviously, the potential for ongoing intimidation, "mind-forged manacles," as Blake would later put it, was great, especially in view of the range of errors that could be cited:

> for a badly made border, 10 sous
> for dirt in their work, 2 sous
> for each hole or burn, 5 sous
> for each cat's paw (a wide place in the weave), 5 sous
> for each open weave, 1 sou 6 deniers
> for defects arising from looseness of the warp, 6 sous
> for unequalness in the weave beyond the claims that a
> fabricant might make regarding general quality, 20 sous

34. One of the most interesting books focusing on the problem is Jonathan Prude's *The Coming of Industrial Order: A Study of Town and Factory Life in Rural Massachusetts* (Cambridge, Mass., 1986).

This is a realm of semiprivate law, not that dissimilar to the world portrayed by Douglas Hay in analyzing the operation of the criminal law in eighteenth-century England: patronage and "mercy" are forthcoming for the "respectable" common folk—those who kowtow to the powers that be.[35]

While the weavers' fate was sealed, the règlement of 1740 touched the situation of the pareurs rather lightly, decreeing a different and more time-consuming method of teaseling to improve the luster of the finished cloth and prohibiting the use of *cardes à fer* at any point in the operation. Fabricants' rights to police their work, however, was significantly enhanced. The pareurs' recompense was the stabilization of the mode of payment, a tactic not unknown in more recent efforts to offset discontent over the loss of workers' power in the workplace.

The other reason that 1740 marked Lodève's great turning point was that it ushered in a twenty-three-year period of nearly constant international warfare, with a short respite after 1748. During the forties, trends already in motion intensified. Rural weaving of broadcloth expanded rapidly as the army orders poured in. Whatever claims the city weavers made against abuses of the process were largely ignored by authorities. Moreover, the demand for labor was such that fabricants paid advances to rural weavers to come to the city itself; many were not properly apprenticed, many worked inside the bosses' mills, and all took lower wages. Certainly they were resented, but most Lodève weavers had food on the table. The city's cloth production leapt from about eight thousand bolts in 1739 to more than twenty thousand in 1747. When peace came in 1748 production plummeted.[36] Only at this point did the woolen workers seem to realize what had happened. Several petitions were sent to the Estates of Languedoc pleading for assistance and complaining about various aspects of the work regulations. Physical conflicts also occurred. The worst was during Carnival in 1748, when a weaver was murdered by Sauclières, the inspector, after a burlesque con-

35. Douglas Hay, "Property, Authority, and Criminal Law," in *Albion's Fatal Tree: Crime and Society in Eighteenth-Century England*, ed. D. Hay et al. (London, 1975), pp. 17–63.

36. The key studies of production in the 1740s are Appolis, *Un pays languedocien*, pp. 479–94; Martin, *Histoire de Lodève*, vol. 2, pp. 250–60; and Dutil, *L'état économique du Languedoc*, pp. 420–26. On the regulation of the industry see especially the correspondence and reports of Henri Sauclières and J. B. Tricou, the local inspectors of manufactures during the 1740s and 1750s, ADH, CC 2500, 2501, 2502. See also Appolis, *Un pays languedocien*, pp. 534–54.

frontation turned grim. Sauclières, an aristocrat, was not charged, though he did give some money to the widow and left Lodève for another post.[37] We can only imagine the aftertaste, for further documentation on Lodève's mood is nonexistent.

In 1751, however, the pareurs' guild petitioned the inspector-general in Montpellier to put an end to the emerging practice of hiring nonguildsmen as planquets and violating their rights to control apprenticeship and journeyman recruitment. The inspector-general refused to send the request further. "Contract, day, and piece workers of the province," he said, "would like to lord it over those who give them subsistence."[38]

The official mentality revealed here speaks to a new era. Master pareurs, the most prestigious of woolens artisans, thirty years before were members of a corps treated, outwardly at least, by the Parlement of Toulouse as an equal to the corps of fabricants. They were now lumped with all other workers, including those, largely women in the textile industry, paid by the day. The authority of capital was not to be challenged, and here was the state pronouncing on its behalf.[39] Entrance into the fabricants' guild also became increasingly difficult as the century progressed, due primarily to the skyrocketing cost of the mastership fee: 300 livres in 1708, it rose to 1,050 livres by 1749, with the crucial proviso that the sons of fabricants would be required to pay only 200.[40]

Fabricants increasingly operated as they wished. Rural carding and spinning were perfectly suited to army production, virtually disappearing in slack time, ballooning in boom periods. This does not seem to have created great hardships in rural areas. The rural population in the diocese of Lodève remained stable during the first two-thirds of the century (26,700 in 1698; 28,521 in 1761, with the city of Lodève accounting almost entirely for the total increase). Inten-

37. Appolis, *Un pays languedocien*, pp. 556–68 and ADH, C 148.

38. ADH, C 2792.

39. Thomson examines the process of producer subordination in *Clermont*, pp. 348–56. This same trend forms the principal theme of Maurice Garden's fine study, *Lyon et les lyonnais au XVIIIe siècle* (Paris, n.d.), esp. pp. 582–92. In woolens the struggle to overwhelm the croppers of Sedan and Verviers was completed at about the same time as Lodève. See G. Gayot, "La longue insolence des fondeurs de draps dans la manufacture de Sedan au XVIIIe siècle," *Revue du Nord* 63 (1981) 248:105–34.

40. ADH, C 2792; Appolis, *Un pays languedocien*, p. 491. As Thomson shows (pp. 320–21), similar blockage took place in Clermont. On the uses of guild privilege to enhance the power of capital elsewhere in eighteenth-century France, see Gail Bossenga, "Protecting Merchants: Guilds and Commercial Capitalism in Eighteenth-Century France," *French Historical Studies* 15 (1988), 693–703.

dant Balainvilliers gives a probably inflated figure of 40,000 for 1788; much of the growth stemmed from the agricultural prosperity of the eastern and southern areas of the diocese. Hence, protoindustrializa- tion apparently did not provoke a dangerous population explosion, as was often the case elsewhere.[41] The irregularity of industrial work remained largely supportable among a rural population whose ex- pectations may have risen, but whose ability to survive was not seri- ously impaired by a periodic loss of income that was considered a bonus in the first place. Moreover, the general demand for wool and its rising price in the later eighteenth century possibly provided more income for *caussenards*, while good markets for olive oil and local wine undoubtedly contributed to marginally increasing local prosperity, offsetting any potential disaster.[42] In any case, the city of Lodève itself served to drain off excess rural population. Forty per- cent of all people marrying in the city between 1730 and 1789 were born elsewhere, and the city's total population expanded from four thousand to more than eight thousand during that period.[43]

Rural weaving, however, posed a problem. In most of the nearby villages, the expensive broadlooms were provided by the fabricant. To leave them in place during slack times was inefficient; to cart them back and forth a cumbersome and potentially ruinous job. There may have been pressure to sell them to the sometime rural weaver, but success was limited. The more logical orientation would be to abandon rural weaving altogether. This happened in the de- pressed 1760s, and that resolve was maintained through the boom period of 1778 to 1783. Several things, in fact, came together during the American War that gave Lodève an organization of production as sophisticated as any woolens center in Europe.[44]

We know, by virtue of a census taken in 1798 that gives occupa-

41. See Rudolf Braun, *Industrialisierung und Volksleben* (Winterthur, 1960) and David Levine, *Family Formation in an Age of Nascent Capitalism* (New York, 1977). Bal- ainvilliers, "Mémoire," p. 174.

42. Balainvilliers remarked that the Lodève hills are "cultivated in olives and vines to the summits." "Mémoire," p. 176.

43. C. Rolland, "Recherches démographiques et sociales sur Lodève au XVIIIe siè- cle," D.E.S. Histoire (Montpellier, n.d.). This is confirmed by my own research using the remarkable *Recensement de l'An VI* of Lodève, Archives Communales de Lodève (hereafter ACL), 1 F 2.

44. For a comparable development see Pierre Lebrun, *L'industrie de la laine à Ver- viers pendant le XVIIIe et le début du XIXe siècle* (Liège, 1948).

tion, place of birth, and date of arrival in Lodève,[45] the city drew heavily on qualified weavers and other woolens workers from distressed Levant-trade towns during this new war boom. Most arrived in Lodève as single young adults and had doubtless passed their apprenticeships in their hometowns. At the same time, the fabricants avoided putting-out the weaving of military cloth to rural areas. Thus, reurbanization of the industry occurred. Manufacturers, having broken the guilds with ample help from the state, now reduced their reliance on a more distant and less stable work force and increasingly sought experienced weavers willing to accept proletarian status, which many Lodève weavers were willing to do. More and more also went to work in the damp lower levels of the fulling mills or in newly built weaving sheds.[46]

Why would weavers, long accustomed to regulating their own work-pace and the way their family participated in the process, voluntarily trudge off to the fabricant's terrain? The answer, especially in slack times, was simple: to avoid the expenses of home work, regardless of whether one owned one's own loom. Clearly, for new arrivals or poor Lodève journeymen, to be set up with work at low cost was a good opportunity.[47] But even well-established artisans were faced with costs that made the prospect of space and equipment supplied by the fabricant attractive. After the Seven Years' War, army orders dwindled and many small fabricants and master weavers went out of business. Under these conditions, the consumer—in this case the state—found it opportune to demand a higher quality product (this coincides with a variety of proposals for military reform at this time), and a proposal was made that Lodève increase the warp density of its cloth and use a finer grade of weft thread or lose army business. Lodève's principal manufacturers complied, but refused to grant wage increases to warpers and weavers. A home-weavers' petition of 1771 speaks to the problem of why one might at this point opt for the "factory." Because they now worked longer hours for the same pay, their costs had increased, especially that of lamp oil. Night work was slowed by the growing demand for

45. ACL, 1 F 2.

46. "Etat de fabrique," October 2, 1824, ACL 2 F 6; Plaintes et Pacets, ADH, C 6766, 6767; "Les tisserands de Lodève aux citoyens composants la Commission des subsistances à Paris" (An II), AN F12 1389–90; "Vols de fabrique," ACL 2 I 10.

47. "Tisserands de Lodève à M. le Prince de Beauveau," ADH, C 6766.

blue and green cloths, the threads of which were difficult to see. Moreover, given this work with dyed yarn

> the weaver is constrained not only to moisten the weft but also the warp which harms the heddles, the fittings, and the shuttles and causes rot in the workshop, a considerable loss to the worker. . . . And how is one expected to live since out of the 8 livres, 10 sous one receives per piece, the master weaver must pay a third to his *compagnon* leaving only two-thirds for him from which he has to pay the warper, the bed and board of the compagnon, the upkeep of the shop, and lamp oil?

Increasing numbers of the shop-owning weavers could not pay their taxes. Several, the petition concluded, were now "à charge à l'hôpital et à la miséricorde."[48]

The heavy demand during the American War caused fabricants to provide still more looms in their ateliers for immigrant weavers. This also was the era that women began to be employed as *tisserandes*. Forty-three are listed in the census of 1798, undoubtedly lower than the actual number, for only single women's occupations were given.[49]

Thus, well before the Revolution and without the least change in machine technology, Lodève was moving toward the factory system. After a period of industrial dispersion, which served to undermine the power of the urban guilds, its manufacturers were able to concentrate much of their production again in the city. Complex manufacturing establishments had grown around fulling mills. The only elements in the process that now fell outside the direct oversight of the fabricant were carding and spinning, and perhaps half the weaving, and both operations were so carefully regulated that little could happen without the boss's knowledge. Independent dyeworks were a thing of the past, though master dyers in the employ of fabricants still made their way into the latter's ranks.[50] Finishing operations, still contracted by master pareurs, took place according to quite specific work rules advantageous to the fabricants' authority and in buildings they owned. Up and down the Lergue and stretching back into the narrow valley of the Soulandres the *usines* of the Lodève's captains of

48. Ibid.
49. *Recensement de l'An VI*, ACL, 1 F 2.
50. See especially the report on dyes, 7 Germinal An 2, ACL, 2 F 6.

industry dotted the landscape. Images of the Colne valley, of the West Riding, or of the Vesdre and Verviers come to mind.[51] But in the Languedoc case the leading force in this industrial revolution came from a state bent on considering power and profit jointly.

And without Lodève, the product of this eighteenth-century variant of state capitalism, the plight of the southern textile industry would have been sorry indeed. By the 1780s nearly half of the forty thousand-plus broadcloth production of Languedoc was in army cloth. Lodève led the way, but other centers had applied for military contracts and, at the price of modernization, won them. Bédarieux's largest houses provided several hundred bolts, but the major beneficiaries were Manufactures Royales and new establishments. Villeneuvette, an old royal manufactory close to Clermont, worked exclusively for the army; developed a highly efficient, concentrated operation; and hired workers, many from distraught Clermont, willing to put up with a regime that provided cradle-to-grave benefits in return for subservient hard labor. It was Robert Owen's New Lanark before the fact. Saptes and Montesquieu were less idealistic but no less authoritarian as they moved from draps de Levant to government work. The village manufactory of Riols, a new facility in the Saint-Ponais, aped Lodève with considerable success and during the Revolution became an important defense contractor.[52] Workers from the older centers flocked to the new, then returned as spurts in peacetime private commerce coincided with declines in military demand.[53] Although state contracts did not fully offset the losses in the Levant trade, they held Languedoc's head above water, at the same time bringing advanced practices of capitalist labor organization to the region. And a working class was formed.

In other works I examine that process in detail and deal with the ways in which the French Revolution first offered hopes of a kind of democratic free enterprise, especially in the Jacobin era, then gave

51. It is not at all farfetched to liken the situation of Lodève to that of Verviers or Huddersfield in the late eighteenth century either in terms of output or population. See the excellent studies by Pierre Lebrun, *L'industrie de la laine à Verviers*, and D. T. Jenkins, *The West Riding Wool Textile Industry, 1770–1835: A Study of Fixed Capital Formation* (Edington, Wilts., 1975).

52. See B. Devic, *L'industrie de la laine dans la vallée du Jaur 1789–1851* (Saint-Pons, 1968).

53. This ongoing symbiotic relationship is demonstrated in Johnson, *Industrial Languedoc*, chaps. 2 and 3.

way to renewed state support for a fabricant elite under the Consulat and Empire. These concerns, although relevant, go beyond the focus of this essay. It is my hope, however, to have shown, especially through the detailed analysis of the transitional moment of 1740, the centrality of the eighteenth-century state in the early emergence of capitalist practices in textiles and in the proletarianization of an artisan population.

Haim Burstin

3 Unskilled Labor in Paris at the End of the Eighteenth Century

Unskilled labor was an essential element of the preindustrial city and its economic life. If one studies the working world only from the point of view of guild structures, one risks only partially grasping the role of unskilled workers.

Indeed, one of the characteristics of such labor is its fluctuation among employment, unemployment, and semi-indigence, as well as—from another angle—among regulated, corporate, and unrestricted work. It is a dynamic element that must be traced through varying conditions.

Unskilled labor is often studied in relation to the broader process of forming a "reserve army" of labor as a prelude to the birth of factory economies and is, therefore, a key element in the complex transition to advanced industrial capitalism. Here, however, I consider the role of work in its continuity rather than as a factor of change. And in this case the principle of continuity is fully justified because the more or less wide fringe of unskilled labor was a presence in eighteenth-century Paris independent of any transformation of the productive structure.

If we consider some especially evocative excerpts of nineteenth-century literature we might note that some typical figures of popular Old Regime iconography reappear there with characteristics more like those of their ancestors of a century earlier than those of the factory proletariat alongside which they are placed. The long-term survival of a given level of the socioprofessional hierarchy can be traced to some Parisian peculiarities. In the first place, the city's unique demographic scale must be mentioned. With a population of about six hundred thousand at the end of the 1780s, Paris was exceptionally large and densely populated. When the delay in the development of urban manufacture in the capital is considered, this level of concentration takes on a more particular significance. Trading activities and the presence of the main administrative, bureaucratic, financial, cultural, and ecclesiastic organs caused a continuous influx of individuals, which produced a growing demand for every type of service and attracted a large labor force to perform them. The uncontrolled population growth was in itself a stimulus to hypertrophy because of the increasing need for hands for the general maintenance of the city and the satisfaction of its inhabitants' demands. Consequently, unskilled laborers swarmed into Paris looking for work and found enough occasional commissions, services, or tasks to survive.

The picturesque eighteenth-century literature dedicated to the capital describes in great detail the activities of unloaders, dock workers, laborers, porters, road sweepers, water carriers, and navvies. These were just some of the innumerable jobs carried out in Paris by unskilled labor. This category with its many nuances included, in the lower-class neighborhoods, the street trades involved in petty commerce and peddling: street vendors, rag-and-bone men, scrap-iron dealers, second-hand clothes peddlers, and so on. The noisy spectacle of Parisian streets, where each kind of seller was recognized by a particular call, later registered in the *Cris de Paris*, creates a well-known picture that needs no further explanation.[1]

The image becomes less picturesque when the socioeconomic conditions of this population are investigated, starting with the emblematic figure of the *gagne-denier* (penny-earner), an essentially untranslatable term that epitomizes the category of unskilled labor. Behind its generic name is hidden a complex and diversified reality, which we are far from understanding completely and regarding which I will limit myself to certain aspects.

1. See Marguerite Pitch, *La vie populaire à Paris au XVIIIème siècle* (Paris, 1949); Jeffry Kaplow, *The Name of Kings: The Parisian Laboring Poor in the Eighteenth Century* (New York, 1972).

First, unskilled labor included those who specialized in not specializing in anything. As already indicated, their labor entailed that toilsome work, elastic in its application, especially directed to all types of transport, loading, and unloading. Within this field we find not only those who lived on casual labor, but also those who, although unskilled and executing the same sort of work, had cornered a specific task creating a spontaneous division of labor. They held a semimonopoly made legitimate by habit of practice and implicit recognition in the city. A starting point for a study of the long-term situation could, therefore, be to discover how a given group of workers was able to obtain, consolidate, and defend this privilege. In the absence of corporate bylaws, either the *Traités de police* or the municipal administrative guides could be references. But it is also probable that, where disputes and legal battles were concerned, information could be obtained from the inexhaustible judicial records of Paris's Châtelet.[2]

One of the more meaningful standards of division of unskilled labor is region of origin. It is well known that Auvergnat immigrants were traditionally water carriers, the Lyonnais porters, the Savoyard shoe shiners and chimney sweeps, the Normand stone-breakers, and so on. Here the socioprofessional analysis merges with the demographics of large-scale immigration and highlights one of the fundamental characteristics of Paris at the end of the eighteenth century, that is, the numerical predominance of the provincially born with respect to the Parisians and—among the immigrants—the weight of the fluctuating part of their population.[3] That contradicts the conclusions of Louis Chevalier in his famous and fundamental work *Classes laborieuses et classes dangereuses*.[4] In the light of more recent research, it is no longer possible to affirm that the town developed mainly owing to the larger number of births than deaths and that, therefore, the newcomers were a small portion of the total population. Actually, it is a fact that Parisians by birth were a minority. However, the immigrants were not homogeneously distributed among all trades; often weak in the prestigious crafts, this group expanded in the poorer jobs that also absorbed immigrants from rural areas who came to the city hoping for better living conditions.

2. Archives Nationales, Series Y.

3. Daniel Roche, *Le peuple de Paris: Essai sur la culture populaire au XVIIIe siècle* (Paris, 1981), pp. 11–37.

4. Louis Chevalier, *Classes laborieuses et classes dangereuses* (Paris, 1958).

Unless equipped with a solid, specialized craft, poor laborers who settled in Paris permanently or seasonally drifted toward unskilled activities typical of their region of origin or acquired by the previous generation of compatriot immigrants.

From a strictly economic and social point of view, the condition of the unskilled workers could have been shared by several groups of skilled ones whenever there was a crisis in a sector, such as luxury production during the Revolution. Generally speaking, however, skill was a factor of dignity and distinction that conferred a certain status in urban society, besides defining a specific network of solidarity. The consciousness of having a definite place in the world of production gave the skilled worker the confidence to assume an identity in the urban division of labor.

At any rate, beyond the simple choice or acceptance of unspecialized work that accompanied individuals for their entire lifetime and made possible their survival, another aspect should be understood—the movement toward unskilled work as a result of cyclic deterioration of socioeconomic status, which affected Parisians as well as provincials. As far as this crucial point is concerned, our sources are limited. Better, descriptive sources may exist, along with quantitative data inferred from registry-type documents (birth, death, marriage) that can serve to check events or develop certain hypotheses. It is more difficult to work on levels of wealth and mechanisms of impoverishment. The notarial records I was able to consult while studying the Faubourg Saint-Marcel in 1789, although containing a discreet contingent of journeymen, confirm and testify to the consolidation of wealth or social advancement (a fortunate marriage, bequests, etc.) but not to downward economic mobility and social derogation. Unskilled work was not listed. This also emerges from Daniel Roche's study of the people of Paris, based on the examination of notarial records, which emphasizes household servants and certain relatively comfortable journeymen.[5] To avoid this pitfall and in lieu of parish registers, I have turned to the *carte de sûreté*—an identification document issued during the revolutionary period containing demographic and professional data on the adult male population. In the Faubourg Saint-Marcel unspecialized jobs, accounting for about 10 percent (1,642 individuals) of the registered

5. Roche, *Le peuple de Paris*, passim.

population, were the best represented occupational element.[6] In this group, where the percentage of immigrants was high, especially from the Parisian region, Bourgogne, and Lorraine, there was a considerable presence of relatively old workers, a measure of social decline, at an age when the possibility of recovery was scarce. Double entries, where the same individual declared himself a gagne-denier or performed a qualified job alternately, also attest to probable declassation. This is further supported by the fact—not at all rare—that next to the registration of an unskilled job, traces of literacy appear with the signature.

Although these data probably hold true for other quarters as well, we are nonetheless dealing with clues that do not satisfactorily answer our question: How does one become a gagne-denier? The downward push could correspond to a general crisis, or a particular sector's crisis like that provoked by the trade agreement of 1786 with England, or a crisis in the professional career of an individual, such as illness or an accident suffered on the job.

The dynamics of declassation (the process that threw many into the already teeming ranks of the unskilled) consisted of a complex chain that was articulated between two extremes: engagement in a qualified activity with guild membership, and the neediness of the Hôpital tenants. The reconstruction of the intermediate steps between the two would be important. And a point, albeit precarious, of resistance along the way was unskilled labor, where, as we have seen, a notable contingent of the Parisian population settled, avoiding a further decline thanks to the abundant demand for services by the city.

Despite the diversity of identity within this group, it was relatively homogeneous in terms of activity. From the social point of view, however, this same group had much in common with those who performed the lowest task levels within the professions. Here I refer to auxiliary or simple functions, upon which even the highly skilled crafts depended.

The huge army of manual laborers used in construction, who appeared at the first glimpse of sunrise at the Place de Grève to be hired for the day, comes to mind. The various roles they performed—digger, hodcarrier, stonecutter—actually defined several

6. See Haim Burstin, *Le faubourg Saint-Marcel à l'époque révolutionnaire: Structure économique et composition sociale* (Paris, 1983).

functions of auxiliary unskilled labor, interchangeable according to the circumstances. The work of the hands, employed by every journeyman mason, was also an auxiliary occupation, as well as the *alloués*, auxiliary workers used by printers, hired outside of the guild system, and often used in competition with the same journeymen.[7] Many jobs had a double definition, such as the *tonnelier*, at once a cooper and unloader of wines in the harbor. When the guild structure in Paris at the end of the eighteenth century became more rigid, this sector of the work force, integrated with the skilled crafts, yet clearly subordinate and unskilled, was certainly faced with ceilings to its social mobility. So, in all probability a certain osmosis existed between heavy manual labor within and outside of this system; the already considerable unskilled workforce was enriched by another contingent.

Under favorable economic conditions, vertical divisions existed within the sector of unskilled work, imposing distinctions dictated by the complex hierarchy of social dignity intrinsic to Old Regime society. To be engaged in an occupation was more socially reassuring than being simply an Auvergnat or Savoyard manual laborer and, thus, positionless and nomadic. (We can compare this to the status of the migrant worker in the rural social hierarchy.)

When employment conditions deteriorated, however, and the city entered a crisis period, unskilled work tended to become more homogeneous. Blocking every hope for promotion and causing unemployment, the crisis acted as a social leveller, diluting occupational distinctions. Yet, once entered in the Bicêtre register, it did not make much difference whether one was listed as gagne-denier, boy, or journeyman!

These two worlds of work—skilled and unskilled, incorporated and unincorporated—coexisted in eighteenth-century Paris. Yet they were fundamentally distinct. Despite moments of necessary, mutual dependence in the labor process, their characters and organizations differed in several respects.

First, a certain geographic stability was characteristic of the corporate world. The *tour de France* was an exception, and it remains to be seen how many experienced it. Master craftsmen were usually well

---

7. See Paul Chauvet, *Les ouvriers du livre en France des origines à la Révolution de 1789* (Paris, 1959); and more recently, Philippe Minard, *Typographes des lumières* (Seyssel, 1989).

anchored to the city where their occupational and institutional affiliations endured. As a matter of fact, a good bit of parochialism was ingrained in the corporate ideology, and this joined monopolistic considerations to resist competition by outsiders. Evidence of this attitude can be found among the bylaws of most guilds, in the clauses limiting the assignment of a mastership or employment of journeymen and apprentices. Turgot himself, in the edict of February 1776 that abolished the guilds, condemned this practice: "Among the unreasonable and infinitely diversified provisions of these statutes, always dictated by the major interest of the masters of each guild, there are some . . . [that] refuse all those who were born in another town."[8] The decree of August 1776, which restored the corporations, still allowed access by foreigners. But the stubbornness of the corporate mentality on this point is surprising. Unfortunately, no *cahiers de doléances* of the Parisian guilds exist; they no doubt would have reflected the split in temper within the corporations on the eve of the Revolution. In fact, the electoral bases for the Estates-General in 1789 were the districts not the guilds; a few cahiers were presented unofficially by some crafts, and they were representative only to a certain degree. Where, on the other hand, the guild cahiers were regularly written, as in Marseille, the position against foreigners was taken up again with a vengeance. For example, they contained express prohibitions against the masters of Aix—particularly feared in some crafts—and the fishermen of Catalonia.[9]

A second aspect that characterized corporate work was the role of the family and family strategies in artisanal careers. Thanks to family connections, which offered an effective means of naturalizing quickly in Paris, provincials could become masters regardless of protectionist clauses. Thus, despite a well-established parochialism, the guilds of Paris were not impenetrable by outsiders.

The world of unskilled labor was quite different. Neither geographic stability nor family strategy played an essential role. It was

8. A.-R.-J. Turgot, *Oeuvres*, vol. 2 (Paris, 1844), p. 305: "Parmi les dispositions déraisonnables et diversifiées à l'infini de ces statuts, mais toujours dictées par le grand intérêt des maîtres de chaque communauté, il en est qui excluent entièrement tous autres que les fils de maîtres, ou ceux qui épousent des veuves de maîtres. D'autres rejettent tous ceux qu'ils appellent étrangers, c'est-à-dire ceux qui sont nés dans une autre ville."

9. See Joseph Fournier, *Cahiers de doléances de la Sénéchaussée de Marseille pour les Etats généraux de 1789* (Marseille, 1908).

typified by migration, relative nomadism, elasticity of employment, and occupational mobility; the family was often absent or far away in the town of origin. Therefore, the presence of two tangential areas destined to be nonintersecting can be recognized: corporate work and unskilled labor.

To privilege stable, institutionally defined occupations obscures a consistent part of the real situation in Paris. Despite the diversity between these two sectors, however, it would be wrong to state that unskilled labor completely excluded any organizational or regulatory mechanism. The situation was more complicated, because this large group of workers on the fringe of the guild system also experienced a strong need for social protection of its requirements for survival in the city. These forms of tutelage were based on those already dominant and were, therefore, imitative, in a general sense, of the family and the guilds. Immigrant workers in Paris without their relatives were received by the *chambrée*, an association based on rigid living rules, an agreement of reciprocal aid, and an established hierarchy with the eldest as leaders.

Piganiol de la Force described the organization of the Savoyards: They were distributed in chambrées, each formed by eight or ten of them, and were directed by a chief or old Savoyard who was the treasurer and the tutor of the young boys, until the age of autonomy. Each Savoyard had his marked place in Paris, where he went in the morning to serve the public. They returned in the evening, each bringing his little money and putting it into a community box called the *tirelire*. The box was opened only when it contained enough money to give meaning to the advice of the chief of the chambrée.[10] As Louis-Sébastien Mercier observed: "The oldest have right of inspection on the younger; there is a punishment against those who misbehave; they have been seen to judge one of them who had stolen; they put him on trial and they hanged him."[11]

In the absence of a true family structure, a group of immigrants devoted to hard labor gave themselves a semifamilial code of behavior. Their hopes for survival within a city as brutal and unrelenting as Paris were based on the safeguarding of certain customs concern-

10. J.-A. Piganiol de la Force, *Description historique de la ville de Paris et de ses environs* (Paris, 1765), vol. 6, p. 8.

11. Louis-Sébastien Mercier, *Tableau de Paris* (Paris, 1853), p. 179: "Les plus âgés ont droit d'inspection sur les plus jeunes; il y a des punitions contre ceux qui se dérangent: on les a vus faire justice d'un d'entre eux qui avait volé; ils lui firent son procès et le pendirent."

ing work, discipline, and economy around which their existence was regulated. Again, Mercier recalls the Savoyards: "They economize on the necessary, to send money to their poor parents every year."[12] Sources permitting, it would be extremely interesting to attempt a reconstruction of this type of ersatz family, beginning with the place of emigration and leading to the new settlement, possibly following the vicissitudes over several generations. It would allow us to understand how a nuclear family is transferred, transplanted, and in turn serves as a bridge for new immigrants. This is the same task that Louis Chevalier proposed many years ago for nineteenth-century Paris.

Regarding work organization, a division of labor quite understandably characterized unskilled work, where groups of workers controlled separate tasks, often exclusively.[13] A standard of monopolistic protection applied that was similar to that of the guilds, though based on unformalized custom. The penny-earners theoretically had different areas of competence defined according to the type of merchandise they transported or unloaded. In the same way, the privilege of unloading certain articles was the exclusive right of certain groups of workers. This privilege constituted a form of regulation of heavy manual labor. In the ports of the Seine, where daily merchant traffic was heavy, a network of diversified functions corresponded to the same number of exclusive or semiexclusive groups of workers. Though informal, these rights assumed the status of property. Even the water-carriers, upon retiring from their occupation, would sell their business to a comrade.

Like their skilled neighbors, unskilled laborers defended their acquired prerogatives obstinately. Perhaps the most sensational example is the uprising of the penny-earners in January 1786 against a new company destined to monopolize package delivery in the city to the detriment of the porters and others traditionally engaged in this activity.[14] Although they lost, this significant battle mobilized hundreds of individuals in the Place Maubert quarter and testified to the type of rights claimed: the more general right to work and the par-

12. Ibid.: "Ils épargnent sur le simple nécessaire, pour envoyer chaque année à leurs pauvres parents."

13. See Alfred Franklin, *Dictionnaire historique des arts, métiers et professions exercées dans Paris depuis le XIIIème siècle* (Paris, 1906).

14. Marcel Rouff, "Une grève de gagne-deniers en 1786 à Paris," *Revue historique* 635 (1910), 332–47; Haim Burstin, "Conflitti sul lavoro e protesta annonaria a Parigi alla fine dell'Ancien Régime," *Studi Storici* 19 (1978), 735–75.

ticular right to exclude others from the practice of certain kinds of labor.

Corporate arguments were used against competitors even though unskilled work was outside the guild context. An important example—although not Parisian—is that of the dockhands in Marseille. United in a fraternity, trusted by the merchants, and strongly self-disciplined, they maintained exclusive labor rights in the port. Their chronic antagonists were cut-rate competitors, the *robeirols*, dock-hands who were not members of the fraternity. We find a trace of this time-worn conflict in the cahiers de doléances, where the dock workers requested the formal prohibition of work by the robeirols, whom they considered foreigners and unworthy of the merchants' trust.[15]

The dockworkers of Marseille formed a well-described group, relatively settled, with solid family structures and were, therefore, dissimilar to their Parisian brethren. Other associations of unskilled workers can be found in Paris through the records generated by the defense of their prerogatives. The case of the domestics and their uprising in August 1789, when the Revolution was already under way, is typical. Hit by unemployment caused by the first wave of aristocratic emigration, the abandoned servants had nothing better to do than demand the expulsion of the Savoyards and other foreigners responsible for stealing work from Parisians.[16] Such corporate tactics, taken up by unskilled workers, testified to the strength and influence of certain reference models and the ability of the corporate world to dominate and condition the working environment outside of its own confines. An ideological homogeneity between skilled and unskilled, which was greater than the objective distance separating them, had emerged.

This conclusion, together with the comments preceding it, are no more than hypotheses in a complex and still poorly explored area of study, an area which—as I hope to have succeeded in demonstrating—is no less essential for an understanding of eighteenth-century Paris.

15. Fournier, *Cahiers de doléances*.
16. *Les Révolutions de Paris*, August 28, 1789.

Susan C. Karant-Nunn

4   From Adventurers to Drones:
     The Saxon Silver Miners
     as an Early Proletariat

The concepts of Marxism have long been part of bourgeois everyday conversation. Perhaps ironically, then, my topic, the Saxon silver miners as an early proletariat, is one that until recently has been addressed chiefly by Marxist historians in the former German Democratic Republic. To the question, whether in fact the fifteenth-, sixteenth-, and seventeenth-century miners of Saxony actually did constitute an early proletariat, we might expect their answer to have been categorically affirmative. The truth is, however, that their views have varied. The position of the silver miners in early modern society and economy has been a besetting and befuddling problem.[1] In the nineteenth century Karl Kautsky regarded the miners as proletarians even though during the great German peasants' uprising in 1525 the miners and peasants did not close ranks.[2] In the mid-twen-

1. See Karl-Heinz Ludwig's critical review of Marxist historiography, "Bergleute im Bauernkrieg," *Zeitschrift für historische Forschung* 5 (1978), 24–47. More recently George Waring has examined the literature in "The Silver Miners of the Erzgebirge and the Peasants' War of 1525 in the Light of Recent Research," *Sixteenth Century Journal* 18 (1987), 231–47; and I have done likewise in "Between Two Worlds: The Social Position of the Silver Miners of the Erzgebirge, c. 1460–1575," *Social History* 14 (1989), 307–22.

2. Karl Kautsky, "Die Bergarbeiter und der Bauernkrieg," *Die neue Zeit* 7 (1889), pp. 289–97, 337–50, 410–17, 443–503, 507–15. See also Kautsky's numerous refer-

tieth century, after the founding of the German Democratic Republic, Johann Köhler, lacing his commentary with the requisite citations of Lenin and even Stalin, labeled the miners as proletarians as early as the fifteenth century.[3] More circumspect scholars—those more familiar with the archival sources, however ardent their political commitment—could not go beyond calling the miners a "preproletariat" (Vorproletariat) as of 1525. To this group belong Ingrid Mittenzwei, Horst Carlowitz, and Adolf Laube.[4] Particularly Mittenzwei and Laube have explored with sensitivity the differences between most peasants' and most miners' interests at the time of the peasant revolt.

For our purposes here, I want to disregard these historians' possibly ideologically influenced conclusions and sift through the evidence afresh. In doing so I shall look not just at the miners' unrest coinciding with the Peasants' War but also at their broader circumstances, over a longer period of time. I shall take up not only their physical and fiscal condition but also the evolution of a miners' mentality. Marxist colleagues would surely agree that class identity is as important to genuine proletarians as the objective terms of their employment. The historical situation was more complex than we have usually been led to think. A proletarian mode of work tended to precede the evolution of a shared self-image among the miners.

The Erzgebirge is a hilly region in the southern part of eastern Germany that extends over into the Czech Republic. During the Middle Ages, miners on either side of the border with Bohemia were German, and they came and went freely, as working conditions and the presence of silver, a little gold, and other less valuable minerals like copper and tin fluctuated. Freiberg in the eastern Erzgebirge

ences to miners in Communism in Central Europe in the Time of the Reformation, trans. J. L. Mullikan and E. G. Mullikan (New York, 1959), passim.

3. Johann Köhler, Die Keime des Kapitalismus im sächsischen Silberbergbau (1168 bis um 1500). Freiberger Forschungshefte D13 (Berlin, 1955).

4. Ingrid Mittenzwei, Der Joachimsthaler Aufstand 1525, seine Ursachen und Folgen (Berlin, 1968), for example, p. 5; Horst Carlowitz, "Die revolutionäre Bewegung der Bergleute in den Silberstädten Annaberg, Marienberg und Geyer während des Bauernaufstandes 1525," Sächsische Heimatblätter 16 (1970), 15–21; Adolf Laube, "Zum Problem des Bündnisses von Bergarbeitern und Bauern im deutschen Bauernkrieg," in Der Bauer im Klassenkampf, ed. Gerhard Heitz, Adolf Laube, Max Steinmetz, and Günter Vogler (Berlin, 1975), p. 87. Cf. Siegfried Sieber, "Die Teilnahme erzgebirgischer Bergleute am Bauernkrieg 1525," in Bergbau und Bergleute, Freiberger Forschungshefte D11 (Berlin, 1955), pp. 83–106. Essential on the general topic of Saxon silver mining is Laube's Studien über den erzgebirgischen Silberbergbau von 1470 bis 1546 (Berlin, 1974).

was the only silver-mining center of midmedieval foundation, arising out of a boomtown (Sächsstadt) in 1186. As minerals near the surface quickly became exhausted, mining operations declined. The technological means of aerating and draining water out of deep tunnels were as yet unknown. During the fifteenth century, the essential mechanisms for pumping air into the shafts and water out were gradually developed.[5] A money economy and the costly undertakings of expansive states now increased the incentive to find more of the shiny metals. From about 1450, a new silver rush was on. This time it permeated the entire Erzgebirge, producing in succession the founding of new cities as centers of mine administration and metal processing. Schneeberg received its charter in 1479, Annaberg in 1496, Buchholz in 1501, Joachimsthal (in Bohemia) in 1516, and Marienberg in 1521. Many smaller towns filled in the interstices, and all interrupted the stable repetitiveness of the peasant agriculture that had existed there since the Germans pushed out the Slavic Sorbs in the twelfth century.

In thinking about mining as labor and of its organization, we cannot dispense with this recapitulation of events. Labor is dynamic; it changes as the conditions change in which it is embedded. One of the shortcomings of existing scholarship on the silver miners is that it has tried to grasp them as they were at one particular moment, nearly always 1525 when the German Peasants' War erupted. In fact, up to perhaps 1550, the miners' circumstances were continually changing, though not consistently at the same rate. Even in 1525, as I have shown elsewhere, their situation was by no means uniform throughout the Erzgebirge. For the first century, from about 1450 to 1550, the conditions of work and the structure of organization varied both in time and from place to place.[6]

With that fundamental qualification in mind, we can proceed to summarize the evolution that occurred in every locale that proved to be a good source of silver. In the silver-rush phase, men and some women, of diverse backgrounds and statuses, hurried into this comparatively wild part of Germany in the hope of becoming rich. No generalization can capture the social or cultural essence of these

5. K. Schwarz describes the changes in mining technology during the late Middle Ages in *Untersuchung zur Geschichte der deutschen Bergleute im späteren Mittelalter*, Freiberger Forschungshefte D20 (Berlin, 1958), pp. 15–17.
6. Karant-Nunn, "Between Two Worlds," passim.

throngs. This was equally true in the California gold rush. In Saxony in the fifteenth century, with Germany's population expanding rapidly by all accounts, many people no longer felt constrained to stay where they were. Artisans, laborers, shopkeepers, peasants, and their families hurried away and thrust their picks and shovels into the topsoil whether or not it was planted with grain; neither peasants nor any other occupants of the surface had the right to prevent digging on their lands. Life was initially precarious because neither markets, housing, nor handicrafts existed to sustain life. The hopeful adventurers huddled under trees and in caves and bought or stole food from the peasants. These rushes were repeated whenever a major new vein of silver appeared, the last time being in the vicinity of Marienberg just before the Peasants' War.

The local peasants themselves were in an enviable position from the perspective that they could temporarily maintain an "amphibious" existence. They could hunt for precious metals, but if they failed to find any—as was usually the case—they could walk home to enjoy food and shelter. This became a bone of contention between peasants and full-time hewers, and the hewers occasionally tried to exclude peasants from the mines. But whether of peasant or other provenance, all ran the risk of impoverishment if not starvation. The footloose subsisters gave rise to the image of the volatile, uninhibited, amoral hewer that settled folk needed to beware of. James Bryce, the historian of the Holy Roman Empire, sized up the situation after traveling in the California mining fields in the mid-nineteenth century. He called mining "an industry which is like gambling in its influence on the character, with its sudden alternations of wealth and poverty, its long hours of painful toil relieved by bouts of drinking and merriment, its life in a crowd of men who have come together from the four winds of heaven, and will scatter again as soon as some are enriched and others ruined, or the gold in the gulch is exhausted." The miners at this stage were individualists and opportunists. They were untrammeled by the conventions of stationary society. They daily confronted the notorious dangers—the gas, the cave-ins, the floods—of the pits.[7]

By way of recompense for these risks, authorities acknowledged

7. On conflict between hewers and peasants, see Hermann Löscher, "Die erzgebirgischen Knappschaften vor und nach der Reformation," *Blätter für deutsche Landesgeschichte* 92 (1956), 184; James Bryce, *The American Commonwealth* (London, 1889), vol. 2, p. 372.

the miners' right—they could not stop them in any case—to move around (*Freizügigkeit*), to bear arms, to avoid much taxation, to form a hewers' brotherhood (*Knappschaft*), to meet, and to administer their own relief fund.[8] This was possibly the advantageous side of the miner's vocation in the early and prospecting phase. Peasants who stuck to their agrarian activities and adhered to their traditional feudal dependency are alleged to have envied the miners their liberties.

The apparent copiousness of the gleaming mineral in the Erzgebirge and the princes' incipient efforts at the expensive enterprise that we call state-building contributed both to the steady curtailment of miners' freedoms and to the imposition of order from above. The rulers were deeply interested in the output of the mines, and they saw in discipline an antidote to the miners' fractiousness, and a guarantee of steady, sizable augmentation of their treasuries. Both branches of the Wettin family, the Albertines and the Ernestines,[9] shared equally the ducal tenth of the mines' yield, and they cooperated in drafting mining ordinances for each area.[10] These constituted the basic law setting the terms of extraction. Each successive generation of princes either modified or reconfirmed these ordinances. In them, wages, working hours, duties of each level of a more closely defined mining bureaucracy, procedures, prohibitions, and punishments for infractions were set down. These ordinances, their detailed content, and, more to the point, their *effect* represent a milestone in the transformation of silver miners from freewheeling, more or less self-employed small entrepreneurs to employees of the rulers. In theory, and indeed in practice, the hewers and their helpers were not working in the pay of the duke and the elector, but the realistic consequence of the formulation and enforcement of

8. Before the beginning of the sixteenth century, the smelters broke away from the comprehensive brotherhood and formed their own fraternity, its German name, *Rosenkranz* (rosary), bespeaking the religious component of its existence. In general, the smelters, whose skills were more specialized, had a higher status in mining society than the hewers.

9. After the land division of 1485 between the brothers Albrecht and Ernst. The Ernestines held the electoral honor until 1547, when it was seized by the Albertine duke Moritz, and the title and the electoral district were formally conferred upon him by Emperor Charles V in 1548.

10. See, for instance, Dresden Staatsarchiv (hereafter DSA), loc. 4494, "Annabergische Bergordnungen . . . 1499–1539."

these ordinances at the end of the fifteenth century was that the miners became princely employees—or very nearly so.

At least until the middle of the sixteenth century, every stage of the mines' evolution could be found somewhere in the Erzgebirge; as long as there was the possibility of finding new veins of ore, prospecting was encouraged. But as soon as it became evident that little new metal-bearing rock was likely to be uncovered, the administrative emphasis was entirely upon strict oversight and consistent practice. The prince headed the state bureaucracy, of which the miners had become, in their niches and crevasses, small cogs.

Another element fostering the advance of miners' subjection to those above them was the necessity of financing deep mining. Small investment corporations called *Gewerkschaften* were formed, made up of persons usually unacquainted with each other and residing in different, often far-removed, places. They took out shares (*Kuxe* or *Berganteile*), each shaft being divided into about 128 shares. Many people of modest means purchased fractions of shares. Hewers themselves could be members of Gewerkschaften, either where they were engaged in mining or elsewhere. Peasants who occupied the surface were ipso facto entitled to a $1/32$ share—if they were prepared to join in bearing the considerable expenses of mining. City councils, individual burghers, big speculators from Nuremberg and Augsburg, including the Fugger, and the princes bought shares. The city and the citizens of Leipzig were important investors.[11] As Laube notes, some individuals, like the wealthy Römers of Zwickau and the princes, owned many Kuxe in different places. Some peasants did manage to invest in the mines, and the Peasant Woman, a shaft near Annaberg, was one of the few returning a profit in 1531. We might recall that Martin Luther's father, Hans, although in Thuringian copper mining, had risen from landless peasant son to hewer to member of a Gewerkschaft to shaft lessor to city councilman in Mansfeld. It could be done. However, Paulus Niavis was correct when he wrote, "If one person gets rich, one hundred work in vain. They put gold and silver in and get stones and filth out . . . and if we observe the matter rightly, people have put much more money into

11. Theodor Gustav Werner, "Das fremde Kapital im Annaberger Bergbau und Metallhandel des 16. Jahrhundert," *Neues Archiv für sächsische Geschichte und Altertumskunde*, part 1, 57 (1936), 113–79; part 2, 58 (1937), 1–47; part 3, 58 (1937), 136–201; Ernst Kröker, "Leipzig und die sächsischen Bergwerke," *Schriften des Vereins für die Geschichte Leipzigs* 9 (1909), 25–77.

that Schneeberg and the hills around than they have taken out in profit."[12]

Far more investors of every station lost money than made any. Most vulnerable were those with little or no excess capital out of which to pay the wages of hewers, shaft managers (*Steiger*), and overseers (*Schichtmeister*) and to buy all the requisite equipment and supplies.[13] Picks and shovels would no longer suffice. By the early sixteenth century, the majority of miners were not either entrepreneurs or investors, but were wage-earners. They had reached what I shall call the second phase in the evolution of their profession. It is just at this point that Laube, Carlowitz, Siegfried Sieber, and Mittenzwei detect the emergence of their "early proletariat," and it is in this transitional setting that the Peasants' War burst forth.[14]

What were the miners' working conditions? The work day was divided into three seven- or eight-hour shifts. In cities and towns a church bell pealed one hour before the start of the next shift, which, if audible, also signaled the end of the current one. Shaft entryways were distributed all across the landscape, and the hewers often boarded with peasants, or occupied rural smithies or the equipment huts that stood at each point of entry. The galleries had been braced with timber; as they were extended, carpenters went down and added new beams. Very few shafts employed more than ten hewers; the majority had from one to six. Of those few shafts actually yielding silver, most had from six to thirteen workers. Hewers brought along their own *Arschleder* ("arse leathers," garments for protecting their backs from the low, rough ceilings underground, which alone speaks eloquently of their cramped work environment); they donned the traditional miner's pointed hat, which can be seen in many of the illustrations of Georgius Agricola's *De Re Metallica*. They picked up their "metal," the implements of their trade, their "frog

12. On the Annaberg shaft, see DSA loc. 4506, "Bergwercks sachen zu Sangerhaussen, Freyberg, Annaberg, Schneeberg, Geyer, Glasshütte, Hockendorff, Altenberg . . . 1530–1," fol. 165; on Luther's father, see Hanns Freydank, "Martin Luther und der Bergbau," *Zeitschrift für das Berg-, Hütten-, und Salinenwesen im Preussischen Staate* 81 (1933), B311–19; the quotation is from *Judicium Jovis oder Das Gericht der Götter über den Bergbau*, trans. and ed. P. Krenkel, Freiberger Forschungshefte D3 (Berlin, 1953), pp. 39–40.

13. Laube, *Studien*, gives a concise summary of the types of officials and their duties, pp. 54–59.

14. See n. 4 above.

lamps" and the tallow to burn in them, and descended by ladder and sloping gangway to their tasks.[15]

Lesser-paid workers, called generically *Knechte*, hauled the broken rock up and out in carts, assisted occasionally by dog teams. Knechte performed much other miscellaneous work in and around the mines. Before the ore could be smelted, male and female washers cleaned it in half-barrel tubs, and pounders of both sexes broke it into smeltable chunks, discarding any plain rock that they could.[16]

It is hard to say how many workers were in each mining field. Laube sums up the primary and secondary literature, and his figures reveal considerable seasonal fluctuation. In Annaberg in 1514, there were a maximum of about 3,400; in Joachimsthal in 1524 about 4,000; in Marienberg during 1538–39, between 1,750 and 3,350. In the small centers there were fewer.[17] These numbers represent not just hewers but paid workers of every type, including unskilled and occasional labor.

The overseer, who might have two or three shafts in his charge, paid out wages to all workers on Saturday at midday.[18] If a shaft was yielding no ore, hewers might have to go for four weeks or even longer without pay, or receive lower remuneration than that set in the ordinances. The various *Bergordnungen* prescribed from nine *Groschen* per week in Annaberg to ten and one-half Groschen a week

15. See the tables for Annaberg in Laube, *Studien*, pp. 112–14; and for Joachimsthal in Mittenzwei, *Der Joachimsthaler Aufstand*, p. 17. *Georgii Agricolae De Re Metallica Libri XII. . . .* (Basel, 1556). The modern reader should consult instead *De re metallica libri XII*, trans. and ed. Georg Franstadt and Hans Prescher (Berlin, 1974), or *De Re Metallica*, trans. and ed. Herbert Clark Hoover and Lou Henry Hoover, first published by *Mining Magazine* (London, 1912) and reprinted by Dover Publications (New York, 1950). There is a photograph of a frog lamp in Friedmar Brendel, "Über das alte bergmännische Geleucht," Freiberger Forschungshefte D11 (Berlin, 1955), p. 129.

16. On women at the mines, see my "The Women of the Saxon Silver Mines," *Women in Reformation and Counter-Reformation Europe: Private and Public Worlds*, ed. Sherrin Marshall (Bloomington, 1989), pp. 29–46. Early twentieth-century photographs of boys and men pounding ore in the same old way in Freiberg are in *Reymann: Fotodokumentaristen der Bergstadt Freiberg 1865–1945*, ed. Günther Galinsky (Leipzig, 1985), pp. 70–71. Many thanks to Michael Oertel for bringing this to my attention.

17. Laube, *Studien*, p. 115.

18. Occasionally workers were paid on Friday. Many Schichtmeisters' pay rosters dating from the later sixteenth century are preserved in the Freiberg Bergarchiv (hereafter FBA), a branch of the DSA. The princes insisted that detailed records be kept, specifically requiring the use of first and last names.

in Schneeberg, a discrepancy that annoyed the laborers.[19] Why such a difference should have arisen is unclear. In 1520 delegates of the Bohemian Schlick earls met with advisers of Duke George the Bearded and Elector Frederick the Wise and agreed not to raise miners' wages so that the workers could no longer put pressure on their lords by moving from one site to another.[20] The miners' right to move freely had become a thorn in the princely side. In the end, however, depleted minerals were decisive as to whether miners stayed and mined, stayed and changed their means of earning a living, or went elsewhere, such as to the Harz region.[21]

As the hewers increasingly worked only for their pay and as (from about 1525) prices rose throughout Germany, laborers tried to make ends meet by working double shifts and by taking on special assignments (*Gedinge*) for a sum agreed on in advance. The princes outlawed double shifts on the grounds that sixteen hours of arduous exertion was more than one man could well continue, and men were likely to sleep on the job. Gedinge were tolerated. The mining ordinances always left the shaft overseers, and certainly the higher officials, some leeway in permitting overtime or raising wages, if conditions truly warranted extraordinary measures.[22] The overriding consideration was to harvest the silver.

The miners' source of cohesion was the Knappschaft, a brotherhood that sprang into being as each new mining site opened. The oldest Knappschaft was that of Freiberg, which was originally a religious confraternity.[23] It retained some religious, welfare, and philan-

19. For wages in Joachimsthal, see Mittenzwei, *Der Joachimsthaler Aufstand*, pp. 65–66.

20. Weimar Staatsarchiv (hereafter WSA) reg. T 1556. They never could physically prevent them from moving, of course.

21. Max Möckel, "Berbauliche Zusammenhänge von Oberharz und Erzgebirge," *Sächsische Heimatblätter* 12 (1966), 72–83, esp. 74, 77.

22. WSA reg. T 1, fol. 87, part of mining ordinances for Schneeberg, 1500; DSA loc. 4494, "Annabergische Bergordnungen . . . 1499–1539," fol. 9, which leaves open the small possibility of double shifts and higher wages under extenuating circumstances. But it outlaws *Gedinge* (fol. 10).

23. "Bergamtsrat" Wappler, "Über die alte Freiberger Berg-, Knapp- und Brüderschaft," *Mitteilungen vom Freiberger Altertumsverein* 37 (1900), 48–71. Originally all full-fledged mine workers were members of the Knappschaft, but in the late fifteenth century, the smelters founded their own "rosary" societies (*Rosenkranzbrüderschaften*). Bernhard Wolf states that the Dominican Jakob Sprenger, of *Hammer of Witches* fame, founded the first Rosenkranz brotherhood in Cologne in 1475 ("Aus dem kirchlichen Leben Annabergs in vorreformatorischer Zeit," *Mitteilungen des Vereins für die Ges-*

thropic characteristics when it was reformed in 1537 by fiat of Duke Heinrich, George the Bearded's younger brother and heir. Until then the Freiberg fraternity had numerous women members ("old sisters")—a peak of eighty-seven in 1522—and did not exclude hewers if they were too poor to pay their dues.[24]

In the western Erzgebirge these brotherhoods reflected circumstances prevailing at their inception. They may have taken their basic form from Freiberg, but they quickly came to represent the local mining collectivity. They tried to rectify the corruption and neglect that funneled silver and advantage into illegitimate hands and that did not insist on adequate safety in the galleries. Miners' lists of grievances, delivered through the Knappschaften, ever reflected susceptibility and anger in the face of abuse. At the time of the Peasants' War, the miners' demands did not at all resemble those Twelve Articles of Memmingen that became a veritable symbol of the restive peasantry. The Joachimsthal rebels of May 1525 set out their dissatisfaction in seventeen articles.[25] Some of these complaints sound as though they came from members of mining corporations, but it should be remembered that Joachimsthal had got underway only in 1516, and at this stage some miners were investors.

The earls of Schlick had promised the hewers the traditional freedom of the mines (*Bergfreiheit*) and many other (*mannigfältige*) things that were not subsequently carried out. The hewers took exception to silver being exported for minting and demanded that the minting be done there. Another denomination, the *Guldengroschen*, being minted there was improperly taken away, and the miners declared that this was disadvantageous to their pay. Presumably they were being forced to take Bohemian pennies, which were unacceptable in the neighboring Saxon marketplaces. The men of the Joachimsthaler mines wanted to choose their own tithe master (*Zehntner*) to

chichte von Annaberg und Umgegend 11 [1910], 85). Consult also Hermann Löscher, "Die Anfänge der erzgebirgischen Knappschaft," *Zeitschrift der Savigny-Stiftung für Rechtsgeschichte*, Kanonistische Abteilung, 71 (1954), 223–38.

24. FBA, "Brüderregister I, 1519–1545," no call number, no pagination. The contents of this and the subsequent volume are discussed in Johannes Langer, "Die Freiberger Bergknappschaft," *Mitteilungen des Freiberger Altertumsvereins* 61 (1931), 18–92, esp. the chart on 20; and 62 (1932), 68–88 for later periods.

25. Walther Peter Fuchs, *Akten zur Geschichte des Bauernkrieges in Mitteldeutschland*, vol. 2 (Jena, 1942), doc. 1591, pp. 388–91; Johann Karl Seidemann, "Die Unruhen im Erzgebirge während des deutschen Bauernkrieges," *Abhandlungen der historischen Klasse der königlichen Bayerischen Akademie der Wissenschaften* 10 (1867), 173–76.

assist and check up on *Graf* Schlick's official. These and other articles concern suspected dishonesty among the officers and the miners' desire to participate in mine administration. The only request that resembles one of the peasants' is that they be given the prerogative of hiring and firing their own pastor and preacher, "inasmuch as [they] are supported from the community chest" into which all residents paid their alms.[26] The miners too had heard of Luther's tract of 1523. Nonetheless, the Schneeberg miners' grievances of April 1525 had only to do with mining.[27]

In Saxony the hewers' brotherhoods won no concessions to speak of. They continued to exist, even into the nineteenth century, as a vestige of the past and as the focus of members' social life. One by one, in the aftermath of the peasant unrest, their privileges were taken away or severely restricted: their right to administer their own funds for sick and injured brothers; to meet without permission or supervision; to choose a preacher for their own chapel. In 1537 Duke Heinrich in effect dissolved the venerable Freiberg Knappschaft, eliminating the women and all impecunious members. He made its reincarnation an elite and ceremonial society, to which Elector Johann Friedrich and Dukes Moritz and August were admitted in 1542.[28] In 1539, by contrast, Heinrich granted the Marienberg Knappschaft's request for an official seal. He also allowed them to administer their own fund for the relief of ill members. He did this "in the furtherance of mining."[29] But he made sure that his officials supervised all that was done. He was careful not to compromise the control that he sought over all his subjects.

Were the miners turning into an early proletariat by Heinrich's death in 1541? By then most miners identified themselves as part of

26. Fuchs, *Akten*, pp. 388, 389; the quoted material is from ibid., article 12, p. 390.
27. *D. Martin Luthers Werke* (Weimar, 1883–), vol. 11, pp. 401–16: "Dass eine christliche Versammlung oder Gemeine Recht und Macht habe, alle Lehre zu urteilen und Lehrer zu berufen, ein- und . . . abzusetzen, Grund und Ursach aus der Schrift"; on the miners' grievances, see WSA reg. T 91, fols. 5–32; DSA loc. 4490, fols. 67–70.
28. FBA, "Brüderregister I, 1519–1545," no pagination, but under entries for 1542.
29. DSA loc. 4504, fols. 28, 46–47. Both Heinrich and Moritz let the Annaberg *Knappschaft* retain *jus patronatus* in their own chapel (Annaberg Stadtarchiv [hereafter ASA], "Die hiesige Bergkapelle," II 20H). This was now practically an empty privilege, as it increasingly was for noble and other patrons, inasmuch as all clerical candidates were examined and supervised after the Reformation by their district superintendent and by the parish visitors. The Schneeberg *Knappschaft* lost its corresponding right.

a profession that was surviving despite the decline in silver.[30] They were now less often former craftsmen, former monks, or present or former peasants; both they and members of those other groups felt miners to be a distinct category. Peasants and miners were estranged, and only those hewers who resided in towns were really integrated into the urban collectivity.[31] They labored for others, even if overwhelmingly in small groups; they used the implements provided by the Gewerkschaften, though as a cost-cutting measure the hewers increasingly had to bring their own lamp tallow. They were skilled wage laborers with no access to the finished product, minted coin, except in their modest pay. Their frustration resulted from their inability to control crucial aspects of their work and of their affairs. As the aggrandizing state tried to reduce all subjects to the same manageable level in the sixteenth century, no segment of society was exempt from interference. The Schneeberg Knappschaft lost its house during the first parish visitation in 1534, and the miners were compelled to put their weekly pennies for the relief of ill brothers into the community chest. The smelters' brotherhood of Annaberg in 1543 objected strenuously to Moritz's outright confiscation of the house the membership had bought forty years earlier to accommodate sick and injured brothers. The smelters told him, to no avail, that they had paid for that building with their own "sour sweat and blood" and desired to pass it on to the next generation.[32]

In some respects, then, mine workers do resemble an early proletariat. They increasingly had nothing but their wages and were exploited to the full by those above them. Their efforts at collective representation of their interests met defeat at nearly every turn. Their social ties to other established groups, such as the peasantry and the satisfactorily off burghers, were weak. But there is nothing inherently progressive or unique, or anything really new in this con-

30. See Laube, *Studien*, pp. 268–69 for a table of silver production from 1470 to 1546.
31. Karant-Nunn, "Between Two Worlds," pp. 316–19; cf. Wieland Held, "Soziale Herkunft und Situation der Mansfelder Bergleute in der ersten Hälfte des 16. Jahrhunderts," *Jahrbuch für Wirtschaftsgeschichte* 4 (1982), 115–27; and Karl-Heinz Ludwig, "Neue Quellen zur Bevölkerungsentwicklung in der ersten Hälfte des 16. Jahrhunderts, die Salzburger Mannschaft von 1531 und 1541," *Mitteilungen der Gesellschaft für Salzburger Landeskunde* 117 (1977), 201–15.
32. On the community chest, see WSA reg. Ii 7, fols. 419, 420, 422. DSA loc. 9827, "Die Stadt Annaberg und besonders deren Privilegia belangende de anno 1529–1710," vol. 2, fols. 189–90, 196–97.

figuration. Indeed, the miners very much looked either backward or outward to their contemporaries in their aspirations. They came to model their craft on the guild structure in evidence all around them.[33] The Knappschaft was responsible for ensuring quality of work and the moral behavior of the brothers. Men coming from elsewhere were to present a letter testifying to their legitimate birth and upright character. Upon admission, the members had to obey the elected leaders. Before the Reformation the entire Knappschaft convened on the morning of Corpus Christi Day in June and ate a common meal (*Frühsuppe*). It then heard allegations of dishonorable behavior that ranged from the personal (adultery or having sex with virgins) to the professional (stealing ore). If found guilty, the culprit was banned from the fellowship until he had made satisfaction.

The Knappschaft also provided for the training of new hewers through apprenticeship. These *Lehrhäuer* were often very young, even nine years old. Juvenile mine workers have long been the objects of Marxist and bourgeois sympathy, especially of scholars writing from the socialist perspective who have noted disparagingly that capitalists did not shrink back "even" from exploiting women and children.[34] These accusations fail to take note of the fact that medieval guilds absolutely depended upon the work of masters' wives, and that sons were put out to apprenticeship at about nine. Indeed, children of both sexes, even if not apprenticed, regularly went out to serve in other people's households. Elector Moritz specified in 1543 that people renting rooms from others could not keep with them children above the age of nine but had to send them out to work or the parents would be punished.[35] This was neither cruel nor unusual. Child labor and female labor were typical and indispensable in the crafts, not to mention the entire agrarian world, throughout the Middle Ages.

As soon as apprentice hewers learned the basic processes of digging out the ore, they could expect promotion to regular hewer sta-

---

33. Simon Bogner's redaction of the Freiberg mining customs is particularly revealing of guild similarities at midcentury, and the word *Zunft* even appears in them (Hermann Löscher, *Das erzgebirgische Bergrecht des 15. und 16. Jahrhunderts*, part 1 [no more appeared], *Die erzgebirgischen Berggebräuche des 16. Jahrhunderts und ihre Vorläufer seit etwa 1450* [Berlin, n.d. but approx. 1957], pp. 141–210, use of *Zunft*, p. 186).

34. For example, Mittenzwei, *Der Joachimsthaler Aufstand*, pp. 72–73.

35. ASA, "Ordennung der Handtwergk wie sich ein itzlichss haldten soll," 1543, no pagination.

tus and a correspondingly higher wage. There was no journeyman level in mining. Mining was palpably a dangerous activity, and though statistics are lacking, a high death rate very likely opened up positions regularly. It is well known that both Paracelsus and Agricola saw much "miners' sickness."[36] Many widows with young children lived in the chief mining towns, which placed a heavy burden on public assistance.[37]

The miners, then, had links to the past as well as the future. They worked in small groups rather than gangs, but there were lots of them. They resembled other late medieval workers, such as journeymen, mercenary soldiers, and day laborers, who earned their pay for an agreed-upon task and often had to fend for themselves in off seasons.[38] If the miners were in any sense proletarians, then so, perhaps, were these; and if we concede this, our definition of proletarian may become exceedingly diffuse and lead us ever farther back into the Middle Ages. Modes of production are hardly discrete, nor are the periods in which they have been said to prevail.

The second phase, of mixed type, shades almost imperceptibly into the third, that of professional miners with a clear if humble identity, far fewer in number than at the turn of the century, rigorously overseen by bureaucratic representatives of the aggressively state-building Albertine electors.[39] They still rented beds from peasants and burghers alike. If they lived in the towns, it was largely in the suburbs and the poorer quarters.[40] No more major deposits of silver were to be found, and prospecting was generally fruitless.

36. Joachim Vetter, *Die soziale und hygienische Lage der bergbauenden Bevölkerung des Erzgebirges in der ersten Hälfte des 16. Jahrhunderts*. Schriften für Heimatforschung, vol. 4 (Berlin, 1950), pp. 40–41.

37. DSA loc. 10600, "Supplication Bericht vnnd Missiven an die herrn Visitator [sic] auss den Gebürgischen Embtern . . . 1557," for Buchholz in 1555, reports only 350 hearths (in another place, 400) including 107 poor widows, most with young children, who had to be supported (fols. 68, 69, 73). In Geyer in 1533, there were 241 hearths, in 45 of which lived poor widows (Johannes Falke, *Geschichte der Bergstadt Geyer* [Dresden, 1866], p. 53).

38. On Saxon journeymen, Hellmut Bräuer, *Gesellen im sächsischen Zunfthandwerk des 15. und 16. Jahrhunderts* (Weimar, 1989). There is an amusing analysis of sixteenth-century depictions of the mercenary soldier (*Landsknecht*) in Keith Moxey, *Peasants, Warriors, and Wives: Popular Imagery in the Reformation* (Chicago, 1989), pp. 67–100.

39. The Ernestine branch of the Wettin family was defeated in the 1547 War of the League of Schmalkald and excluded from the silver-mining regions.

40. Ulrich Thiel, "Untersuchungen zu den wirtschaftlichen und sozialen Verhältnissen Freibergs um die Mitte des 16. Jahrhunderts und die Freiberger Volksbewegung vom April 1547" (Master's [*Diplom*] thesis, Humboldt University, Berlin, June 1981), pp. 21–22.

Many women who stayed in the towns turned to making bobbin lace; men turned to the cottage-industry manufacture of braids and trims.[41] Nevertheless, a number of men stayed with mining.[42] Women were now completely excluded except as occasional ore pounders and day laborers.[43]

The numbers of hewers per shaft continued to be few, but their self-definition was clearly that of miner. They now took pride in what they regarded as their craft. One way they showed this was by dressing up once a year—before the Reformation on Corpus Christi Day, the second Thursday after Pentecost; after 1537 on Pentecost itself—in festive mining garb, taking up their tools, the symbols of their livelihood, and marching in the annual procession of city fathers and craftsmen. In Freiberg, and probably in the other silver cities, the Knappschaft had pride of place, marching before the other craft guilds.[44] The *Bergmeister* went first, then other officers, then the eight elected candlebearers, then the rank-and-file hewers.[45] The future electors Moritz and August are said to have possessed the Knappschaft retinue in miniature when they were boys.[46]

Miners' chances of social mobility and political participation were now limited, and their vulnerability to lung diseases and accidents was as great as before. Their discontent over inadequate pay, administrative corruption, and dangerous neglect of the shafts and implements occasionally flickered into a work stoppage, but full-scale revolt was a thing of the past. This was in part because the electors of Saxony, like their princely contemporaries elsewhere, were perfecting and strengthening their methods of control.[47] It was also because

41. Herbert Zimmerman, "Die Posamenten im Erzgebirge," *Vom silbernen Erzgebirge*, vol. 2, ed. Friedrich Köhler (Schwarzenberg, 1939), pp. 68–77; also Christian Meltzer's description of the many intricate lace patterns in *Historia Schneebergensis* . . . (Schneeberg, 1716), p. 883.

42. To a limited extent, silver mining continued until the 1960s, though not without interruption as European silver prices declined.

43. Karant-Nunn, "Women of the Saxon Silver Mines," 37, based on *Schichtmeisters'* pay records in FBA.

44. Freiberg Stadtarchiv (hereafter FSA), "Hant Buch im 1500 Jare," insert between fols. 73–74.

45. Not even the Hoovers were able to come up with an apt translation of *Bergmeister*. The *Bergmeister* governed the production of silver, including the approval of mining claims. See Laube, *Studien*, pp. 55–56.

46. Heinrich Gerlach, "Kleine Chronik von Freiberg," *Mittheilungen von dem Freiberger Altertumsverein* 12 (1875), 95.

47. There is a growing literature on the religious and cultural aspects of the princely imposition of control. Fundamental to any discussion of confessionalization

the era of impassioned adventurism was past. Those who remained were willing to make do with a modest scale of life and the camaraderie of their peers. They were neither as ambitious nor as transfixed by fantasy as their predecessors.

As the transition from the second to the third phase got underway, what was lacking among the hewers was a strong and consistent sense of their common identity, a new self-definition, though it existed at an embryonic stage. The Reformation proved to be a significant aid in forging a miners' mentality from what were originally disparate ingredients. Word of Martin Luther's insubordination filtered into an Erzgebirge that was as anticlerical as any other part of Germany.[48] The rousing sentiments of Luther and others created unrest and disorientation. Rebel voices articulated various messages, in addition to those of Luther and his scrupulously loyal followers such as Johannes Bugenhagen, Nicolaus Hausmann, and Friedrich Myconius.[49] The teachings, even if not the person, of Andreas Bodenstein von Karlstadt appeared. The Erasmian, Johannes Sylvius Egranus, preached there intermittently. Thomas Müntzer is alleged to have had a following, but Siegfried Hoyer (who has tried harder than I) cannot verify that Müntzer was ever there.[50]

---

are Gerhard Oestreich, *Geist und Gestalt des frühmodernen Staates* (Berlin, 1969), esp. pp. 179–97, translated as *Neostoicism and the Early Modern State* (Cambridge, 1982); Heinz Schilling, "Die Konfessionalisierung im Reich. Religiöser und gesellschaftlicher Wandel in Deutschland zwischen 1555 und 1620," *Historische Zeitschrift* 246 (1988), 1–45; idem, "Between the Territorial State and Urban Liberty: Lutheranism and Calvinism in the County of Lippe," in *The German People and the Reformation*, ed. R. Po-chia Hsia (Ithaca, N.Y., 1988), pp. 263–83; Wolfgang Reinhard, "Zwang zur Konfessionalisierung? Prolegomena zu einer Theorie des konfessionellen Zeitalters," *Zeitschrift für historische Forschung* 10 (1983), 257–77. A recent summary of the literature may be found in R. Po-chia Hsia, *Social Discipline in the Reformation: Central Europe 1550–1750* (New York, 1989), including the annotated bibliography at the back, pp. 188–212.

48. For insight into one major episode in Buchholz, see R. W. Scribner, "Reformation, Carnival and the World Turned Upside Down," in his collected essays, *Popular Culture and Popular Movements in Reformation Germany* (London, 1987), pp. 71–101, esp. pp. 74–75; originally published in *Social History* 3 (1978), 235–64.

49. Bugenhagen (1485–1558) spent most of his career as pastor in the Wittenberg city church, though he spent some time on leave in Braunschweig, Hamburg, Lübeck, and Denmark. Hausmann (1478–1538) preached in Schneeberg from 1419 to 1521 and then became pastor in Zwickau. He died in Freiberg in 1538. Myconius (1490–1546), also called Mecum, was a Franciscan in Annaberg who preached there, in Buchholz, Zwickau, and elsewhere before becoming pastor in Gotha, where he lived out his days.

50. On Egranus, see Heribert Sturm, *Skizzen zur Geschichte des Obererzgebirges im 16.*

Among the nonorthodox individuals were Hartmann Ibach in Buchholz, who lost his post in 1525 and later came to be seen as a Zwinglian; Wolfgang Ackermann in Schneeberg, a Catholic clergyman who preached against other members of the clergy and against the magistrates; and Georg Amandus, an outspoken and irrepressible Karlstadtian who preached in Schneeberg during 1524 and 1525 and was dismissed by Elector Johann.[51] Amandus was antigovernment, iconoclastic, and mystical. Later on, rumors of an Anabaptist presence circulated, but the parish visitors who hastened forth to investigate rarely found any.[52]

The conflict between Lutheran sympathizers, Johann and Johann Friedrich, and their ardent Catholic cousin, George the Bearded, is well known. Until George's death in 1539, their wounded relationship threatened periodically to draw them into war. George's brother, Heinrich, was persuaded by his wife, Katherine of Mecklen-

Jahrhundert (Stuttgart, 1965), pp. 31–37. Vaclav Husa, *Thomás Müntzer a Cechy* (Prague, 1957), pp. 52–54; personal communication from Siegfried Hoyer.

51. L. Bartsch, "Kirchliche und schulische Verhältnisse der Stadt Buchholz während der ersten Hälfte des 16. Jahrhunderts," *Beiträge zur Geschichte der Stadt Buchholz* 3 (1897), 25–72; 4 (1899), 73–216; on Ibach, 4 (1899), pp. 82 and 89–117. Ackermann's identity is never clear. Could he have been the "Herr Wolffgang," an evangelical preacher, whom, according to Christian Meltzer, the miners of Schneeberg maintained even before Hausmann arrived in 1519 (*Historia Schneebergensis . . .*, p. 296)? Felician Gess, *Akten und Briefe zur Kirchenpolitik Herzog Georgs von Sachsen*, vol. 1 (Leipzig, 1905), pp. 527–73, 580, 636. On Amandus, see Fellician Gess, "Die Anfänge der Reformation in Schneeberg," *Neues Archiv für sächsische Geschichte und Altertumskunde* 18 (1897), 37–49; Otto Clemen, "Georg Amandus," *Beiträge zur sächsischen Kirchengeschichte* 14 (1899), 221–23; WSA reg. Ii 131, fols. 1–31; WSA reg. N 35 and N 35a; WSA reg. T 90, fols. 28–33, 96–166; WSA reg. T 116, fols. 131–75.

52. See, however, WSA reg. N 1032, about Anabaptist journeyman Peter Pestel who said he had visited Joachimsthal and Schneeberg briefly during 1535–36; WSA reg. N 1033, concerning three others, Hans Stensdorf, Heinrich Tritzschel, and Hans Hamster. There is much evidence of Anabaptists in Thuringia from 1527. In a rather ideological piece, Helmut Bräuer says that from 1528 there were Anabaptists at work (*tätig*) in Annaberg, Buchholz, Freiberg, Plauen, Schneeberg, Wiesenthal, and Zwickau ("Das Erzgebirge und die Einführung der lutherischen Reformation," *Erzgebirge Jahrbuch* [1983], p. 37.). *Tätig* may be too strong a word. The visitors in Buchholz were told in 1529, "Secten oder yrthumb Im glauben yst uns nicht bewust Einicherley bey vns" (DSA loc. 10598, "Meysnische Visitation 1529 ff, 1531 ff," fol. 162). The first parish visitors in Schneeberg reported that the city was "von Sacramentirern vnd widerteuffern vnbeschmitzt befunden" (WSA reg. Ii 7, fol. 418). In ASA, "Die erste Kirchen Visitation alhier gehalten zu St. Annaberg Anno 1539," which also contains the results of the second (1540) visitation, the visitors said, "Der secten halben, sey es wol Im geruchte gewhesen, das Wider Teuffer seyn solten, Es hab sich auch nach fleysiger Erforschung nicht aber eyner sey vorhanden, des sacrament halben, befunden" (fol. 30).

burg, and by Johann Friedrich to accept Lutheranism. Heinrich was increasingly attracted to it during the 1530s and declared a policy of "religious toleration" in 1536. By the following year, toleration had turned to enforced Lutheranism.

It would be interesting to know whether in private conversations in Torgau and Freiberg, Johann Friedrich ever intimated to Heinrich that advantages accrued to princes in adopting Lutheranism, such as the consolidation of power over any of the previously exempted corporations ranging from the church to the knights. Whether or no, Heinrich made a start at exercising de facto headship over his territorial (Lutheran) church just as fully as Johann Friedrich did until his capture at Mühlberg in April 1547. After Heinrich's death in 1541, his sons, Moritz and August, continued in the same pattern: they turned their authority over religious institutions into a key component of administration, integrating ecclesiastics into the growing bureaucratic apparatus. Whatever spiritual motives or higher passions impelled them, the princes used the Reformation to expand their hegemony dramatically. Lutheranism was a magisterial creed, regardless of the fact that its dispersed territorial setting did not allow it to be so in the same way that Zwinglianism was in Zurich, or Calvinism in Geneva. Differences in geography rather than ideology dictated the structure of the new church. Princes, not urban magistrates, sat at the head of the earthly ecclesiastical echelons in Saxony. They made use of all the techniques employed by city fathers in other milieus, but in forms suited to a body of subjects spread out over the land. Moritz, August, and Christian I (r. 1586–1601) employed synods, visitations, consistories, and secular jurisdictions and personnel to attain their goals.[53]

Coercion was inadequate to the task of subordinating all corporations and persons to the state. Molding a popular mentality conducive to the same end was essential—all the while, I must reiterate,

53. See in the newer literature, on Moritz, Günther Wartenberg, *Landesherrschaft und Reformation: Moritz von Sachsen und die albertinische Kirchenpolitik bis 1546* (Weimar, 1988), idem, "Die Entstehung der sächsischen Landeskirche von 1539 bis 1559," in *Das Jahrhundert der Reformation in Sachsen,* ed. Helmar Junghans (Berlin, 1989), pp. 67–90; in the same volume, Michael Beyer, "Die Neuordnung des Kirchengutes," pp. 91–112, esp. 109–12; also there, Ernst Koch, "Ausbau, Gefährdung und Festigung der lutherischen Landeskirche von 1553 bis 1601," pp. 195–223. Still valuable is Thomas Klein, *Der Kampf um die zweite Reformation in Kursachsen 1586–1591* (Cologne, 1962).

fostering the genuine spirituality and neighborly Christian demeanor of all citizens. Whether authorities consciously, cynically set out to marshall the church and religion for statist purposes, they used these for their secular purposes. Four major tools of public indoctrination were the sermon, the catechism, the songbook, and the education of children.

Such means were adopted across the land. What have any of them to do in particular with helping to form the Saxon silver miners' emerging collective identity? I suggest that Wolff Meyerpeck, the Zwickau and then the Freiberg printer, and Johannes Mathesius, the charismatic Saxon preacher in Bohemian Joachimsthal, are representative of a type of man who was shaping popular mentality in all urban centers. In part these two directed their attention to miners and promoted the development of an essential psychosocial component of any proletariat.

Wolfgang Meyerpeck printed in Zwickau from about 1525 until his departure for Freiberg in 1550, from 1529 in his own establishment.[54] Zwickauers were deeply interested and involved in the mining to the south of them. Schneeberg, only twelve miles away, was originally a colony of Zwickau, the parent providing food and manufactured goods, as well as investment, until the child was equipped with its own market and guilds. Meyerpeck's shop thus brought out to an enthusiastic local audience, as well as to residents of Schneeberg, several pertinent items. In 1531 a booklet of supposed mining songs appeared under the title, *Some Pretty Mining Songs, Spiritual and Worldly Combined*.[55] In reality most of the lyrics betray a folk origin and are not miners' songs at all. The two major themes of the thirty-six songs in this first edition are love, including sex, and reli-

54. Helmut Claus, *Die Zwickauer Drucke des 16. Jahrhunderts*, part 2, *Wolfgang Meyerpeck 1530–1551* (Gotha, 1986), pp. 10–15. Meyerpeck's firm may have continued to print on a very modest scale after his departure. One publication in 1551 is certainly his. See also Reinhard Kade, "Geschichte des Freiberger Buchdrucks," *Mitteilungen des Freiberger Altertumsvereins* 30 (1893), 7–23.

55. *Etliche hübsche bergkreien geistlich vnd welt-lich zu samen gebracht. M. D. XXXI*, in Zwickau Ratsschulbibliothek, XXX. 5. 20/1. This anthology may have had a predecessor; see Gerhard Heilfurth, Erich Seemann, Hinrich Siuts, and Herbert Wolf, *Bergreihen. Eine Liedersammlung des 16. Jahrhunderts* (Tübingen, 1959), xiii. A new edition followed in 1533–34 under the title *Bergkreihen. Etliche Schöne Gesenge newlich zusamen gebracht/gemehret vnd gebessert. M. D. XXXiij*. In Helmut Claus, *Die Zwickauer Drucke*, part 2, items 192 (68–69) and 208 (77), respectively.

gion.[56] Most of the new songs are easily recognized, for they are candidly labeled "a pretty new song about. . . ." Rigid orthodoxy, including very straight and narrow moral standards, had not yet been formulated in 1531, or at any rate not stringently imposed; and some of the market for this small volume of verses lay in still-Catholic Albertine lands and ever-Catholic Bohemia. This helps to explain why the second piece, "Maria Lob," is a hymn of praise to the Virgin. The typical love song included here draws on familiar strains of courtly love—except that the part of the knight is played by a hewer who persuades a fair blond maiden with rose-red lips to sleep with him. In this variation on the alba, the next morning he bids her a fond adieu and moves on.[57]

In later sixteenth-century editions, songs of love remained prominent even though Lutheran authorities took an increasingly harsh view of promiscuity.[58] If publishers had removed such songs entirely, sales would surely have declined. Reflective of the longing of the poor for economic success and the entree into elite circles that wealth made possible, a common Annaberg hewer, in the edition of 1547, sleeps with a rich burgher's daughter, who finds him eminently appealing. She regrets that he does not speak to her of marriage.[59]

It is striking that of those songs labeled "new," the majority convey to readers recently formulated Lutheran doctrines. Printers conveyed their enthusiasm and spread the faith by inventing instructive lyrics for the public. Gerhard Heilfurth, the noted expert on miners' songs, refers to Meyerpeck as the "compiler" of these earliest songs, but it seems more likely that either he or someone in his employ composed new lyrics.[60] Purposely put in first place in 1531 is a thirteen-verse song entitled "A Pretty New Song about the Word of God and Faith." It was to be sung "to the tune of the mining song of Saint Joachimsthal," which is evidence that the miners in that town

56. Gerhard Heilfurth, *Das Bergmannslied: Wesen, Leben, Funktion* (Kassel, 1954), chap. 2, "Themen und Motive," pp. 75–209.

57. For example, 1531 *Berggreihen*, song 7 (no title).

58. *Bergliederbüchlein. Historisch-kritische Ausgabe*, ed. Elisabeth Mincoff-Marriage (Leipzig, 1936), discusses seventeenth- and early eighteenth-century efforts to prevent miners from singing "coarse obscenities and shameful songs that only infuriate God and annoy listeners" (introduction, xvii). At one point, the songbook was banned.

59. "Wär ich ein wilder Falke," Heilfurth, *Das Bergmannslied*, p. 532. No example of the 1547 edition has survived.

60. Heilfurth, *Das Bergmannslied*, pp. 39, 63–65.

had one song of their own. A rare, existing miners' song is thus adopted as a vehicle for the new teaching. The first, third, and tenth verses may be translated as follows:

> Ah, God in Heaven's kingdom
> Please graciously confer
> Thy Holy Spirit upon me
> Through Jesus Christ, thy son,
> That I may sing with happy heart
> About thy holy Word,
> Which now doth spread forth mightily
> To many a place on earth. . . .
>
> Thy Word remains eternally,[61]
> Just as Isaiah says,
> It can be banned by no one,
> No power in the world.
> Though people rail against it,
> As some will often do,
> Jesus Christ, thy holy Son,
> Defeats them every one. . . .
>
> And he who has no faith
> Is even now condemned,
> Of heaven's bliss is robbed,
> His works avail him naught.
> Where truly good works come from,
> Those show us with their deed,
> Who serve their neighbor for *his* good,
> As stands in Matthew's Word.[62]

Meyerpeck calls another song "A Pretty New Song about the Sybil's Prophecy." Here allusions are made to the medieval themes of a "Frederick" who will win the holy grave, by which a leafless tree stands, sucked dry (*aus gesogen*) by the pope. Frederick shall hang his shield on this tree. This particular Frederick, it turns out, is neither Barbarossa nor Frederick the Second, but Duke Frederick of Saxony, Frederick the Wise.

---

61. "Verbum Dei manet in aeternum" was a Reformation slogan; it was displayed in public places by those who adopted Luther's belief in the primacy of Scripture.
62. Zwickau Ratsschulbibliothek XXX, V, 20/1.

> Frederick of Saxony is his name;
> God sent him to the world
> For our own good to plant the tree
> That was so long dried out.
> It bears again both leaf and grass,
> And for us is made fruitful.
> The tree it is God's holy Word,
> It blossoms out in every place.
> Whoever will receive its fruit,
> Which tastes so very lovely,
> His heart will surely be at peace,
> His life will pass without unease.[63]

These sentiments might have been directed to any person or group being wooed to Lutheran belief. There is nothing specifically about miners here. But other items were interspersed among love songs, and these contain occasional references to miners. In one, a young woman finds a wounded man in a forest, and he dies. Two hewers bear the body to the grave:

> Ah, the hewer lads are pretty and fine,
> They hack the silver from hardest stone.
> They hew the silver and reddish gold.
> Would God they were my own men bold.[61]

Another popular song similarly adapted for this book has nothing to do with mining except that the singer is a wanderer. Its real subject is the plight of a peasant who cannot survive on so small a plot of land. He praises the self-indulgent, carefree life, which of course cannot be his.[65]

At this early stage, the only song that genuinely has a mining provenance recalls a battle between hewers and peasants at Kutten-berg in Bohemia. Underlying the story is the perennial tension between peasants and prospectors. Four hewers are sent into a field planted in legumes (*schoten*). The village mayor challenges them, and in the ensuing fray, two are killed, one is wounded, and the fourth

63. 1531 *Bergreihen*, song 11, verses 6 and 8.
64. 1531 *Bergreihen*, song 34, verses 11 and 12.
65. Included in August Sach, *Deutsches Leben in der Vergangenheit*, vol. 2 (Halle, 1891), esp. chap. 5, "Deutsches Leben im Volksgesange der Reformationszeit," p. 97.

runs to the Bergmeister. At the village celebration of its church's founding (*Kirmes*), the miners take their revenge, slaughtering 350 peasants. The king of Bohemia tells the peasants to leave all mining personnel alone as they are carrying out his wishes.[66]

One other song has entirely to do with mining. We may be sure, however, given its Lutheran nature, that it was of recent origin. It is an eloquent metaphor, comparing human beings to miners, the earth to a mine shaft, and God to the overseer.

(1)
I know the richest mine of all;
All earthly others must make way.
I lift my eyes with yearning heart;
God shows this site to searchers few. . . .

(5)
He will not let your foot to slip
If, Christians, you're at risk.
He guards you with paternal love
As you descend the shaft.

(6)
He is our proper overseer (*Hütmann*);[67]
He never sleeps, but saves
Each one who trusteth in his Word
With constant hope and love.[68]

By contrast, the much-expanded edition of 1574 includes songs in which hewers praise themselves and their way of living.

We hewers are a courageous lot,
In the hills lie riches great
—We want to praise all mining—
We harvest them with hammer and pick,
The silver and the reddish gold.

66. 1531 *Bergreihen*, song 25, no title.
67. Possibly a play on the verb *hüten* (to guard; to tend livestock, i.e., to shepherd) and *hütmann* (the keeper of the shack where mining tools were kept); probably also *Hütte* (the smelting house).
68. 1531 *Bergreihen*, no. 17, no title except "Ym thon Lobt Gott ihr fromen Christen etc." The allusions are to Psalm 121.

> God grant us all the tender maids
> Where we the metal dig;
> They love us hewers well.

The subjects lament their periodic hunger, the torments of winter, and the decline in silver production. They praise their profession, nonetheless, and frankly enjoy their drink.[69]

Taken as a group, the songs of the first edition are rarely, and in their origins only once, about miners. Meyerpeck astutely sensed the emerging image of a new group as well as the widespread public attraction to the romantic aspects of that image—the wanderlust, the love of beautiful young women, the flirtation with danger, the closeness to nature. One could ask, indeed, whether he intended this little volume for mining folk at all or whether it was exclusively for the entertainment of peripherally involved burghers.[70] Perhaps it was really they whom he hoped to educate and persuade of the correctness of Lutheran teaching about the Bible, faith, and works. We are certainly aware today of the possible discrepancy between the views of those who write books and those who are represented in them. Miners themselves would not have objected to the attribution, and with the passage of time, they may have come to regard both old and new as their own. A bourgeois compilation, and in part a bourgeois creation, encountered an identity in formation and interacted with it, conceivably to the benefit of both participants. The gradual effect of the songs was to focus and reinforce the miners' perception of themselves, which was taking shape independently. By the end of the century, the miners had adopted *Bergreihen* as their own genre and self-expression.

69. Heilfurth, *Das Bergmannslied*, pp. 549–51, "Wir Häuer führen einen freien Mut." According to the last verse (p. 551), the composer was "Hensel Seliger," who was imprisoned for a year by the knights of "Newenberg." The edition of 1547 (Heilfurth, *Das Bergmannslied*, p. 40) was published by Hans Daubmann of Nuremberg and contained a number of "new *Reihen*," including some "from Schneeberg, Marienberg, Annaberg, Freiburg [*sic*], and St. Joachimsthal." With these additions, there were now one hundred songs. This anthology was reissued in 1574 by Valentine Fürmann. It is essential to consult Heilfurth, Seemann, Siuts, and Wolf, *Bergreihen*.

70. Heilfurth, *Das Bergmannslied*, pp. 477–79, records a piece with twenty-one verses glorifying miners and mining town by town in the Erzgebirge. The date given is 1545. The words contain a number of proofs of bourgeois composition. In verse 14 the poet speaks of paying much *zubus*, that is, the costs of mining a claim that yields little or no silver. In verse 17, the teller mentions owning shares (Kuckis). By 1545 the hewers themselves were less frequently, and certainly not typically, investors.

Sermons on the subject of mining were another means of cultivating identity and inculcating belief. The devout Lutheran pastor Johannes Mathesius (1504–65), a Saxon residing in Joachimsthal, is a leading example of mining homiletician. He grew up near the mines and easily assumed the persona of a miners' preacher. He became pastor in Joachimsthal in 1545, after having served there as schoolmaster from 1532 and preacher from 1541. Every carnival time between 1553 and 1562, this prolific sermon writer dressed up in miner's costume and preached on mining, using as his texts various pertinent scriptural passages. The sixteen sermons thus produced were published in 1562 in Nuremberg under the title *Sarepta*, the Greek rendering of the name of the village of Zarephath (today, as Sarafand) in I Kings 17. By tradition Zarephath was a mining town; its name meant "refinement." Mathesius calls Joachimsthal "our Sarepta."[71] These sermons are on multiple topics, and they are rich in metaphor. They could be analyzed for their theological content, their social views, their classical allusions. In the twelfth sermon, Mathesius holds forth against consulting cunning people who purport to reveal where silver lies. Such people are in league with the devil, as is the mine spirit (*Berggeist*), in whom many believe.[72] He does not confine himself to silver mining but expounds on gold (sermon 4); copper (7); iron (8); tin, lead, bismuth, antimony (9); flint, cobalt (10); saltpeter, borax, alum, and salt (11), among others.

These sermons convey to listeners not only broad religious and moral instruction but also a sense of their calling. One comes away from reading them, as one surely did from hearing them, with an impression of the respectable niche in the world occupied by the people of the mines. Miners and all who participate in exploiting underground riches are depicted as highly skilled, knowledgeable, and as favorably regarded by God as the practitioners of any other trade. Being given at carnival, their presenter uncharacteristically attired, these sermons were designed to appeal to a large popular au-

71. The definitive biography of Mathesius remains G. Loesche, *Johannes Mathesius, ein Lebens- und Sitten-Bild aus der Reformationszeit* (Gotha, 1895), vol. 1, "Lebensgeschichte," pp. 1–258. Johannes Mathesius, *Sarepta, Darinn von allerley Bergwerck vnnd Metallen, Was jr eygenschafft vnd natur, vnd wie sie zu nutz vnd gut gemacht, guter bericht gegeben* (Nuremberg, 1571). I have not yet located a copy of the first printing. Mathesius, *Sarepta*, sermon 1, p. 6; see *Sarepta*, sermon 2, p. 13, for Mathesius's explanation of the origin of the name.

72. Mathesius, *Sarepta*, sermon 12, pp. 144–45. In the same sermon, he lists the Joachimsthal pastors from 1521 on (pp. 135–36).

dience. Mathesius drew on the ancient practice of changing identities on *Fastnacht*—an activity that for secular purposes was now discouraged. But still the need for a break from the ordinary must have been felt, and the community must have attended with special interest, though Mathesius seems to have been a beloved figure at all times.

Both songs and sermons simultaneously tapped and strengthened the miners' identity. They articulated what was only sensed before; they also moderated and shaped a collective temperament reputed to be all too volatile. Meyerpeck and Mathesius interacted creatively, purposively with their audiences. It is hard to say whether they succeeded. In 1555 the parish visitors reported that in neither Annaberg nor Marienberg did miners or their children come to church regularly.[73] Certainly other incipient forces aided them at their task—especially the integration of towns into the territorial state and the thoroughness with which princes now oversaw their subjects. Where precious metal was at stake, rulers took a keener interest than where it was not. Another factor in the calming of the miners was the precipitous decline in the output of the mines. There were consequently fewer miners than before, and those who stayed knew their position would be little better elsewhere. Miners became more sedentary—thereby giving up one of their much-touted liberties. The miners' being effectively place-bound contributes to their proletarian aspect. As workers they had little choice but to stay where they were and accept their vacillating wages.

Absentee financing also helped to set the miners apart from those craftsmen who were accustomed year after year to practice their trade on their own or a neighbor's premises. As the sixteenth century wore on, hewers were probably less likely to be acquainted with their employers than in the prospecting and boomtown years. They still worked in small groups in dispersed shafts, but their strictly wage labor resembles that of a later proletariat.

Nevertheless, the great accumulations of capital of the eighteenth and nineteenth centuries would be needed to convert the silver miners into a mature proletariat. Our sixteenth-century miners' descendants would take with them into the age of the Industrial Revolution

73. DSA loc. 2001, "Visitation des Gebirgischen Kreisses 1555," fols. 240, 305. Miners had their weddings on Sundays; other people often held theirs during the week (fols. 240–41, 595–96).

the basic working conditions and an essential concept of themselves that cohered and ripened out of diverse ingredients in the Reformation and post-Reformation eras.

Mathesius composed a miners' hymn. Five of the verses are as follows:

(1)

In the Garden of Eden, God made red gold
As adornment, pleasure, and to gain him praise.
Adam, the very first miner true
Without divining rod found iron and gold.

(2)

Metal is a blessing and a gift from God
To all who use it without deceit,
Who make no idols, fix their hearts not on it,
But use it for their God and everyone.

(3)

He who sees God in a beautiful rock,
Works faithfully, calls on God alone,
Through Scripture believes in Jesus Christ,
That miner is a blessed man.

(4)

Oh, God, who makes flint, lead, and quartz,
Convert these stones to silver ore,
With all thy skill turn plain to precious,
And through thy Spirit our sins destroy. . . .

(8)

Lord, let be recommend' to thee
The Church of this Sarepta small.
She houses thy Word and keeps it pure;
Reward her with Elijah's pay.[74]

74. Added on at the back of Mathesius, *Sarepta*, the edition of 1571, p. 226.

Christina Vanja

5 Mining Women in Early Modern European Society

In contemporary Western civilization women's work and mining seem to be very different concerns. As early as the nineteenth century, western European women working in mines were considered "unfemale." In 1869 a German trade-union official regarded mining as solely male work; if it was done by women the degenerate nature of females would ruin the foundation of state and society.[1] Consequently, in western Europe and in many other areas of the world, women were forbidden to work underground or to perform heavy labor on the surface.[2]

Under the influence of this rejection of women's work in the mines, the historiography of mining has largely ignored mining women, as well as the wives of the miners. Descriptions of the historical development of mining usually mention female workers only in passing or deny their existence by citing official regulations.[3] The

1. Adolf Frantz, *Die Beschäftigung der Frauen und Mädchen beim (belgischen) Bergbau unter Tage* (Beuthen, 1869), p. 10.
2. Christina Vanja, "Bergarbeiterinnen: Zur Geschichte der Frauenarbeit im Bergbau, Hütten- und Salinenwesen seit dem späten Mittelalter, Part II," *Der Anschnitt. Zeitschrift für Kunst und Kultur im Bergbau* 40 (1988), 128–43.
3. For further information, see Helfried Valentinitsch, *Das landesfürstliche Quecksilberbergwerk Idria 1575–1639* (Graz, 1981); Susanne Gröbl, *Der Kupfererzbergbau in der Radmer von den Anfängen bis 1650* (Graz, 1986).

historiography of women's labor concentrates on urban crafts and trades.[4] Women's contributions to capitalist production during the eighteenth century have received due attention, but women's labor in preindustrial trades and rural enterprises, such as mining or smelting, has been largely ignored.[5] Yet, we cannot assume that the division of labor implied by this silence corresponds to the reality of women's work. In all industries women were involved in a range of tasks. So it was in mining. Only in the late seventeenth century did the assumption of craft organization and the development of labor-saving technology eliminate most women from the mining and metallurgy industries.

The early studies of Ivy Pinchbek and Alice Clark clearly show a broad range of women's work. Whether married, unmarried, or widowed, women worked as employees and as independent employers on farms, in crafts, in trades, and in the civil service. Clark and Pinchbek also point out that women often did unregistered and unpaid work and occupied subordinate positions of every kind.[6] Subsequent studies confirm the impression that in preindustrial times work determined the daily life of almost every woman, regardless of her social status. Although the type and character of work changed over the centuries, working women remained indispensable. Only a very small group of elite wives and daughters enjoyed leisure time. At the end of the early modern period most women were burdened by increased work and longer working days than ever before as a result of new social demands and economic requirements.[7] We must not assume mining was an exception. Nineteenth-

4. *Women and Work in Preindustrial Europe*, ed. Barbara A. Hanawalt (Bloomington, 1986); Merry Wiesner, *Working Women in Renaissance Germany* (New Brunswick, N.J., 1986); Martha C. Howell, *Women, Production, and Patriarchy in Late Medieval Cities* (Chicago, 1986); *Die Frau in der deutschen Wirtschaft*, ed. Hans Pohl (Wiesbaden, 1985); *Sisters and Workers in the Middle Ages*, ed. Judith M. Bennett, E. A. Clark, J. F. O'Barr (Chicago, 1989).

5. Rudolf Braun, *Industrialisierung und Volksleben. Veränderungen der Lebensformen unter Einwirkung der verlagsinternen Heimarbeit in einem ländlichen Industriegebiet (Zürcher Oberland) vor 1800* (Winterthur, 1960); Paul Fink, *Geschichte der Basler Bandindustrie 1550–1800* (Basel, 1983).

6. Ivy Pinchbek, *Women's Work and the Industrial Revolution 1750–1850* (London, 1981, reprint of 1930 edition); Alice Clark, *Working Life of Women in the Seventeenth Century* (London, 1919).

7. Heide Wunder, "Frauen in der Gesellschaft Mitteleuropas im späten Mittelalter und in der Frühen Neuzeit (15. bis 18. Jahrhundert)," in *Hexen und Zauberer. Die große*

century prints portray husbands in this industry returning from the pits to hearth and home, where their wives and children wait. But mining did not create a modern family type nor observe a strict division of labor for men and women.[8] The early study of mining women in Great Britain and Belgium emphasized the nineteenth and early twentieth centuries. Starting in the 1980s, however, research reached into earlier periods with particular attention to German women.[9] Many sources remain still unresearched, and the subject awaits integration into the historiography of women's work and mining. With this in mind, I offer the following foray into this unexplored facet of the history of women and women's work.

In western Europe since the fifteenth century, more men than women have performed wage-labor as miners. Nevertheless, women worked outside the pits until the nineteenth century. Expanding our attention to female activities opens a view of the combined industries of mining and metallurgy. It addresses the various jobs necessary to provide the final product.[10] As Georgius Agricola maintained: "since Nature usually creates metals in an impure state, mixed with earth, stones, and solidified juices, it is necessary to separate most of these

---

Verfolgung—ein europäisches Phänomen in der Steiermark, vol. 2, ed. Helfried Valentinitsch (Graz, 1987), pp. 123–54; idem, *Er ist die Sonn'—Sie ist der Mond: Frauen in der frühen Neuzeit* (Munich, 1992); Christina Vanja, "Zwischen Verdrängung und Expansion, Kontrolle und Befreiung. Frauenarbeit im 18. Jahrhundert im deutschsprachigen Raum," *Vierteljahrschrift für Sozial- und Wirtschaftsgeschichte* 79 (1992).

8. Michael Mitterauer, "Produktionsweise, Siedlungsstruktur und Sozialformen im österreichischen Montanwesen des Mittelalters und der frühen Neuzeit," in *Österreichisches Montanwesen. Produktion, Verteilung, Sozialform*, ed. Michael Mitterauer (Munich, 1974), pp. 235–315.

9. Susan C. Karant-Nunn, "The Women of the Saxon Silver Mines," in *Women in Reformation and Counter-Reformation Europe: Private and Public Worlds*, ed. Sherrin Marshall (Bloomington, 1989), pp. 29–46; Christina Vanja, "Bergarbeiterinnen. Zur Geschichte der Frauenarbeit im Bergbau, Hütten- und Salinenwesen seit dem späten Mittelalter, Part I," *Der Anschnitt. Zeitschrift für Kunst und Kultur im Bergbau* 39 (1987), 2–15; idem, "Frauenarbeit in der vorindustriellen Gesellschaft. Fragestellungen-Quellen-Forschungsmöglichkeiten," in *Frauenalltag-Frauenforschung*, ed. Arbeitsgruppe Volkskundliche Frauenforschung Freiburg (Frankfurt, 1988), pp. 261–73; *Frauen und Bergbau: Zeugnisse aus Funf Jahrhunderten*, ed. Deutsches Bergbau-Museum Bochum (Bochum, 1989).

10. Helmut Kirchberg, "Erzaufbereitung im XVI. Jahrhundert," in *Georgius Agricola 1494–1555. Zu seinem 400. Todestag*, ed. Deutsche Akademie der Wissenschaften (Berlin, 1955), pp. 31–91.

impurities from the ores as far as can be, before they are smelted."[11] These tasks fell frequently to women as did unrelated responsibilities—especially the organization of the food supply—which enabled the miners' society to survive.

Many indications survive of women's work in small pits, owned and run by families, and in leased enterprises (*Eigenlöhnersystem*) in the late medieval period.[12] Women's work in self-managed mining was such strong competition to mining based on wage-labor that as early as 1545 it was a main point in the miners' complaints in Schwaz in Tyrol.[13] Wives working in the mines are mentioned in the numerous fairy tales and legends about rich discoveries of ore. For example, a woman bumped her head on a rock in a mine. After her husband removed the rock they could see the gleaming metals.[14] In the eighteenth and early nineteenth centuries, mining officials designed work programs for the wives; at the time women were completely integrated in the mining industry, although they were not officially employed.[15] Working teams of husbands and wives lasted until the nineteenth century. In 1870 a miner claimed that with the death of his wife, who transported the ore to the city, he lost his horse.[16] Apparently mining could be a form of household enterprise similar to farming or many crafts.[17]

The place of mining women among large-scale enterprises, where the miners and metal workers were wage-laborers paid by businessmen or aristocrats, was far more complex and peripheral. This sys-

11. Georgius Agricola, *De Re Metallica*, trans. Herbert Clark Hoover and Lou Henry Hoover (New York, 1940), p. 267.

12. Karl-Heinz Ludwig, "Aspekte der Arbeitsverfassung im Europäischen Bergbau des Mittelalters und der Frühen Neuzeit," in *Bergbau und Arbeitsrecht. Die Arbeitsverfassung im europäischen Bergbau des Mittelalters und der frühen Neuzeit,* ed. Karl-Heinz Ludwig, Peter Sika (Vienna, 1989), pp. 11–36; Otto Hue, *Die Bergarbeiter. Historische Darstellung der Bergarbeiterverhältnisse von der ältesten bis in die neueste Zeit,* vol. 1 (Stuttgart, 1910).

13. Erich Egg, "Schwaz ist aller Bergwerke Mutter," *Der Anschnitt. Zeitschrift für Kunst und Kultur im Bergbau* 16 (1964), 3–63.

14. Hue, *Die Bergarbeiter,* p. 154.

15. Gerhard Pferschy, "Versuche zur Einführung der Spinnereilohnarbeit bei den Frauen und Kindern der Erzbergarbeiterschaft," *Mitteilungen des Steiermärkischen Landesarchivs* 19/20 (1970), 173–80.

16. Hue, *Die Bergarbeiter,* p. 153.

17. Wunder, *Frauen in der Gesellschaft Mitteleuropas,* pp. 123–54; see also Wiesner, *Working Women in Renaissance Germany*; *Women and Work in Preindustrial Europe,* ed. Hanawalt.

Women rinsing and sorting ores, illustrated in the "Annaberger Altar" from the mining town of St. Annaberg in the Harz Mountains. By permission of the Deutsches Bergbau-Museum, Bochum, Germany.

tem obtained from the late fifteenth century in the ore mines and huts of the Erzgebirge, in Bohemia and Poland, in Tyrol and Styria as well as in the salterns (a place where salt is rendered by boiling) of Lüneburg and the salt mines of Salzburg. Based on the very few archival and pictorial sources available we can recognize a strict, gender-specific division of labor in large-scale mining enterprise. Women did not enter the pits, nor did they engage in highly specialized metallurgy. Their tasks were limited to low-skilled, physical labor: hauling and transporting materials; breaking and rinsing ore. Though their domestic tasks and by-employments supported mining households and communities, the role of women in the mines seems not to have differed greatly from that in organized crafts. Their gradual exclusion may be symptomatic of a process of proletarianization, in which all miners were transformed from independent, petty producers, operating small pits, to wage-dependent specialists, participating in large-scale industry.

Woman transporting ore at a stamping works in Alsace. Reproduced from Heinrich Winkelmann, *Der Bergbuch des Lebertals* (Wethmar/Post Lünen, 1962).

Given the general lack of traditional archival sources, we must turn to nontraditional materials to learn about women miners. The illustrations of ore mining from the fifteenth and early sixteenth centuries show several women on the surface of the mines torrefying, pulverizing, rinsing, sorting, and transporting the products. On the title page of the famous *Kuttenberger Kanzionale*, a collection of

Women culling ore in Alsace. Reproduced from Heinrich Winkelmann, *Der Bergbuch des Lebertals* (Wethmar/Post Lünen, 1962).

religious songs composed in Bohemia around 1490, one woman is washing the ore contained in a basket and shaking it in a big tub of water. Comparable pictures are found on the altarpiece of Saint-Annaberg in the Harz Mountains (1510), in the technical books of Agricola and other authors, and on the title pages of mining rules.[18]

18. *Meisterwerke bergbaulicher Kunst vom 13. bis 19. Jahrhundert*, Veröffentlichungen aus dem Deutschen Bergbau-Museum Bochum, number 48 (Bochum, 1990), 180–84, 212–15; Agricola, *De Re Metallica*, pp. 292–93.

Other women shown on the *Kuttenberger Kanzionale* are involved in the strenuous work of sorting ore and are illustrated transporting baskets with pieces of ore to the sorting areas. The separating of the ore (*Klauben*) is also a frequently pictured women's job. It is shown, for example, in Sebastian Münster's *Cosmographia* (1544); in a picture from a series of drawings of the "Red Pit Saint Nicolas" in a valley in Alsace in the middle of the sixteenth century; in the *Münz- und Mineralienbuch des Andreas Ryff* printed in Basel during the second half of the sixteenth century; and, of course, in one of Agricola's several illustrations of women's work.[19] The written documents show that in Poland also several women worked as ore sorters. The work was usually done on a table in a hut that served as a shelter from rain and wind. Sometimes the women had tools to remove the dead rocks and the earth from the ore. Mostly they did the work with their hands, sorting the pieces in different containers according to quality and size.[20]

Another late fifteenth-century painting, the *Siegerländer Randleiste*, probably originating in Bohemia, depicts a woman with a big hammer breaking the ore and a second torrefying it to make it more brittle.[21] The pounding of ore by women is also the subject of the Alsatian drawings mentioned earlier and of a seventeenth-century pen-and-ink drawing in the State Archives of Nürnberg.[22]

Women also engaged in rinsing and separating small types of ore such as tin and gold, a more complicated work process. As Agricola explained, the mixture of ore, earth, and dead rocks was thrown into chests where it was cleaned by running water. The miners helped in the process by pushing the ore with wooden paddles. The lightweight, dead material was washed off the heavy metal, which

19. Helmut Wilsdorf, *Präludien zu Agricola*, Freiberger Forschungshefte, D5 (Berlin, 1954), pp. 69–75; Heinrich Winkelmann, *Bergbuch des Lebertals* (Lünen, 1966); Eugen A. Meier, *Basler Erzgräber, Bergwerksbesitzer und Eisenhändler* (Basel, 1965), illus. 12; Agricola, *De Re Metallica*, p. 268.

20. On Polish women in mining, see Danuta Molenda, "Die Arbeitsverfassung im Erzbergbau Kleinpolens und Oberschlesiens vom 15. bis zum 17. Jahrhundert," in *Bergbau und Arbeitsrecht: Die Arbeitsverfassung im europäischen Bergbau des Mittelalters und der frühen Neuzeit*, ed. Karl-Heinz Ludwig, Peter Sika (Vienna, 1989), pp. 253–74, 289; Agricola named seven sizes of ore pieces which were filled in different barrels: Wilsdorf, *Präludien*, p. 177.

21. Karl-Heinz Ludwig, "Umschlagbild. Die Pergament-Randleiste aus dem 15. Jahrhundert in Siegen mit einem böhmischen Bergbaumotiv," *Technikgeschichte* 56 (2/1989), 133–37; *Meisterwerke bergbaulicher Kunst*, p. 176.

22. Winkelmann, *Lebertal*; *Meisterwerke bergbaulicher Kunst*, pp. 198–99.

Women separating ore. A: long table; B: tray; C: tub. Georgius Agricola, *De Re Metallica* (Basel, 1556). Special Collections, Van Pelt Library, University of Pennsylvania.

was gathered in canvas, nets, or pieces of turf. These the women washed out for reuse. They also cleaned the entire installation, especially the water channels. Sometimes they even worked at the washing chests with or in place of the men.[23]

The physically demanding job of working the windlasses is rarely mentioned as work for women. The larger mines of the early mod-

23. Agricola, *De Re Metallica*, pp. 317, 325, 332, 333, 340.

ern period used horse whims.[24] In smaller operations, however, the miners, including the women, probably shouldered this task when necessary.

Once rinsed and freed of earth and dead rock, ores were further purified through smelting. In the smelting huts women did various transport jobs. They carried wood and coal to heat the furnaces. They also transported the cold iron, as shown in the painting *Landscape with Mining*, by the Flemish artist Henri met de Bles (circa 1540).[25]

In addition to transporting materials, women produced briquettes for fuel. Agricola described this activity in a separate chapter illustrated with working women. Coal and loam were mixed with water and formed into balls that were dried in the sun.[26] The same motif appears in two paintings from eighteenth-century Belgium, in which a group of women are mashing the coal by foot and another group are forming and burning the briquettes.[27]

Salterns provided work for a significant number of women. The transport jobs were portrayed for the first time by Agricola's illustrator. Women hauled the baskets of salt, which were to dry in the sun.[28] According to sixteenth-century illustrations, women hauled coal to heat the salt solutions at the Lüneburger salterns.[29] They handled the windlasses, and they also helped in the graduation houses of the salterns.[30] Women often transported the extracted salt from the mountain mines to the valleys in baskets on their backs, and in pic-

24. Irmgard Lange-Kothe, "Fremde Bergleute an der Ruhr," *Der Anschnitt. Zeitschrift für Kunst und Kultur im Bergbau* 7 (1955), 16–19, 17.

25. F. Toussaint, "Ein frühes Industriebild mit den Augen eines Ingenieurs gesehen," *Der Anschnitt. Zeitschrift für Kunst und Kultur im Bergbau* 13 (1958), 20–23; *Meisterwerke bergbaulicher Kunst*, pp. 215–21.

26. Agricola, *De Re Metallica*, pp. 367–68.

27. Fritz Wündisch, *Von Klütten und Briketts. Bilder aus der Geschichte des rheinischen Braunkohlenbergbaus* (Brühl, 1982), p. 47; *Frauen und Bergbau*, p. 135 n. 55. Wündisch erroneously identified the pictures as coal mining in southern France, but they originate from the mining area around Lüttich in Belgium from the year 1777 and show the production of hard coal briquettes.

28. Agricola, *De Re Metallica*, p. 553.

29. Lothar Süss, *Die Nauheimer Saline im Mittelalter* (Frankfurt, 1978), illus. 4b.; H. Durtz, *Die Soleleitung von Reichenhall nach Traunstein 1617–1619. Ein Beitrag zur Technikgeschichte Bayerns* (Munich, 1978), p. 80.

30. Claus Proesner, *Das deutsche Salinenwesen im frühen 17. Jahrhundert* (Munich, 1980); women in salterns documented, for example, around 1800 in the saltern of Kötzschau in Saxony—kindly pointed out by Hans-Henning Walter, Freiberg.

Women rinsing ore. A: basket; B: basket handles; C: dish; D: back of dish;
E: front of dish; F: dish handles. Georgius Agricola, *De Re Metallica* (Basel,
1556). Special Collections, Van Pelt Library, University of Pennsylvania.

tures of towns women are shown bringing the refined salt to the
ships or carriages.[31]

Beyond transporting raw and finished materials, heating the
ovens in the salterns was also work often done by women. In the
salterns of Hallein in Austria the women who ensured a constant

31. Friedrich Morton, "Die Hallstätter 'Kerntrageweiber'," *Der Anschnitt. Zeitschrift
für Kunst und Kultur im Bergbau* 14 (1962), 49. The transport of rock salt (*Kern*) in
Hallstatt by women continued until the end of the nineteenth century when young

heat were called wind pullers (*Windzieherinnen*).[32] At Hallein women also stamped the salt to small pieces, hooped the salt barrels, and drew water by walking on a treadmill.[33] An illustration done at Traunstein, Bavaria, in 1780 shows women assisting in the construction of a salt drier.[34] In salt mines as in other mines women apparently took part in all associated tasks outside the pits themselves.

Illustrations show various forms of work undertaken by women in the mines, smelteries, and salterns. But determining the exact number of women in mining is generally impossible. At our disposal are only individual references. In the gold mines in Lavanthal, owned by the Fugger family, one-third of the employed miners were women (96 out of 299 workers).[35] In all the other mining areas—as far as we know from the archival material—women were named only sporadically in shift slips, accounts, and food registers: in the mercury mines of Idria; the copper mines of the Radmer in Styria; in the gold mines of Salzburg; and in the silver mines of the Upper Harz Mountains.[36] In other parts of Europe, such as France (except Alsace) or Italy, women are not known to have worked in mining.[37] If women were named at all, usually no more than three or four were listed in a single working group.[38]

These laboring women were mostly paid at the lowest level of the

---

men began to move it on sledges. The weight of the filled baskets was about eighty pounds. For pictures of women hauling salt, see *Hall und das Salz. Beiträge zur hällischen Stadt- und Salienengeschichte*, ed. Kuno Ulshöfer and Herta Beutter (Sigmaringen, 1983), pp. 60, 70.

32. Heinrich Winkelmann, *Das Halleiner Salzwesen und seine bildliche Darstellung in den Fürstenzimmern des Pflegamtsgebäudes zu Hallein* (Lünen, 1966), illus. 29.

33. Winkelmann, *Das Halleiner Salzwesen*, illus. 33.

34. J.-F. Bergier, *Die Geschichte vom Salz* (Frankfurt, 1989), p. 78.

35. Mitterauer, *Produktionsweise*, p. 305.

36. Valentinitsch, *Das landesfürstliche Quecksilberbergwerk Idria*, p. 200; Karl-Heinz Ludwig, "Einkommen und Löhne von Knappen und Arbeitern in der europäischen Montankonjunktur des 15./16. Jahrhunderts," *Zeitschrift für historische Forschung* 14 (1987), 385–406; Ekkehard Henschke, *Landesherrschaft und Bergbauwirtschaft. Zur Wirtschafts- und Verwaltungsgeschichte des Oberharzer Bergbaugebietes im 16. und 17. Jahrhundert* (Berlin, 1974), pp. 263, 266.

37. Adolf Laube, *Bergbau und Hüttenwesen in Frankreich um die Mitte des 15. Jahrhunderts. Eine Studie über die Entstehung kapitalistischer Produktionsverhältnisse in den Gruben des Lyonnais und Beaujolais*, Freiberger Forschungshefte D38 (Leipzig, 1965). I thank Roberta Morelli, Rome, for information on the situation in Italy.

38. This, for instance, is well documented in a grain register for the miners in the Upper Harz Mountains in 1622, where all people were listed by name. See *Frauen und Bergbau*, pp. 109–10.

Women washing canvas ore catches. A: launder from the screen of the mortar box; B: three-toothed rake; C: small settling pit; D: canvas; E: strakes; F: brooms. Georgius Agricola, *De Re Metallica* (Basel, 1556). Special Collections, Van Pelt Library, University of Pennsylvania.

wage scale.[39] A calculation of the usual wages in the Alps in the mid-sixteenth century specifies five shillings for the female washers and twenty *Kreutzer* (approximately 4.2 shillings) for the female sorters. Male washers received seven shillings and more, male sorters four shillings and eight pennies and more, and the hewers six to nine shillings.[40] In the Upper Harz Mountains women received 3.35 pennies; boys in the mines received a wage of 4.5 pennies and male day-laborers in the summertime 6.5 pennies. Only the ordinary helpers (*Handlanger*) were paid one penny less.[41] In sixteenth- and seventeenth-century Poland, women and young people received wages 40 percent lower than men for the same tasks.[42] Susan Karant-Nunn found that in sixteenth-century Saxony "wherever wives worked directly alongside their husbands, the husbands got a full wage and the wife a much smaller sum or a gratuity."[43] In the copper mines of the Radmer in Austria the wages of women were lowered after 1619. Then only small piece-wages were paid.[44]

In general the women were employed only for single days or limited shifts. More women were employed when men were scarce, such as during the Thirty Years' War. On the other hand, women were discharged first when there were a sufficient number of male workers.[45] Young women in the mines of the Upper Harz Mountains in the first half of the sixteenth century were named lace-maids (*Knüppelmägde*), because they usually worked in the home making lace when no work in the mines was available.[46]

Wives could replace or support their husbands on the job; they also found independent labor directly or indirectly related to the mining and metallurgy industry. The former included handling ores. The latter extended to sewing the bags for salt and ore and breading the wicks for the candles.[47] The women in mining towns

39. Vanja, *Bergarbeiterinnen*, part 1, p. 9.

40. Karl-Heinz Ludwig, "Einkommen und Löhne von Knappen und Arbeiter in der europäischen Montankonjunktur des 15./16. Jahrhunderts," *Zeitschrift für historische Forschung* 14 (1987), 385–406.

41. Ostmann, *Codex Rerum Metallicarum Herzyniae*. tom 2, vol. 4 (Nachstunden, 1928 and 1933).

42. Molenda, *Die Arbeitsverfassung im Erzbergbau*, p. 267.

43. Karant-Nunn, "The Women of the Saxon Silver Mines," p. 38.

44. Gröbl, *Der Kupfererzbergbau in der Radmer*, pp. 128–32.

45. For example, small piece-wages were paid after the Thirty Years' War and in the eighteenth century when the population was growing.

46. Herbert Dennert, *Kleine Chronik Oberharzer Bergstädte* (Clausthal-Zellerfeld, 1974).

47. Kurtz, *Die Soleleitung*, p. 80.

Women cleaning sluices. A: head of sluice; B: riffles; C: wooden scrubber; D: pointed stick; E: dish; F: cuplike depression; G: grooved dish. Georgius Agricola, *De Re Metallica* (Basel, 1556). Special Collections, Van Pelt Library, University of Pennsylvania.

and villages also performed various tasks outside the mines that were essential for the existence of mining communities and households. Located near the pits, these communities were frequently isolated from local exchange networks. Therefore, women provided the needed connections. They did wage-labor on the farms in the neighborhood and tended their own livestock. They carried food from the valleys up to the mountains, where crops did not thrive.

They also worked in home industries, spinning or making lace, jobs which provided critically needed income in times of crisis.[48]

The collaboration between women and men was essential at small pits run by families or small groups of independent miners. By the eighteenth century at the latest, women had largely disappeared from mines, as well as from the large smelteries and the salterns. We do not yet clearly understand the reasons for dividing the work by gender, the character of women's work in mining, or the causes for replacing women with men and machines.

All the activities of women in mining were unskilled. They held jobs for a day, a week, or a season. Yet women were not hewers, smelters, or glassblowers. As a rule they were not involved in underground tasks. Women generally shared the work of children; their labor was physical and unskilled. There was no promotion possible in the world of women's work. Employment for a girl in the mines was not the start of a career. As a consequence, women had no craft-consciousness. Accordingly, in all the illustrations, they wore no particular, identifying work costume.[49]

During the early modern period, the small mining operations, to which women had contributed their labor, were gradually absorbed into larger, more complex, capitalistic enterprises that were vertically organized. Mining work was transformed, too. Starting as stamping boys, men worked their way up through a well-organized hierarchy of tasks until they became hewers. In this context the status of men was different; all activities were steps in the life cycle of work. In a strict hierarchy of laborers, men were able to develop a sense of craft solidarity and identity and to create their own fraternities—fraternities from which women were usually excluded.[50] This process reached its conclusion in the late seventeenth and eighteenth centuries and had many similarities with the earlier development of the

48. Bernd Schöne, "Posamentierer-Strumpfwirker-Spitzenklöpplerinnen," in *Volksleben zwischen Zunft und Fabrik. Studien zu Kultur und Lebensweise werktätiger Klassen und Schichten vom Feudalismus zum Kapitalismus*, ed. Rudolf Weinhold (Berlin, 1982), pp. 107–64.

49. Karl-Ewald Fritzsch and Helmut Wilsdorf, "Die bergmännische Kleidung im Berufsleben und in ihrer gesellschaftlichen Funktion," *Sächsische Heimatblätter* 3 (1973), 106–17; Vanja, *Bergarbeiterinnen*, part 2, pp. 128–30.

50. For example, Susan Karant-Nunn, "The Women of the Saxon Silver Mines," p. 39, found that in the Erzgebirge only the Freiberg associations seem to have had female members.

Women at the washing chests. A: wooden dipper; B: cask; C: tub; D: master; E: youth; F: wife; G: wooden spade; H: boards; I: baskets; K: hoe; L: rake; M: straw; N: bowl; O: bucket containing blood; P: tankard containing beer. Georgius Agricola, *De Re Metallica* (Basel, 1556). Special Collections, Van Pelt Library, University of Pennsylvania.

urban crafts and their guilds.[51] Women were all but excluded from every aspect of mining as a craft and its associated craft-consciousness.

In the mining industry women took no part in the process of the maturation of the craft.[52] Excluded from most career avenues, such as apprenticeship or study, women were also excluded from training as professional miners. Therefore, women assumed peripheral tasks and by-employments to support their families and to aid their husbands in their labor.[53]

Technological change gradually eliminated unskilled jobs in mining, which affected women in particular. For example, horse whimsies replaced the hand windlasses, stamping machines replaced stamping by hand, washing machines replaced handwashing. Competition for jobs in mining and technological advances during its transformation into a capitalist industry promoted a masculinization of mining.

States, as entrepreneurs, supported the exclusion of women from this important industry. During the eighteenth century mining developed a military-like, disciplined character that excluded females as irregular and unskilled workers.[54] Administration officials also shared a new bourgeois ethos that minimized the role of women in manual labor. They saw only men as supporters of the families. These authorities were later among the first to demand a legal prohibition of females in mining.[55]

Nothing is reported about women's protests against their exclusion from training or work in mining. Perhaps women did not consider themselves to be the victims of occupational segregation. Not until the nineteenth century had it become so clear that the division of labor by gender during preindustrial times paved the way for discrimination against women in general.

51. Christoph Bartels, "Der Bergbau vor der hochindustriellen Zeit—Ein Überblick," in *Meisterwerke bergbaulicher Kunst*, pp. 14–33.
52. Heide Wunder, "Zur Stellung der Frau im Arbeitsleben und in der Gesellschaft des 15.-18. Jahrhunderts. Eine Skizze," *Geschichtsdidaktik* 6 (1981), 239–52.
53. Michael Mitterauer, "Geschlechtsspezifische Arbeitsteilung in vorindustrieller Zeit," *Beiträge zur Historischen Sozialkunde* 3 (1981), 77–87.
54. Bartels, "Der Bergbau vor der Hochindustriellen Zeit," p. 28.
55. Vanja, *Bergarbeiterinnen*, part 2, p. 136.

Thomas Max Safley

6 Production, Transaction, and Proletarianization: The Textile Industry in Upper Swabia, 1580–1660

In 1924 a historical newsletter in the south German city of Memmingen published the following, elegiac description of weaving before the factory:

> Thus the loom was in its simplest form a universal, household tool, and it was really something beautiful when the entire cycle of work, the sowing and harvesting of the flax, the crushing, the drying, the breaking, the winnowing, the spinning, the winding, the warping, the weaving, was carried out within the family circle, when one process flowed into another and one member worked hand-in-hand with another, until something finished came into being, a bolt of fine, durable cloth. In a weaver household this wonderful cooperation occurs even today.[1]

The manufacture of cloth before industrialization would seem to have formed a seamless web. All production happened within the

---

1. Hans Reyhing, "Ein untergehendes Handwerk," *Westallgäuer Heimatblätter* 40 (1924), 196. "So war der Webstuhl in seinen einfachsten Art ein allgemeines Hausgerät, und das war wirklich etwas Schönes, wenn die ganze Ring der Arbeit, das Saen des Hanfes, das Hanfrupfen, Spreiten, Dörren, Brechen, Schwingen, Spinnen, Spulen, Zettlen, Weben in einer Familie sich vollzog, wenn eine Arbeit in die andere überging und ein Glied der Familie dem andern in die Hände arbeitete, bis etwas Fertiges entstanden war, ein Ballen feinen, habhaften Tuches. In einem Weberhause kommt diese schöne Zusammenarbeit auch heute noch vor."

bounds of the household; all transactions occurred within the circle of the family; all conflicts yielded to the common purpose. The unit of production was independent, and the market disappeared in a rose-colored autarchy. This romanticized nostalgia for a lost unity of work and family, a forgotten self-sufficiency of production and household, reveals far more about the author than about the craft he described.

In fact, for Swabia, and especially for the Allgäu, that part bounded by the Alps in the south and the Lech River in the east and extending north to the city of Memmingen and west to the upper tip of Lake Constance, the manufacturing of linens was an important export industry that produced huge volumes of cloth for the markets of Switzerland, Italy, and Bohemia. Rather than a harmonious activity among family members, cloth manufacture was a series of often discordant exchanges between various productive sectors, no more than one of which could be executed ordinarily within the domestic economy. These exchanges or transactions between spinners, weavers, finishers, and merchants determined prosperity and proletarianization within the cloth industry.

A combative image of artisanal families and their work emerges from events in the free, imperial cities of the Allgäu. Periodic dearth and inflation pressed the urban artisans of that region; political and military upheavals further reduced their incomes by rendering many cloth markets inaccessible. A series of uprisings between 1580 and 1660, emphasizing the organization of production and the transactions that marked its various stages, revealed the paramount concerns of weavers.

In the Allgäu weavers were independent, petty producers, operating one or two looms within their households. Because they owned their tools and materials and paid all costs of production, these masters were caught in a network of market transactions and expressed consistently the same set of concerns in crisis and conflict. They bemoaned the quantity and quality of thread, the finishing of foreign cloth in local works, and the access of foreign producers to local markets.

At issue were the costs and profits of production, a constant struggle to reduce the former without jeopardizing the latter. Sufficient supplies of thread reduced the expense of manufacturing linen. Though ideally inexpensive, thread could not be cheap. Adequate quality, achieved only at cost, guaranteed the eventual price linen commanded on the market. The same calculation marked finishing processes. High-quality finishing increased the value of cloth, but it required time and care in the hands of skilled dyers, bleachers, fullers, and cutters. Foreign cloth raised the costs of production by competing for access to finishing works. Moreover, foreign goods, if sold on domestic markets, might lower prices by raising supplies. Weavers in the Allgäu were subject to all the market pressures of workers caught in a "production network."[2]

Craft unrest in the Allgäu raises profound questions about the organization of preindustrial weaving and its impact on the well-being of weavers. Given that production was apparently in the hands of independent or semi-independent masters and journeymen, it begs an examination of the exchanges between craftsmen at the various stages in the creation of cloth. Because exchanges loomed large in the consciousness of weavers, it requires an investigation of the system of transactions.

As the relationships between craftsmen in different sectors of production take on greater importance, those between craftsmen and merchants seem less so. This is particularly ironic given the household basis of linen production in the Allgäu, in which masters commanded limited capital resources and depended on local markets. The reason lies in the paradox of production, the costs of which were so debilitating to artisans, while the organization of which was the basis of their independence. To dispossess the master craftsmen of control over their own skills and resources and, so, promote proletarianization, the merchant capitalist had to establish vertical control over the entire series of discrete production processes or dominate the market transactions that linked them. Neither occurred in the Allgäu. In fact, as a region it demonstrated surprisingly few of the integrative characteristics emphasized in the literature on protoindustrialization and, more recently, on regions and industries.[3] The

2. Michael Sonenscher, *Work and Wages: Natural Law, Politics, and the Eighteenth-Century French Trades* (Cambridge, Eng. 1989), p. 140.

3. Maxine Berg and Pat Hudson, "Rehabilitating the Industrial Revolution," *Economic History Review*, 2d ser., 45 (1992), 24–50; *Markets and Manufactures in Early Industrial Europe*, ed. Maxine Berg (London, 1991); *Regions and Industries: A Perspective on the Industrial Revolution in Britain*, ed. Pat Hudson (Cambridge, Eng., 1989), esp. pp. 1–40; Pat Hudson, *The Genesis of Industrial Capital: A Study of the West Riding Wool Textile Industry c. 1750–1850* (Cambridge, Eng., 1986); Maxine Berg, *The Age of Manufactures: Industry, Innovation, and Work in Britain, 1700–1820* (London, 1985), L. A.

counterpoise to capitalist enterprise was the master's own capacity to manipulate production transactions to his own advantage. By no means absent, the merchant appeared neither as the scourge of artisans nor as the agent of progress, but rather as a customer, a middleman, and a competitor. Thus, the organization of production, the system of transactions, and the relationship between producers all played a role in the course of proletarianization in the age of manufacture.

The production of linen may be divided into four general processes. First, flax was spun into linen thread. Second, thread was woven into raw linen of various sizes, patterns, and qualities. Third, raw linen was finished: fulling, dyeing or bleaching, and cutting constituted these finishing touches; the actual process depended on the quality of the raw linen. Fourth, the finished cloth was inspected and marketed. Municipal officials examined the cloth and gave it a seal as a guarantee of quality and origin. Sales usually occurred at the *Schau*, where goods were inspected and duties were assessed, as soon as the city seal was in place. Seen in this manner, textile manufacturing was a system of transactions binding together the various production processes.

Weavers required thread in a number of forms—and acquired it through a number of means, nearly all of which were controversial in the sixteenth and seventeenth centuries. Although not limited to the countryside, spinning seems to have been predominantly a rural by-employment. Few references to urban spinning, except as a livelihood for individual poor families, survive in the archives of any of the free, imperial cities of the Allgäu. One exception is the 1571 *Schneiderzunftordnung* of Lindau, in which weavers were permitted to spin a maximum of four *Ballen* annually for sale.[4] But, this does not seem to have been a common practice, especially in the major textile centers. A weavers' petition in Memmingen notes that much thread

---

Clarkson, *Proto-Industrialization: The First Phase of Industrialization* (London, 1985); *Manufacture in Town and Country before the Factory*, ed. Maxine Berg, Pat Hudson, and Michael Sonenscher (Cambridge, Eng., 1983); D. C. Coleman, "Proto-Industrialization: A Concept Too Many," *Economic History Review*, 2d ser., 36 (1983), 435–48; *Industrialization before Industrialization: Rural Industry in the Genesis of Capitalism*, ed. Peter Kriedte, Hans Medick, and Jürgen Schlumbohm (Cambridge, Eng., 1982); Sidney Pollard, *Peaceful Conquest: The Industrialization of Europe, 1760–1970* (Oxford, 1981); Franklin F. Mendels, "Proto-Industrialization: The First Phase of the Industrialization Process," *Journal of Economic History* 32 (1972), 241–61.

4. Stadtarchiv (hereafter StA) Lindau, 113,7. Schneiderzunftordnung, 1571.

was once spun in the city but increased demand for different kinds of cloth forced weavers to seek larger sources of supply *extra muros*.[5] As a result domestic spinning dwindled, and weavers purchased their thread on the market. Not surprisingly, efforts to regulate transactions in thread in order to control its quality, quantity, and cost to the advantage of local weavers were unending.

Allgäuer cities universally mandated that thread, whatever its form or origin, be sold only on the open market and only at carefully prescribed times. The legal, public sale of thread was carefully choreographed. When thread was sold in an authorized location— "inn der Waag, oder am Marckht, unnd Baumgarten alhie"—seller and buyer proceeded together to the municipal scales to have the thread weighed and its tariff assessed.[6] Certain steps in this dance were common to all cities in the Allgäu. Sales could only occur at specified times and in public places. This was intended to provide equal access for all weavers to the supply of thread and prevent hoarding or speculation. Sales occurred through direct contact of buyer and seller. Municipal mandates usually encouraged market transactions to be direct transactions between producer and consumer. Such face-to-face exchanges were held to offer the maximum supply of thread at the lowest possible cost to the weaver. Sales were immediately subjected to official scrutiny. The city was concerned not only to collect its revenues but also to protect the quality of local products and the livelihood of local artisans.

Traditionally, thread was sold by weight measured in *Pfund*, which varied from roughly 472 to 491 grams. This method of sale had the virtue of preventing variation in amount if not in quality. Sometime during the sixteenth century, however, spinners and middlemen began to sell several new linen threads: *Fäden, Leipziger,* and *Wepfen.* The first term referred to thread sold according to the number of strands, or Fäden, rather than by weight. Leipziger, also known as *Schlesischer* or *lange Garn*, was a linen thread of exceedingly poor quality imported from the eastern Empire. Wepfen, or warp threads, were semifinished goods, consisting of prestrung threads wound on the warp axis and ready to be mounted on the loom.

To the weavers who purchased them, these goods shared certain virtues and vices. They were usually less expensive than high-quality

5. StA Memmingen, A475/3. *Supplikation an ein ersamen Rat.* s.d., s.a.
6. StA Lindau, 54,1. *Garnhausordnung*, 1594.

linen thread, thus lowering production costs and yielding a less expensive, more competitive product. They were also less durable and open to variations in length, however, which resulted in inferior cloth and depressed demand.

The new types of thread stirred controversy in the Allgäu during the 1500s and painfully and persistently raised production issues. The relative advantages and disadvantages could divide the community of weavers.[7] Poorer weavers probably advocated the purchase and use of less expensive threads and ready-made Wepfen because of their lower cost and higher efficiency. They permitted increased productivity through the speedier completion of cloth and promised a marginal gain because of lowered costs. More substantial masters usually focused on the marginal costs resulting from poorer quality and lost reputation. Memminger weavers made the issue crystal clear when they mandated minimum lengths for salable Fäden.[8] Moreover, weavers in some cities were liable for goods that incorporated inferior materials, such as Fäden or Schlesischer.[9] Wepfen, too, opened the door to variations in the length and quality of thread and inspired concerted efforts to control production and circulation.

Behind these innovations stood the middleman, or *Grempler*. His presence was probably a direct result of the growing volume of cloth production and the inability of spinners to meet demand for thread and weavers to obtain adequate supplies. Given the close connection between these agents and the needs of producers, it comes as no surprise that many Gremplers were themselves weavers, who traded in thread. But they distorted those very transactions that weavers had to control to preserve their economic independence. New forms of thread upset the delicate balance between production costs, traditional quality, and market prices. Moreover, the speculative practice of buying up thread for resale at the highest price, known as *Fürkauf*, intruded into the idyllic, direct-exchange economy, which worked to the advantage of weavers.

Weavers clearly understood the complexities of linen production and the linen market and could use its bottlenecks and transactions profitably. In 1549 the council of Kempten complained to the coun-

---

7. Claus-Peter Clasen, *Die Augsburger Weber: Leistungen und Krisen des Textilgewerbes um 1600* (Augsburg, 1981), pp. 140–209.

8. StA Memmingen, A475/2. *Garnordnung*, 1590.

9. StA Isny, A795/18. *Ratsbescheid*, February 4, 1597.

cil of Memmingen that Memminger weavers were buying up thread
in the countryside around Kempten, hiding it "before the gates of
Kempten and in other secret places" and reselling or weaving it.[10]
The Memminger magistrates replied that their weavers were not allowed to purchase thread within the *Zihl*, the three *Meilen* limit
around their own city, except at public market.[11] They could, however, buy and sell at will beyond this zone. The magistrates further
insisted that weavers bought for their own needs only, but that middlemen who purchased for resale and profit did great damage to the
common good. The activities of these agents, many of whom came
from Augsburg and Kempten, forced Memminger weavers to hunt
for other sources of thread, and their violation of the Kemptener
markets had to do finally with the limit of twenty-four Pfund on
thread purchased by foreigners. The Memminger magistrates concluded disingenuously with the suggestion that the problem in
Kempten would correct itself if the magistrates would open their
markets to outsiders.

To prevent Fürkauf and control the activities of the Grempler, the
cities of the Allgäu undertook extraordinary, cooperative efforts.
The scope and determination of these leave no doubt that weavers
and magistrates understood market speculation to be the greatest
single threat to their prosperity. Speculation violated God's will by
depriving workers of their wages and setting the individual good
over that of the community. Because the Grempler frequently
traded in Fäden, Wepfen, and lange Garn, authorities linked attempts to control these types of merchandise with attempts to control the Grempler themselves.

The single most spectacular regional effort to regulate the thread
market was the *Weberbund* of 1532. The cities of Memmingen, Ravensburg, Kempten, Wangen, Isny, and Leutkirch joined forces to
restrict Fürkauf and to limit competition between members.[12] Henceforth, middlemen would be limited to buying and selling in their

10. StA Memmingen, A475/3. Letter to *Kemptener Rat*, February 19, 1549: "Alls
solten etliche unser Burger des weber handtwercks uff dem land hin unnd wider
gehausiert garen uffkhaufft dasselbig zum thaill unnder jrer statthorn unnd anndern
haimlichen winckeln versteckt unnd zum thaill frevenlich unnd mutwilliger weis one
alles scheuchen an jren wheren getragen unnd dasselbig alles wider die ordnung jre
unsere unnd andere stet diser lanndtsart buergere des weber handtwerckh betref-
fendt auch zu wider jrer stat freihait gethaun."
11. The German *Meil* was roughly equivalent to 7.1 kilometers (4.26 miles).
12. StA Memmingen, A475/1. *Weberbund*, 1532.

native markets, and weavers would be prohibited from purchasing thread outside regulated, public markets. Grempler could sell only locally produced thread, and individual sales could not exceed twenty-four Pfund. Weavers were allowed only one purchase from a Grempler per week and could finish and sell cloth only in their own cities. Nor could they seek new markets outside the Bund. A single exception allowed trade between the cities of Isny, Wangen, and Leutkirch. The importation of lange Garn and the production of Wepfen were also prohibited, with the exception of *Golschwepfen* purchased by Memminger weavers. Finally, the signatories erected trade embargoes against certain cities and territories.

The Weberbund failed almost immediately. Many territorial governments refused to prohibit activities, such as the production of certain kinds of thread, that were profitable to their subjects. In 1536 the Bund met to discuss conditions on the thread market and noted with evident despair that neighboring states had erected finishing works and markets and permitted the use of illegal threads.[13] Though the quality of their cloth was poorer than that of the Bund, their prices were lower, and they were attracting cloth merchants away from member cities. Furthermore, as these products were frequently less expensive than those purchased on regulated markets, many signatories soon broke ranks, too. Urban weavers clearly pursued their own gains by exploiting any available markets, forcing the members to recognize that any effective market control would require the cooperation not only of the member cities but of their neighbors as well.

In 1570 a new attempt was made to regulate the activities of middlemen by enlisting the cooperation of all cities and territories in the region.[14] Though many were willing to prohibit Fürkauf, others raised cogent objections to such a prohibition, pointing out that it worked to the advantage of consumers, most of whom were urban weavers, but placed the rural producers at a disadvantage. Counselors of the Bishop of Augsburg argued that such a policy would be disastrous for poor folk, many of whom lived far from the markets and could not afford the time, exertion, or expense of traveling to

13. StA Memmingen, A475/7. *Weberbund*, 1536.
14. StA Memmingen, A476/1. *Das Fuerkauf betreffend*, 1570.

them.[15] These same poor spinners depended on the credit extended by middlemen; they simply did not earn enough to survive from one market day to the next.[16] Fürkauf was the easiest way for rural weavers to sell their goods. The Ritter Hans Philipp Shad von Mittelbiberach took up the bishop's reasoning and added a further dimension: in difficult times rural weavers had to seek the highest possible price for their thread.[17] Furthermore, urban weavers conspired to wring from rural weavers a price lower than they might get from a Grempler.[18] These princes and authorities did not mention that Gremplers and their custom enriched their own coffers through taxes and duties of various sorts.

Transactions between spinners and weavers were clearly a fluid exchange that could take a number of forms and occur in a number of settings. As long as the transactions remained unfixed, the urban weaver risked potentially higher prices and uncertain supplies. Attempts at regulation, however, might rebound to the disadvantage of the very artisans they were designed to protect. The magistrates of Isny learned this to their cost in 1594, 1596, and 1603, when they prohibited the trade in Fäden as well as Fürkauf only to see all thread disappear from their markets.[19] Driven by the demands of Gremplers, spinners produced Fäden to the near exclusion of all other forms of thread. When these goods were prohibited, there were no other sources of supply. The authorities of Isny, forced to

15. StA Memmingen, A476/1. Letter from *Staathalter und Räte zu Dillingen*, April 26, 1570: "Die armen leut den marckhten mererthails weit entsessen, windters zeit vvere des wegs und shlechter cleidung die nit erraichen ja auch zu zeiten ungewitterss unnd strengen wetters halben nit von oder da sy sich weit davon begeben widerumben shwerlich oder wol gar nit jnn jre heuser khomen dardurch mit ainem shlechten besuoch all jr armuth verlassen und jn gefar stellen messen."

16. StA Memmingen, A476/1. Letter from *Staathalter und Räte zu Dillingen*, April 26, 1570: "Das sy damit des marckhts nit allain it erwarthen sonder kaum ain pfanndt zusammen bringen khinden so sy nit gleich not halben wa sy sich und jre khinder der hungers not erwohnen wollen ja biss weitem zu halben und gantzen fierlingen verkauffen oder darauf entlehnen muessen."

17. StA Memmingen, A476/1. Letter from *Ritter Hans Philipp Shad von Mittelbiberach*, April 29, 1570: ". . . mancher armer mann mit verkhauffung seines garns des wochenmarckhts bey disen theuren jarn nit erwarten kan, sondern wirth dahin getrungen sein aigen garn gegen dem zuverkhauffen der jme zum maisten gelt darumben gibt."

18. StA Memmingen, A476/1. Letter from *Ritter Hans Philipp Shad von Mittelbiberach*, April 29, 1570: "Zu dem ob sy gleich das garn uff die wochen marckht jnn den stetten tragen so seyen die selben weber dermassen aufainander abgericht das sy dem armen mann das garn umb halb gelt abzukhauffen gesinnet."

19. Clasen, *Die Augsburger Weber*, p. 169.

submit to the necessity of ensuring their weavers thread of some kind, withdrew the prohibitions.

While changes in season, supply, form, and quality certainly affected the price of thread, consistent lists of prices are all but nonexistent. Fragments survive. But these figures do not reveal what the spinner earned or what the weaver paid. Prices were subject to change, and information regarding their movements in the sixteenth and seventeenth centuries is inconclusive. Thus, no transaction costs can be derived for these processes. However, related conclusions are possible. No evidence indicates that Allgäuer weavers complained about the supply or cost of thread. If this fact indicates that no natural shortages occurred, then supply and cost were always acceptable unless regulation created some comparative disadvantage in a market, which occurred in Isny in the late 1590s and early 1600s. Taken together, these speculations suggest that the supply of thread, regardless of form, quality, or origin, was probably sufficient and affordable, at least in absolute terms.

Weavers produced a bewildering array of textiles from the thread they purchased in the market or beyond the Zihl. In a linen center, such as Isny, production might be reduced to two categories of cloth, coarse and fine linen. However, within these categories existed a large variety of sorts depending on the thickness and quality of the thread and the type of finishing. Where linen blends were manufactured the number of cloth types could be much greater.

The hand-loom underwent no technological improvement in the sixteenth and seventeenth centuries. Developed in the Middle Ages, it remains a relatively familiar machine today, and its function is reasonably well known. The static technology of weaving prior to the eighteenth century underscores, therefore, the critical importance of work organization and production transactions. Within the shop increased productivity could be attained only by intensification or specialization. The early modern weavers in the Allgäu did both.

Associated tasks consumed the weaver's time or forced a degree of specialization in the workshop. If any spinning were done in the shop, it usually fell to some person other than the weaver: a wife, daughter, or apprentice. Linen thread became brittle when dry; therefore, it had to be washed prior to weaving and kept damp during the entire process. For this reason, linen weavers tended to work in cellars or semisubterranean rooms that remained naturally moist. Like spinning, washing the thread was delegated to a family member, an apprentice, or a servant. Once washed, the weft had to be wound onto the shuttle and the warp threaded onto the loom, both labor-intensive tasks that were entrusted to other members of the household or workshop, thus permitting weavers to concentrate on their essential function.

To produce more cloth, weavers with sufficient capital intensified production by adding looms, usually operated by journeymen or impoverished masters. Unfortunately it is impossible to reconstruct the number of looms operated by master weavers in any Allgäuer city, except Memmingen. A 1595 tabulation of master weavers revealed a total of 231, 90 of whom worked a single loom and 141 of whom worked two. In 1598 single-loom workshops reached a peak, with 106 masters, as opposed to only 65 with two looms. There is no reference to more than two looms in a single shop. By 1601 the relationship of masters with a single loom to masters with two looms was again reversed: of 205 masters 72 had but one loom and 133 had two.[20] By comparison, for the Swabian metropolis of Augsburg figures ranged from one to four per workshop with the vast majority of masters operating two.[21] Only five Augsburger masters operated as many as five looms. The number of looms and varieties of cloth confirm the image of these weavers as independent, petty producers.

Understandably, the price that weavers could demand for their cloth varied according to type. Had weavers been engaged in free market activities, they might have varied the number of looms operated and the types of cloth produced according to market imperatives. Master weavers frequently dedicated all or some of their machines to the production of a single kind of cloth in accordance with

20. StA Memmingen, A478/3. *Zahl der Webermeister.*

Year	One Loom	Two Looms	Sum
1595	90	141	231
1596	135	134	269
1597			
1598	106	65	171
1599	89	106	195
1600	88	120	208
1601	72	133	205
1623			292

21. Clasen, *Die Augsburger Weber*, pp. 54–57.

demand. As a result entire communities specialized. Isny, Leutkirch, and Wangen produced linen to the exclusion of all other textiles.

Master weavers exercised firm control over the structure of their workshops in the early modern period. Still, this independence was never allowed to clash with the greater need to ensure the common good, the livelihood of all. According to demand and prices, the authorities could and did order changes in the structure of the workshop.

Only indirect evidence exists that Allgäuer magistrates ever ordered reductions in the maximum number of looms operated per workshop as a means of curbing production. The weavers of Memmingen noted in a petition to their city council that masters in Kempten were allowed to operate no more than two looms to prevent overproduction.[22] Yet, in cities where the maximum number of looms per workshop rarely exceeded two, radical measures of this sort would have served only to deprive journeymen of their livelihoods and reduce masters to starvation. More selective means to control production were necessary.

One such method specified what sort of cloth could be produced on a given loom. In those cities that produced a variety of textiles, magistrates could mandate production of certain types on certain looms. According to the *Weberordnung* of 1549, no master weaver in Memmingen could produce linen on more than one loom, and the total annual production of linen could not exceed twenty-five pieces.[23]

Magistrates occasionally regulated the production of certain kinds of cloth altogether. In 1540 Graf Anton Fugger petitioned the council of Memmingen to permit his subjects in Babenhausen to bring *Golsch*, a type of linen, into the city for finishing and sale.[24] This marked an expansion of access to Memmingen markets by Babenhausen artisans, but the council wished to grant the request because, as they noted, Golsch was not woven in Memmingen. The weavers opposed Fugger's request and claimed that the lack of domestic Golsch production was the result of a conciliar mandate prohibiting

---

22. StA Memmingen, A475/7. *Supplikation des Weberhandwerks,* July, 18 1583: "Zuo Kempten . . . da er ain maister wiert darff er nhun auf zwayen stielen ettlich jar wurckhen . . . damit dass handtwerckh nit jbersetzt."

23. StA Memmingen, A465/2.

24. StA Memmingen, A475/5. Letter from *Graf Anton Fugger Babenhausen,* September 6, 1540.

it.[25] Were they allowed to produce Golsch, the weavers of Memmingen would do so. The council acceded to the wishes of their weavers, refused Fugger's initiative, and ordered that Golsch be woven in Memmingen.

Graf Fugger's request on behalf of his subjects excited fears that these foreign weavers would consume raw materials and finishing processes, making them unavailable or raising their costs for local artisans. Such concerns inspired the most violent uprisings of Allgäuer weavers between 1580 and 1656. Finishing transactions always inspired greater concern among weavers than thread transactions.

Once their cloth was woven, weavers confronted a classic production bottleneck and with it a series of critical decisions. They could sell their product raw and uncut, or they could finish it. Finishing involved several possible steps: fulling, bleaching or dyeing, and cutting. For early modern weavers in the Allgäu, bleaching was the most desirable and the most problematical finishing process. Its desirability derived from the price of bleached linen, which was consistently higher than either raw or dyed linen. In Memmingen bleached linen was valued at one *Gulden* more than the same type of linen dyed.[26] The problem was the method of bleaching, which was both arcane and risky.

Before the advent in the mid-eighteenth century of chemical agents, such as hydrochloric acid and liquid chlorine, bleaching was not an exact science. No guilds existed to regulate the training of master bleachers or to enforce uniform standards of production. The processes were closely guarded secrets, and varied extraordinarily among bleaching masters.[27] This fact is revealed by the testimony of several experts in Memmingen. City officials asked the bleaching master, Bartholomeus N.; the fulling master, Enderlin Heberlin; the field master, Hanns Kress; and the lye master, Hanns Mayr, to describe the process of bleaching and fulling linen.[28] Though the four masters worked in the same place, their descrip-

---

25. StA Memmingen, A475/7. *Supplikation des Weberhandwerks,* July 15, 1583: "Da ist ain solliche anzal Golschen gemacht worden dass E. E. F. W. bevelch gebem dieselben nit mer zuo beshreiben."

26. StA Memmingen, A134/13. *Verhör der Weber,* October 26, 1586.

27. H. T. Parker, *The Bureau of Commerce in 1781 and Its Policies with Respect to French Industry* (Durham, N.C., 1979), p. 116.

28. StA Memmingen, A476/2. *Anzayg vom Blaich- Walck-, Laug-, und Feldmaister,* 1574.

tions varied remarkably in the amount of heat, water, acid, lye, and exposure given the raw textile.

Generalizing from these four accounts, the method of fulling and bleaching linen emerges. Raw cloth was fulled for one to two hours. Then it was placed in the bleaching field and exposed to the sun for one to two weeks depending on weather conditions and cloth quality. During the fielding the cloth was turned frequently and always kept damp. After the first fielding, the cloth was "bucked," that is, boiled in a lye mixture of water and potash, usually derived from wood ashes, for a period of three to four hours. Bucking removed colored matter from the raw linen. The linen was then removed from the hot alkaline solution to be washed and fulled. Thereafter it was soaked in a warm, alkaline solution the strength of which was made progressively weaker as the cloth became whiter. Bucked linen was again laid in the bleaching field, where it was kept moist and exposed for a week to ten days. After the second fielding, the linen entered the souring process to remove mordants, inorganic substances that would combine with dirt to form insoluble colored matter. For this stage of bleaching, an acid solution was used. Memminger sources do not specify the type of acid, but mixtures of buttermilk, fermented bran, crabapple juice, or lemon juice and water were common elsewhere.[29] The cloth soaked in this acidic solution for two days or more depending on the condition of the cloth itself and was then fulled for thirty minutes to an hour and fielded for a week to ten days again. The entire procedure, which required an absolute minimum of twenty-one days, might be performed once or as many as seven times, depending on the cloth, the weather, and the procedure, to obtain the desired whiteness.

On the basis of work process alone, several observations are possible. All reveal the bleaching works as a protofactory.

Bleaching required a large physical plant. An open field was usually enclosed by fences or hedges with huts scattered about them for guards. Several structures stood more or less in the center. These included the fulling mill, bucking and souring house, and occasionally a pressing house. Canals and pathways crisscrossed the fields to provide essential moisture for the fielded cloth and to allow passage for carts. That these fields were large may be implied from the volume and size of cloth. In mid-seventeenth century Isny the

29. Archibald N. Clow, *The Chemical Revolution* (London, 1952), p. 178.

bleaching fields accommodated hundreds of pieces of cloth simultaneously, each of which were some seventy centimeters wide and several meters long.

Bleaching was labor intensive. Many hands were required to full, buck, and sour the cloth, treating three hundred to five hundred pieces at a time. Many workers hauled cloth to and from the fields, kept the fielded cloth moist over weeks, and turned the unwieldy individual pieces of cloth several times daily. The need for labor varied with the organization of the fields. If they were laid about centrally located works, eight to ten hands might suffice; whereas linear bleaching fields, along a stream, for example, required sixty.[30]

Bleaching was time-consuming. The process described in Memmingen took from three weeks to four months. It was also seasonal. Given the fielding of damp cloth over long periods of time, bleaching could not be efficiently performed in the winter. Probably, for this reason the magistrates of Isny were prepared in 1581 and again in 1597 to restrict foreign linen on the Isnyer bleaching fields to the winter months between October 16 and the first fielding in spring. During this period less local cloth was finished.

Bleaching was complex. Many variables were involved, and each affected the time required to whiten linen and the quality of the finished goods. As might be expected in so complicated a procedure, the various elements of which were set by trial and error, there was much risk of damage. Bleaching masters had to be conscientious and skilled, qualities revealed only through experience over the course of time.

Their task was not simple. Bleaching masters may have been among the earliest factory operators. Because they invested their own resources, exercised a free hand within their business, and pursued potentially unbounded profits, they may also have been among the first industrial capitalists.

Every textile-producing city provided bleaching fields for the use of local artisans. Cities with a growing population of weavers or with a desire to promote themselves as weaving centers might establish bleaching fields as an incentive. Lindau was never a weaving center. Its weavers were too few to warrant their own guild; their craft was

---

30. Clow, *The Chemical Revolution*, p. 179.

subsumed in the Tailor's Guild, among others dealing in cloth.[31] Nonetheless, in 1595 the city decided to open a bleaching field and asked advice of its neighbors, Leutkirch and Wangen, both linen-weaving centers. The information proffered provides a thumbnail sketch of bleaching fields as an enterprise and the transactions that occurred on them.

The city council of Leutkirch reported that the bleaching fields were the property of the city, which rented them to a bleaching master for fourteen Gulden per annum.[32] The city was responsible for the maintenance of all fixed structures, including fences, the fulling mill, and the bucking kettle and stand. In addition, Leutkirch provided all the wood needed for maintaining structures or for hanging linen. The bleaching master paid for all perishable supplies and the wages of his assistants, including the fulling master, the bucking master, the field master, and all servants. The bleaching master also provided three hundred Gulden as security against damage to goods on the bleaching fields. For each piece of linen destined for sale on the open market, the city collected one *Kreutzer* as a toll, and the bleaching master received eleven Kreutzer as his fee. An addendum testified that in 1604 the master's fee rose to fourteen Kreutzer for each piece of linen. These sums were to be rendered by the owner of the linen before it left the bleaching fields.

In 1594 the Leutkircher bleaching works finished thirty-six hundred pieces of linen, excluding those pieces woven for domestic consumption rather than sale.[33] As a result, the bleaching master earned a considerable gross profit of 660 Gulden. Apparently, bleaching could be a lucrative business in Leutkirch.

The agreements struck in Wangen and Leutkirch were virtually identical.[34] Together they reveal much about bleaching as an enterprise and its place in the series of transactions, which constituted linen production. Cities provided fixed capital. Bleaching masters provided the working capital, bore all operating costs, and assumed all risks.

The risks were considerable, and gross incompetence could cost a bleaching master his position. Such was the fate of Bartholomeus

31. StA Lindau, 114,11. *Bericht der Schneiderzunft,* June 28, 1588: "Das Weberwerckh alhie gering."
32. StA Lindau, 54,1. Letter from *Leutkircher Rat,* March 12, 1595.
33. StA Lindau, 54,1.
34. StA Lindau, 54,1. Letter from *Wangner Rat,* March 31, 1595.

Brewer, whose hiring by the city of Wangen was described for the benefit of the city council of Lindau. He was fired in 1597 for damaging numerous pieces of cloth by laying them on top of dung left in the bleaching field by grazing sheep.[35] Evidently the sheep were intended to fertilize the field, the hay from which was Brewer's property.

Haying and bleaching underscore the nature of this work. Though risks were high, an enterprising master could profit handsomely. He had real incentives to hold down operating costs and finish as many pieces of cloth as possible because no limits were placed on the amount that might be earned on the bleaching fields, despite careful, municipal control. This may explain the desire of bleaching masters to keep their fields full and the readiness to finish foreign cloth to the exclusion of local products. Bleaching was in every sense an entrepreneurial form of production.

Spinning, weaving, and bleaching, each a component in the manufacture of textiles, were, nevertheless, distinct processes connected by market transactions. Nothing so clearly underscores the inadequacies of protoindustrial or regional analysis as the almost complete lack of sectorial specialization or regional integration in the Allgäu.[36] Whereas a functional interrelationship between merchant capital and domestic economies emerged in the pursuit of foreign markets, the organization of production resembled a *Kaufsystem* based on local sales. Labor, capital, and credit may have circulated regionally, but were most often purchased locally.[37] Towns and cities replicated much infrastructure, too, without regard for integration, specialization, or capacity. One need only recall the abortive attempts of Lindau and Babenhausen to promote productivity through advance construction of marketplaces, inspection houses, bleaching fields, and fulling mills. In the Allgäu intense competition resulted, driven by price dynamics and comparative advantage. Myriad transactions that occurred during the production process created tensions within industrial sectors and encouraged differential development within the region.

These transactions served as fault lines exerting pressure on the

35. StA Wangen. *Ratsprotokolle*, December 5, 1597.
36. *Regions and Industries*, pp. 15–26.
37. I intend to explore these factors in a more extensive study of linen production in the Upper Allgäu between the collapse of the Great Ravensburger Company in the 1530s and the collapse of the industry itself.

workers engaged in them. By virtue of the closely regulated nature of their craft and their condition as independent, petty producers, weavers found this network of transactions particularly debilitating. Provided they negotiated it successfully, they maintained their status. If they failed to command it, this same network could deprive them of their self-sufficiency.

Nothing so clearly reveals the tenuous situation of linen weavers and the paradox of linen production as the uprisings of Allgäuer craftsmen. Unrest and violence played a part in the negotiations that surrounded production transactions.

On January 8, 1580, the weavers of Isny protested the dyeing of foreign linen in their city.[38] Though details are lacking, the dyeing of foreign cloth posed two possible problems for local artisans. First, foreign cloth competed for the time and materials of the dyers. This made finishing more expensive or more time-consuming, either of which might reduce the weaver's profit. Second, once dyed the foreign linen was inspected by municipal officials and awarded the seals appropriate for those processes carried out in Isny. Thereafter, it could be sold on local markets as locally produced linen, a common practice in most early modern textile centers. Beyond an increase in the volume of cloth for sale, which also depressed prices, many sales of putative Isnyer linen in no way involved or enriched Isnyer craftsmen.

What sort of pressure the weavers exerted is unknown; the council decree referred only to "forbidden and unseemly rioting and unrest."[39] However, the results of the weavers' actions were unequivocal. The council prohibited the fulling or bleaching of all foreign linen, apart from a small consignment already in the works, which would be speedily finished and removed.[40] On the insistence of the weavers, the magistrates altered a situation that would have increased transaction costs between weaving and finishing.

The events of 1580 were not an isolated instance of weavers ready to back economic demands with political actions. Risings occurred

38. StA Isny, A1072/366. *Streitigkeiten des Weberhandwerks*, 1580–98.

39. StA Isny, A795/18. *Extractus protocolli*, s.d. 1580: "Verbottenen ungebuehrlichen rottieren und unrhu."

40. StA Isny, A795/18. *Extractus protocolli*, s.d. 1580: "Alss dann uff solche Zeit einiche frembde Leinwath unangesehen wann sie shon nit gar gefertigget weder gewalcket noch geferbt werden solle."

across the Allgäu between 1580 and 1656: Isny in 1597–98, Memmingen in 1607, Kempten in 1611, Leutkirch in 1620, and Isny again in 1656.[41] Despite variations of time and place, the circumstances of each revolt remained the same. Weavers felt jeopardized by any failure to control the critical transactions that dominated their craft.

The most spectacular of these risings was the so-called Weberkrieg of Isny in 1597–98, which threatened the political order of the city and provoked the armed intervention of neighboring city-states. The intense antagonism of the weavers was unique, but the issues at stake were those of 1580. Once again, the transactions involved in the production of linen created difficulties and uncertainty for weavers.

On January 14, 1597, Isnyer artisans petitioned the council to prohibit the finishing and sale of foreign linen on local markets. They protested that weavers and merchants from Wangen brought their linen to be bleached, inspected, and sold in Isny.[42] Wangen had its own linen works and need not infringe on Isny's.[43] Beyond competition for the resources of the finishing processes, the presence of Wangner linen on Isnyer markets threatened sales of local cloth: "One of our poor journeymen with the same wares must wander the city eight days or longer and in the end not know what to do."[44] Despite the prohibition of 1580, foreign linen was now flooding the city's markets and could be purchased at any time.[45] The result had been especially dramatic in the sale of Isnyer dyed linens, demand for which had fallen to levels lower than that for the traditionally more expensive and less sought after bleached linens.[46] To halt the

41. Franz Ludwig Baumann, *Geschichte des Allgäus* (Aalen, 1973), p. 571.
42. StA Isny, A785/18. *Extractus protocolli*, February 11, 1597. *Supplikation des Weberhandwerks*.
43. Ibid.: "Die Weber von Wangen unangesehen sy eigen Schaw, blaichen, und kauff haben, je laenger ie mehr mit ihren leinwathern an unseren schawtagen grossen ubertranng und uns allso steets uf dem hals ligen."
44. Ibid.: "Unser armen gesellen ainer mit solcher und dergleichen wahr, etwann acht tag oder lenger inn der statt umbgath letstlich dannacht nit waist wa auss oder an."
45. Ibid.: "Dieweil aber angeregte frembde Leinwath ihren gang dermassen widerumb gewunnen allso dass die hauffenweiss herein gebracht wirdt, so und wann ein frembder alher kompt, das die durch das gantz jahr und iederzeit zu bekommen ist."
46. Ibid.: "Dadurch dann unser farbleinwathhandel, der vor diser zeit bey unser eltern etwann in hoechern und mehren werdt dann die blaich leinwath gewesen ietz

tide of foreign linen, the weavers pledged to provide whatever cloth the merchants might demand at the best possible price.[47] Though ambiguous, this offer suggests the ability of weavers to comprehend the market and negotiate shrewdly in it.

Like foreign linen, foreign thread invaded the Isnyer markets and made transactions in raw materials risky. Local thread was more durable but more expensive, and the less expensive import gradually forced it from the market. The weavers expressed concern about the continued sale of Leipziger and other foreign threads that were so poor in quality that they would not endure the standard processes of soaking and bleaching or dying. The use of these raw materials threatened sales of all local cloth. Merchants who merely suspected that such thread was woven in a piece of cloth would refuse to purchase it or demand a lower price.[48] The sale of Leipziger had to be prohibited to keep it out of Isnyer linen.

On the presence of foreign linen in Isny there was no agreement. The magistrates steadfastly refused drastic protectionist measures. Instead they noted that the access of Wangner merchants and weavers to the Isnyer market was a matter of contractual agreement more than fifty years old. Any attempt to abrogate this right could lead to litigation far more damaging than the practice itself.[49] Furthermore, the entire notion of prohibiting foreign linen seemed strange to the council. Many textile centers, such as Memmingen, Ulm, St. Gall, Ravensburg, and Immenstadt, so the magistrates said, sought to attract foreign merchants and linen for the profit of local craftsmen.[50] To forbid this trade altogether would cost the city important sources of income from customs and fees, income that sup-

---

under aber allerdings entzogen, in merckhlichen abgang auch gantz und gar zu grund gehn will."

47. Ibid.: "Dem allem nach erbieten wir uns gantz willig und getrewes vleiss den herrn kaufleuthen wahren zu machen es sey klein, grob, brait, shmall, duenn und dergleichen, wie sie es iederzeit an unss erfordern oder begehren und ihr beste gelegenheit sein wirdt."

48. Ibid.: "Ain Kauffman, etwan ein Stuckh fuergelegt wirdt, an dem er besorgt, gemelten garns darbei sey, sich alssbald ein solchers zu kauffen beshwert auch umb ein ringere bezahlung zu haben vermaint."

49. Ibid.: "Gegen dem Weberhandtwerckh alhie auch erwerungen und gebott fuernemmen moechten."

50. Ibid.: "Allso ueblich und gebrauchig, ia mit sonderm fleiss dergleichen frembde Leinwathshaw an solcher orth gezogen wirdt."

ported public charity, the chief beneficiaries of which were poor weavers themselves.[51] The council was not convinced that foreign—especially Wangner—cloth prejudiced the sale of local goods; Isnyer weavers produced large quantities of linen, had this product readily finished, and never failed to find buyers.[52] Given these arguments, the council was unwilling to abandon traditional practice and close the Isny works and markets to foreign trade. Such actions would awaken hostilities at a time when the city could not afford it.

If the city's decision awakened no hostility among merchants and neighboring cities, it certainly provoked the local weavers. Trapped by their own limited resources, weavers faced ruinous competition if exposed to the open-market transactions advocated by council.

The same day the council's decree was read, February 10, 1597, a large group of what the magistrates later described as "for the most part depraved, reckless, and useless journeymen" gathered in the guild hall to plan further action.[53] As the meeting became more menacing, the council decided to act against the weavers. That evening several persons perceived as ringleaders were arrested; others escaped into the sanctuary of the local monastery. Word of the arrests spread quickly. Fearing violence, the council ordered that the city gates remain closed the next morning. Armed groups of weavers slipped over the wall into the monastery compound to assist their comrades. A mob of between two hundred and three hundred armed suburban weavers, accompanied by their wives and children, approached the city's northern gate and demanded the release of the captives and the acceptance of their demands. Fearing bloodshed and disorder, the council capitulated. In return for the weavers' obedience, they agreed to reinstate the ordinance of 1580 prohibiting all foreign linen in the Isnyer works. The Wangner weavers were required to provide proof of their contractual right to bring their goods to Isny. If such proof was available, then negotia-

51. Ibid.: "Dessen dann gemeine Statt zu den vilen beharrlichen Turggen anlagen und taeglichen underhaltung der Armen darunder dann mehrertheils des Weberhandtwercks hochnotturfftig wie auch inns gemain vast allen andern handtwerckhern zu gutem ufnemmen gedeyen und gelangen that."

52. Ibid.: "Sintemahl der allhiesigen Leinwath vertrib darduch gar nicht gesteckht oder verhindert sonder da sy die weber alhie nur viel Leinwath machen, ihnen daran nichts ueberblibe, sonnder sy alle tag und stund ohne langes herumb tragen oder faylbieten kauffleuth genug darzu hetten."

53. StA Isny, A795/18. *Extractus protocolli*, s.d., 1580. "Etliche unruehigen und meistentheils verdorbnen leichtferttigen und unnutzen gesellen."

tions could proceed. It was a moment of triumph for the artisans of Isny.

The city of Wangen promptly sued the weavers of Isny before the *Reichskammergericht* in Speyer to halt the illegal prohibition of their linen. They claimed the action taken by Isnyer weavers was illegal on three counts: (1) it violated "free trade and handwork;" (2) it constituted a "monopolistic and selfish action;" and (3) it "deprived persons of their livelihood to an unseemly degree."[54] Moreover, since 1532, when the cities of the Allgäu formed the so-called Weberbund to control cooperatively the sale and speculation in linen thread, Isny, Wangen, and Leutkirch alone among all the signatories opened their works and markets to one another.[55] In response the court issued a restraining order in the form of an imperial mandate. The weavers of Isny were ordered to reopen their works and markets to Wangner craftsmen and goods until a legal settlement was reached.[56] Defiance would result in fines against the weavers.

For their part, the weavers of Wangen were less interested in legal niceties than in the sale of their cloth. When questioned, one admitted that 1596 had seen an unusually large amount of cloth exported from Wangen to Isny. However, at no time was the total amount of Wangner linen in Isny more than twenty pieces. These exports were driven by low demand on the Wangner markets; by contrast Isny was "praise God so blessed with merchants that they cannot produce linen enough to satisfy them."[57] Indeed, market scarcity and competition seem to have inspired both sides. The Wangner weavers probably hoped to sell their linen as Isnyer cloth, which enjoyed a reputation for quality. Isnyer masters feared a crisis

54. StA Wangen, VI w 9 nr. 4. *Supplication pro mandato de non impediendo et non offendendo cum annexa citatione*, s.d. 1597: "Freye handels und handtwerckhs gewerbs . . . monopolischer und aigennuetzigen handlungen anmassen . . . iemands sein marung unzimlicher massen abstrickhen."

55. StA Memmingen, A475/1. *Weberbund* 1532: "Dessgleichen soll auch kain Statt sollicher Verainung der andern und jren Webern under jrem gewonnlichen zaichen weder schawen, blaichen, raiffen, ferbn, noch schneiden in kainen weg. Dann allain haben uns den von Ysni unser verwandten diss verstendtnus zugelassen dass wir unsern freunden von Wangen und Leutkierch was sy an unser schaw wurckhen, schawen, plaichen, unser gewonnlich loblich zaichen geben auch raiffen, ferben, und schneiden moegen wie von altter herkommen ist."

56. StA Wangen, VI w 9 nr. 2.

57. StA Wangen, VI w 9 nr. 7. *Interrogatorium*, s.d. 1597: "Dann sy Gott lob mit kauffleutten bei jnen also versahen das sie demselbigen nit gnug Leinwath wirken kinden."

of demand, whether these fears were grounded or not is impossible to determine.

On February 9, 1598, resistance broke out once more in Isny. Foreign linen had appeared in the Isnyer works and markets once again, and the weavers considered themselves betrayed. They threatened to overthrow the present government if the magistrates were not willing to hold to their agreements. The city council called for armed support from neighboring cities to suppress the revolt. Memmingen, Lindau, and Kempten responded to the call. Fifty arquebusiers marched from Lindau on February 13.[58] Another contingent of fifty armed citizens of Memmingen reached Isny in time to prevent violence and force the weavers to negotiate.[59] By February 20 the parties, assisted by arbitrators from Lindau and Kempten, reached a settlement, and the Isnyer weavers returned to their looms.

The new settlement confirmed the victory of the artisans. In addition to many lesser issues, the central point about foreign linen was settled. The city of Wangen agreed to avoid the Isnyer works and markets in exchange for a sum of money to be specified later. Wangner weavers would sell to Isnyer merchants in Wangen.[60] To compensate Isny for this lost source of revenue, the city's weavers agreed to render a duty of three Kreutzer per piece of linen brought to market. All other foreign linen was banned from Isny as per the ordinance of 1581. Henceforth, the weavers of Isny would not be hindered in their access to the finishing resources of their own city. At a price, they secured their ability to control production transactions.

The events and issues in Isny reflect perfectly those in other cities of the region. The uprising of Memmingen weavers on January 30, 1607, began with a petition to prohibit the importation of foreign cloth for the purposes of finishing and sale.[61] In the decade preceding the revolt, the number of masters operating two looms had risen steadily.[62] The events of 1607 may represent a demand crisis, in which producers had overextended their resources and saturated

---

58. StA Lindau. *Ratsprotokolle*, February 10, 1598.

59. A. R. Vincenz, *Chronik der Stadt Isny im Allgäu und Umgegend vom Jahr 200 bis 1854* (Isny, 1854), p. 40.

60. StA Wangen, VI w 9 nr. 1. *Vertrag zwischen Wangen und Isny*, February 19, 1598.

61. StA Memmingen, A477/6.

62. Compare table in n. 20 above.

the market through overproduction. When the city council rejected this appeal for action, weavers, led by the journeymen, staged a work stoppage and paraded through the streets. The chronicles state that 146 journeymen were arrested.[63] A larger group of masters and journeymen met with the council. Several of the detained workers were released, but council and craft reached no agreement on the issue of foreign linen. The weavers returned to their homes; the magistrates prosecuted the ringleaders. The council issued a final decree on July 1, 1607, upholding the right of merchants to import foreign cloth produced outside the Memminger Zihl.[64] As in Isny and elsewhere, craftsmen feared the increased transaction costs associated with high volumes of foreign goods on local markets. For their part, the magistrates upheld—this time successfully—the principle of open markets and unrestricted trade.

In Isny transactions were apparently well regulated for almost sixty years, from 1598 until 1656. Encroachments of foreign linen were carefully scrutinized and permitted only with the approval of the weavers. In 1627 the Bürgermeister of Isny noted that local weavers were disturbed by rumors that the merchant family Eberz was importing foreign linen for finishing and sale.[65] The council warned weavers and merchants to remember the obedience due city ordinances. Two years later the weavers accused the brothers Reiser of purchasing raw linen in Kempten and finishing it in Isny.[66] Worse still, the artisans alleged that the Reisers acquired the city's linen seal from the *Raifer,* Jerg Vogler, and affixed it to their cloth themselves. This was a serious violation of municipal tariff and police authority. The Reisers and Vogler admitted the misdeed, but claimed that they only used the seal on locally produced linen. Unappeased, the council levied heavy fines against all parties. Again in 1631 the Isnyer weavers complained of the presence of foreign linen on the city's bleaching fields.[67] The merchants responsible, Eberz and Wolf, testified that war had deprived them of their access to foreign bleaching fields. Recognizing the difficulty of the situation, the weavers agreed to permit this finishing on an extraordinary basis. A similar accusa-

63. Stadtbibliothek Memmingen, 2° 2, 19. *Erhart Wintergerst Chronik von Memmingen und Johannes Kimpel Chronik,* pp. 288–92.
64. StA Memmingen, A 778/1.
65. StA Isny, A795/18. *Extractus protocolli,* December 8, 1627.
66. StA Isny, A795/18. *Extractus protocolli,* August 10, 1629.
67. StA Isny, A795/18. *Extractus protocolli,* June 17, 1631.

tion in 1632 excited Eberz to reply that the weavers had no grounds for complaint.[68] His family had purchased many hundreds of pieces of raw linen from Isnyer weavers and exported these goods for finishing. That they also imported foreign linen for local finishing should not create problems. Such mercantile activity benefited the entire industry. Indeed, the weavers of Isny were not completely shortsighted or selfish. A request for access to the city's finishing works by merchants from St. Gall was approved by the weavers with the note that they had received assistance from St. Gall in the past.[69] This extended negotiation between artisans and merchants is a salutary reminder of the limits of modern categories. Such early modern exchanges, though controlled by market factors, permitted non-market considerations.

Yet the market was never completely absent. On May 16, 1656, the weavers protested the large quantities of foreign linen again being finished on one of the city's two bleaching fields. Claiming that the foreign goods occupied space that should serve local cloth and, therefore, prevented it from being finished, the head of the weavers, Peter Frickh, requested that the council renew its ban on all foreign linen in the city.[70] The council responded indirectly by summoning the city's bleaching master, Georg Lang, and questioning him about the administration of the process in his charge. He expressed amazement at the weavers' accusations, insisting that his field was by no means full and frequently held several hundred pieces more than at present. Anxious to please the merchants with whom he did business, Lang confessed that he generally accepted cloth for bleaching without asking about its origins. The council warned him to administer the bleaching fields in such a manner as to cause no further complaint, but refused to take any specific action to close the city to foreign cloth. It promised merely to act in such a manner as was consistent with the common good.[71] The council rejected in the strongest possible terms a request by the weavers to inspect Lang's bleaching fields for abuses. Artisans had "nothing to do with these

---

68. StA Isny, A795/18. *Extractus protocolli*, September 7, 1632.
69. StA Isny, A795/18. *Aus den Weberzunftbüchern*, February 6, 1656.
70. StA Isny, A795/18. *Aus den Weberzunftbüchern*, May 26, 1656.
71. StA Isny, A795/18. *Aus den Weberzunftbüchern*, May 23, 1656: "Wegen den frembden Leinwat, keine mehr anzunehmen betrifft, will Ein Ers. Rhat es allso anstellen was sich gebuehren gemainer Statt nutzlich und gueth dem Weberhandtwerckh aber ohnshaedlich sein wurdet."

matters . . . and should consider that inspections of the bleaching fields, the appointment of bleaching inspectors, or anything else pertaining to the bleaching fields is the concern of the council alone."[72] This stern injunction precipitated mob action.

At about 6:00 P.M. on June 2, 1656, some 150 weavers, their wives, and children stormed the house of the Bürgermeister, Caspar Weisslandt.[73] Howling and crying, these poor folk pleaded with the official to prohibit the importation of foreign linen into Isny for the purposes of bleaching. Weisslandt informed them that the decision of the city council to open the Isnyer markets and works to foreign cloth would promote the common good. With that the weavers were shown the door.

After the events of June 2, the artisans submitted a formal petition that went considerably beyond their earlier demand to close the bleaching fields but still voiced the traditional litany of concerns and tensions at work in the craft.[74] Access to the bleaching fields remained an issue; the weavers requested that local products be finished before any foreign goods were accepted. Certain kinds of foreign goods—linens from the distant territory of Silesia and the neighboring city of Wangen—represented unacceptable competition; the weavers insisted that these be prohibited entirely. Schlesischer thread, which was synonymous with poor quality in the sixteenth and seventeenth centuries, had long plagued Isnyer weavers; it must be banned likewise. Clearly, in 1656 the weavers' concerns focused on the same few critical transactions that had occupied them for more than a century: the acquisition of raw materials in the form of thread, the access to limited resources in the form of finishing works, and the sale of cloth to merchants at the local market.

The council had other priorities. Reminding the weavers that it

---

72. StA Isny, A795/18. *Aus den Weberzunftbüchern.* May 26, 1656: "Dass handtwerckh oder jemandt aus demselben habe nichts dabey zuthun . . . solle selbiges den zunfftigen andencken die besichtigung der bleichen und bestellung der bleichenshawer oder was sonsten auf der bleichen zuverfuegen stehe allein einem ers. Rhat zu."

73. StA Isny, A795/18. *Aus den Weberzunftbüchern.* June 2, 1656: "Mit heyllen und shreyen gebetten die frembde Leinwat abzushaffen und nit wie heut dato von Rhat Gericht und Gemaindt beshlossen worden, in die Statt herein oder abblaichen zulassen. Es hat aber her Burgermaister sie berichtet wie der den Webern erthailte beshaidt ihnen ganz nicht zu nachthail sondern vielmehr zum besten gemaint. Sie damit wider abgewisen."

74. StA Isny, A795/18. *Aus den Weberzunftbüchern,* s.d. 1656.

understood the common good and the needs of their craft and would always act accordingly, the council refused to take any new action on their demands.[75] It noted that ordinances existed to control foreign linen and substandard thread, and it refused to restrict access to the Isnyer markets and finishing works in any way.

Against this uncompromising posture the weavers surprisingly showed no more willingness to resist or riot. They rejected the council's decision, but noted that it was too late in the year to effect any change; they hoped that new elections might bring a change of heart.[76] The weavers had lost control of the market and of the transactions that marked production. It was simultaneously a lame ending to the events of 1656 and to more than one century of proudly assertive artisanal politics in Isny.

The failure of 1656 may be traced to the weavers themselves. Isny had suffered dreadfully during the Thirty Years' War. Between 1628 and 1648 the citizens experienced repeated occupations by foreign troops; a harrowing epidemic that killed some eighteen hundred of a possible three thousand inhabitants; and a fire that destroyed 240 houses and 380 stalls.[77] The number of taxpayers fell from 650 in 1628 to 240 in 1648, the majority of whom were *Habnitze*, householders without taxable property. The number of weavers shrank from 350 to 70.[78] As a group the weavers of Isny had lost the ability to organize production beyond the transaction lines that bounded their craft.

Weavers were not proletarians; they did not sell their labor power for wages. But, despite their status as petty, independent producers, they were subject to constraints that rendered them, if not dependent, then certainly vulnerable. This vulnerability derived from the transactions that marked prefactory textile production. On the one hand, middlemen controlled the supply of thread, the costs of which fluctuated according to season, form, quality, and origin of the goods. They maximized their profit by avoiding highly regulated markets and supplying those that paid the best price. On the other hand, bleaching masters operated with fixed prices but the capacity to reduce unit costs. They maximized profits by increasing the num-

75. StA Isny, A795/18. *Aus den Weberzunftbüchern.* s.d. 1656.
76. StA Isny, A795/18. *Aus den Weberzunftbüchern,* June 5, 1656.
77. A. R. Vincenz, *Chronik der Stadt Isny im Allgäu,* p. 41.
78. Immanuel Kammerer, *Isny im Allgäu* (Kempten, 1956), no pagination.

ber of pieces of cloth bleached, at the same time holding down operating expenses. As a result, the weavers found themselves a market-oriented craft unable to exploit the market and sandwiched between two highly capitalized processes, controlled by opportunistic groups. Irregularity in transactions between these stages of production created uncertainty for the master weavers. They survived by successfully negotiating these exchanges and limiting the actions of entrepreneurs. So long as their craft flourished and their numbers were many, they could exert economic and political pressure to regularize economic and noneconomic transactions. As soon as their ranks were decimated by catastrophe and hardship, they ceased to be simply vulnerable and became, for the first time, dependent. No longer able to command transactions in the integrated market of linen production, the petty masters lost their mastery.

Roberta Morelli

7 Men of Iron: Masters of the Iron Industry in Sixteenth-Century Tuscany

(Translated from the Italian by Gabriele Tonne)

The history of the iron industry in Tuscany between the mid-sixteenth and the mid-seventeenth centuries is linked to wide-ranging and ambitious entrepreneurial schemes and to the destinies of a small group of laborers essential to the success of a vital industry.

The entrepreneurial plan, aimed at combining classic production factors—capital, manpower, energy, and technology—in a new and innovative way, was focused on an industry that numerous sources indicate was in rapid expansion. The substantial local demand for iron was a reflection of the growing European demand mentioned by Henry Shubert, John Nef, Jordi Maluquer de Motes, Jean-Pierre Sosson,[1] and others. Under Cosimo I, Tuscany was an established participant on the political and economic scenes that regulated the productive life of Europe. Regional specialization was in its initial stages, and the young sovereign saw his realm as the ideal micro-

1. Henry R. Shubert, *History of the British Iron and Steel Industry* (London, 1957), pp. 332–33; John U. Nef, *Cultural Foundations of Industrial Civilization* (Cambridge, Mass., 1948), pp. 52–53; Jordi Maluquer de Motes, "Le tecniche della siderurgia pre-industriale nell'area mediterranea: Elementi di una comparazione," paper given at the Istituto Internazionale di Storia Economica "Francesco Datini," XVIII Settimana di Studi di Prato, 1986, pp. 3–4; Jean-Pierre Sosson, "Les 'Métiers de la Métallurgie' dans les anciens Pays-Bas méridionaux, XVIIe-XVIIIe siècles: Aspects économiques et sociaux," paper given at the Istituto Internazionale di Storia Economica "Francesco Datini," XVIII Settimana di Studi di Prato, 1986, pp. 11–12.

cosm in which to build—in keeping with the strategy of private business—an economy based on the joint development of agriculture
and industry.[2] The political independence, laboriously gained through
internal wars and clever international diplomacy and sealed by his marriage to Eleonora de Toledo, would be reflected in a kind of economic
autarchy, achieved through intensive use of resources and a strategic
position as the only buyer of the raw materials offered by the mining
industry firmly established in the upper-middle Tyrrhenian region.[3]

In this context, iron was of primary importance. It was in urgent
demand for civilian and military purposes and was also much sought
after for medium- and long-term trade.

Empty galleys and unstocked warehouses in the ports of Pisa and
Leghorn, and ministers who complained about them, were daily fare
for Cosimo; the comprehensive restructuring of coastal defenses undertaken by his son, Ferdinando, only aggravated the situation.[4] References to shortages were sometimes very specific in the private correspondence between the grand duke and local agents. "We are
trying to make do with old cannonballs that are thought to be in
Pistoia," wrote the superintendent of the Arsenal of Pisa in February
1593. Similar appeals to "give orders to the managers of the iron
works" were received from all over the Grand Duchy.[5]

Solutions to the quantitative and qualitative aspects of the problem
called for a dual approach: (1) Cosimo sought privileged access to
iron ore from Elba and (2) he adopted a new technology that would
ensure increased production—almost anticipating large-scale production—and optimum yield.[6] Based on the model of the *manifattura
reale* (royal manufacture), the grand duke's scheme for a large state

2. Roberta Morelli, "Swedenborg and Direct and Indirect Process of Iron Founding in Italy," *Historical Metallurgy* 16 (1982), 621–26.

3. Ivan Tognarini, "Cosimo de'Medici, la guerra di Maremma e la siderurgia cinquecentesca nelle carte di un fondo d'archivio sconosciuto: Le 'Memorie di Casa Ap-
piani'," in *Piombino Storia e Territorio* (Piombino, 1978).

4. Roberta Morelli, "Salario e specializzazione: Tentativo di analisi comparata
nelle comunità minerario metallurgiche della comunità Toscana cinquecentesca," paper given at the Istituto Internazionale di Storia Economica "Francesco Datini,"
XVIII Settimana di Studi di Prato, 1986, p. 2.

5. Archivio di Stato di Firenze (hereafter ASF), Magona, 2251, c. 60: "Si cercha di
accomodarsi con palle vecchie che si crede essere a Pistoia"; ASF, Magona, 2252, c.
92: "Dare ordini alli ministri delle fabbriche."

6. Romualdo Cardarelli, "Le miniere di ferro dell'Elba durante la Signoria degli
Appiano e l'industria siderurgica toscana nel Cinquecento" in *Miniere e ferro dell'Elba
dei tempi etruschi ai nostri giorni* (Rome, 1938), pp. 192–94.

enterprise gradually paralleled the earlier elementary controls on the export and import networks. The *istrumenti* (contracts) signed in 1542 and 1639 show the grand dukes' commitment to purchase substantial quantities of iron ore from the Prince of Piombino, lord of Elba.[7] At the same time, the establishment of the Magona, a state agency for the control and direct and indirect management of all facilities and activities generally referred to as *faccende del ferro* (the business of iron) was an evident epiphenomenon of his political and economic plans. In less than thirty years from these initial steps, the area of the "ancient" iron industry—the southern coastline, the Maremma near Siena, and the long Appennine ridge in the Pistoia area—was modified to meet the needs of the territorial integration required by this widespread industrial venture.[8]

The blast furnaces stood out against a landscape that had been adapted to their requirements. Rivers were rechannelled to provide the water power needed to drive the huge butterfly bellows and the dense forests around the first settlements—Follonica, Massa, and others—were subjected to more frequent and more intensive cutting, map after map, survey after survey.[9]

The inevitable gaps in documentation make it difficult to paint a comprehensive picture. It would seem, however, that existing social and economic conditions in the small communities contrasted sharply with the demands of the state, with the movement of capital, and with the production strategies of the urban entrepreneurs. Taken together, these resulted in the colonization of rural and decentralized areas. Little is known, however, about the people themselves.

This may be so for several reasons. The first is the kind of documentation available: synthetic accounts rather than analytic or descriptive material. The second is that the small number of people employed in the smelting of iron and other metals, in relative and absolute terms, led to the neglect of wages, organization, and social aspects. It is in this vein that Coleman—reflecting on the phenom-

---

7. ASF, Magona, 1617, c. 41; ASF, Magona, 1622, c. 54.

8. Roberta Morelli, "Il passaggio al metodo indiretto di fusione: Cambiamenti socio-economici nella toscana del XXVI secolo," in *Siderurgia e miniere fra età antica ed epoca contemporanea* (Brescia, 1990), pp. 120–22.

9. On the specific characteristics of the bellows used in the Tuscan high furnaces, see Roberta Morelli, "Sullo stato d'infanzia della siderurgia seicentesca: Le ferriere e i forni di Follonica e Cornia (1640–1680)," *Ricerche Storiche* 10 (1980), 486–87; emblematic of the many surveys documented is the one in Campiglia, on May 26, 1636, by Niccolaio, agent of the Grand Duke, ASF, Magona, 2443, c. 11.

ena connected with the preindustrial labor market—singled out the iron industry, emphasizing that "only in a small number of industries using more or less heavy fixed capital equipment, such as iron smelting or paper making, did such other items as fuel or raw materials take precedence over labour."[10] More recently and perhaps more drastically, Landes concluded that while the production unit (in the iron sector) grew under the stimulus of technical progress, the social repercussions of this growth were not comparable to those caused by the transition from cottage industry to factories in the textile sector.[11]

Although the similarities with that situation are obviously not coincidental, the history of the first Tuscan factories suggests a search for bold alternative solutions, which may, to some extent, modify the initial impression of social and economic stagnation given by the ironworkers and more generally by all metalworkers. The combination of a bold and clear entrepreneurial plan and the introduction of a technique that was totally innovative with respect to local know-how and practice gave rise to a new strategy for the use of resources.[12] The effects on labor were explosive, redefining roles and hierarchies in the production process, establishing new positions in the employment structure (see Figure 1) and, above all, altering the relation between merchant-entrepreneur and worker, through the amount, and especially through the form, of remuneration.[13]

A few points of reference are needed to outline a world characterized by a small number of very dissimilar figures.

The first is provided by the time frame considered here: from the mid-sixteenth to the mid-seventeenth century. This period has not been chosen only because of an extremely interesting and fortunate concentration of data—outstanding among which is a rich collection of labor contracts.[14] The choice depends above all on the desire to

10. D. C. Coleman, "Labour in the English Economy of the Seventeenth Century," *Economic History Review*, 2d ser., 8 (1956), 287.

11. David S. Landes, *Prometeo liberato* (Turin, 1978), p. 117.

12. Manlio Calegari, "Origini, insediamenti, inerzia tecnologica nelle ricerche sulla siderurgia ligure d'antico regime," *Quaderni Storici* 46 (1981), 293–94.

13. Morelli, "Salario e specializzazione" pp. 5–11.

14. The contracts referred to were drawn up in the localities of origin of the Bergamascan and Brescian laborers and on some labor markets; besides the names of the employee, the grand duke's agent, and the master, they specify the amount of advance payment, the period of hire, the kind of work to be carried out, and the number of workers making up the team.

study the economic effects and less visible social reactions during such a delicate phase as the introduction of a new technology.

The second point of reference is the geographic area affected by the process in question: a group of territories sharing a common tradition in ironworking but already characterized by product specialization that was to continue up to the beginning of the nineteenth century.[15] The success of the indirect process divided the production cycle of iron into two stages de facto: smelting (from iron ore to pig iron) and refining (from pig iron to wrought iron). Success also called for the coexistence of two technologies: the facilities using the previously unknown technology (blast furnaces), located in strategic positions with respect to the Elban mines—along the coast of the Maremma and in its immediate hinterland—and the structures connected to local and long-established production facilities (iron foundries, nail factories, rolling mills).[16] Although sharing the same spatial and economic isolation from urban trade flows, these production centers and geographic areas met with different social destinies (with respect to the same production).

The last point of reference is the ironworkers themselves. They must be classified by degree of specialization and skill. It is common to keep worker categories distinct in the preindustrial period on the basis of their pay and, broadly speaking, of their chances for economic and social mobility.

Distances and differences in place and status were, of course, perceived and experienced by the people at that time in a much more natural and indistinct manner than is evident from later analysis. The grand duke tried to solve two kinds of problems, the technical aspect of which is summed up well by Landes as reducing the mineral, that is, iron ore, to a metal of convenient purity;[17] and the commercial aspect, the aim of which is described by Calegari as "to become the exclusive merchant of Elban ore . . . and the semifinished product (pig iron) in the entire Mediterranean area." Cosimo intended to fulfill his plan by "preparing financial, contractual, politi-

15. Giorgio Mori, *L'industria del ferro in Toscana dalla Restaurazione alla fine del Granducato (1815–1859)* (Turin, 1966).
16. For a topography of the metallurgical facilities of the Magona from 1594 and 1795, see ASF, Magona, 2394.
17. Landes, *Prometeo liberato*, p. 118.

cal and trade devices" with the more or less explicit intention of "recovering outlays in a relatively short time."[18]

Attention will be focused here on those devices and in particular on the complex pattern of manipulation and subtle pressures to which certain classes of workers were subjected and which in the long term altered labor relations. The managerial, wage, and social devices employed in the Tuscan iron industry responded to the need to unite in a single production scheme technological innovation and established tradition with the least possible waste of resources.[19] In fact, available evidence suggests that wages never required special containment strategies. For example, at a furnace in Follonica, the item "pantry and wages," that is, the total remuneration of labor using the truck system, never accounted for more than 25 percent of the total costs over a span of fourteen years, from 1657 to 1671; whereas the cost of transport and fuel underwent significant fluctuations and increases.[20]

Undeniably, the reign of Cosimo marked a turning point in the world of mining and metallurgy. The flexible new view slowly turned the former structure of a closely knit group of "men who work for little" into a sharply segmented pyramid divided by degree of specialization—and, therefore, by wages, mobility, and autonomy—from the state entrepreneur.[21]

Expertise became the main criterion in hiring for a job that Della Fratta, a writer on metallurgy of the time, described as "the difficult work of the mineralist." The duration of apprenticeship was no longer determined by the guilds, but by an empirical method involving trial and error and by experience gained while working in a team around the blast furnace.[22]

Specialization was another factor used as a criterion for dividing

18. Manlio Calegari, "Forni 'alla Bresciana' nell'Italia del XVI secolo," *Quaderni Storici* 40 (1989), 7.

19. Of particular interest is the work by Paola Massa, "Tipologia industriale e modelli organizzativi: La Liguria in età moderna," paper given at the Istituto Internazionale di Storia Economica "Francesco Datini," XXII Settimana di Studi di Prato, 1990.

20. Roberta Morelli, "Sullo stato d'infanzia," pp. 607–8. A similar view is offered by Ivan Tognarini, "Follonica nell'età moderna" in *Follonica e la sua industria del ferro*, ed. Luigi Rombai and Ivan Tognarini (Florence, 1986), pp. 23–24.

21. ASF, Magona, 1617, c. 28r: "Huomini che con poco obbligano le fatiche loro."

22. Marco Antonio della Fratta et Montalbano, *Pratica minerale*, ed. Marco Cima (Florence, 1985), p. 140: "Li dificili maneggi del mineralista . . . errare molte volte per ben operare."

up the workers into distinct categories and determining their pay. The top of the pyramid was completely transformed as a result of the introduction, from the valleys of Brescia and Bergamo, of the indirect method of smelting and refining iron and as a result of specialized foreign labor brought in to supervise the construction, firing, and operation of the blast furnaces.[23]

The most delicate operation, totally unknown to local labor and, therefore, placed in the hands of foreign specialists, was the first stage of the new production process. After sorting and roasting, the ore was mixed with charcoal and put into the furnace, which Filarete described as "a square building divided in half by a wall about eight ells high, and such was also the width of one of the sides where the bellows were housed."[24] The smelting process was supervised by a furnace master and carried out by an expert laborer, a common worker, and an apprentice. A team was rarely made up of as many as five workers; that number was exceeded only during the preliminary phases of operations, when the choice of leather for renovation of the bellows called for a special master.

Work lasted for a season, which existing contracts would suggest usually started on All Saints' Day and lasted until the end of June. The season was broken down into a series of campaigns, usually no more than one hundred consecutive working days, regulated by the technical limits of the stack.[25]

In the most fortunate cases, a working season consisted of two campaigns, amounting to a total of 200 or 210 working days. But it is difficult to establish the amount of time actually put in by each worker; there were probably pauses between casting, and the whole team may not have worked simultaneously.[26]

The expertise of the furnace masters, placing them at the apex of

23. For details of the technologies used in the modern Italian iron industry, see Domenico Sella, "The Iron Industry in Italy," in *Schwerpunkte der Eisengewinnung und Eisenverarbeitung in Europa 1500–1650*, ed. Hermann Kellenbenz (Vienna, 1974), pp. 103–5; Roberta Morelli, "Human Technology: Lombard Masters Working for Tuscan Mineralogy and Metallurgy in the 16th Century," *9th Congress of International Economic History, Research Topics*, section B-2, ed. H. van Dijk (Bern, 1986), pp. 6–13.

24. The entire quotation, including interesting footnotes, is printed in Calegari, *Forni*, p. 90: "Una casa quadra spartita in due parti per smezzo con un muro alto di qualche otto braccia e cosi di larghezza era da l'una delle parti, dove che stavano i mantici."

25. Calegari, *Forni*, p. 90.

26. The presumed number of working days have been calculated by subtracting holidays from the working period established in the contract.

the employment pyramid, was actually multifaceted. The most easily perceived aspects were related to the acquisition of technical knowledge. In an era in which production was not yet mechanized and standardized, in which know-how had not yet been codified and given precise parameters, individual ability—the feel for a job—which could only be perfected through direct experience, constituted the cornerstone of what councilors defined as *specializzazione*.

"Good order and qualified personnel" was what the expert in mines and metals closest to Cosimo, Cristofan Degler, a German, felt was required in those years to get the industry back on its feet. Only recourse to "men who understand the quality and the nature of the mines and of the ore" could help "to make some profit."[27]

For an understanding of the social and economic status of the furnace masters, it is important to realize that their specialization included a series of managerial responsibilities that were directly linked to the short- and long-term success of operations. Optimal use of resources, increased productivity of individual production factors, and cost control—in short, the economic strategies that combine to maximize profit—were the theoretical problems of politicians. Brescian and Bergamascan masters provided practical short- and long-term solutions, not only through decisions regarding the physical plant—its site, its size, and its construction—but also through shrewd daily management.

The furnace masters, recruited by the agents of the grand duke, chose their own teams, for whom they were responsible. The signatures of masters on almost all contracts show that they belonged to a restricted and educated professional class, able not only to choose "workers . . . who can work at the furnace . . . repair the stack . . . cast cannonballs" but also to adapt, replace, and organize the members of the community to the requirements of production.[28]

In conditions of hard work, but, above all, of social and emotional isolation, rigorous selection guaranteed the "buon ghoverno" frequently invoked. A strongly internalized sense of discipline provided

27. Roberta Morelli, "Argento americano e argento toscano: Due soluzioni alla crisi mineraria del Cinquecento," *Ricerche Storiche* 14 (1984), 199, 202: "Buon hordine e persone qualificate; Huomini che s'intendino della qualità e natura delle miniere, delle vene per fare qualche profitto."

28. ASF, Magona, 1617, c. 28: "Lavoranti . . . per lavorare a[l] forno . . . a esercitarsi in rassettare il canniccio . . . in quello lavorare a palle di ferro."

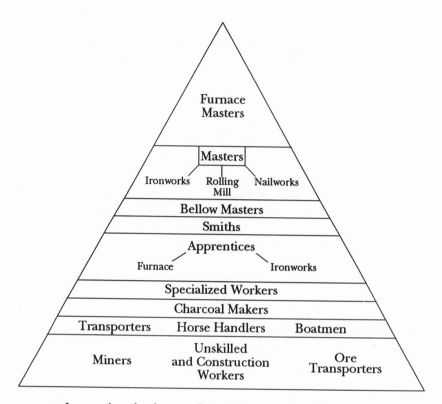

1. Ironworkers by degree of specialization (Tuscany 1550–1650)

the synchrony essential for a production process that was fragmented and called for the participation of several workers.

The excellent pay that the masters enjoyed (and that has been shown elsewhere to fit into a genuine high-wage policy) was the reward for an expertise that was unavailable locally and at the same time a strong instrument of pacification, cohesion, and attraction for the surplus manpower from the north. Unable to find employment in the economies of their native valleys, those workers were willing to stake their future on migration.[29]

High wages bridged the technological gap between Lombardy and

---

29. On high-wage policy, see Maurice Dobb, *I salari* (Turin, 1965), pp. 59–60; on the intertwining of demographic and production aspects of the iron industry in the Brescian valleys, see Domenico Sella, "An Industrial Village in Sixteenth-Century Italy," *Wirtschaftskräfte und Wirtschaftswege* 3 (1978), 37–46.

Tuscany, generated a migratory flow, linked the area of innovation with the area of production, and ensured a remarkable continuity, preserved by the transmission of know-how from father to son to grandson. The stay of the Zeppini family from Lavinone "contrada di Brescia" for several decades had a stabilizing impact on the furnace in Massa where "things have started out well and work goes along cheerfully, producing beautiful and fine stuff."[30]

It is important to point out that the high-wage policy applied to the apex of the labor pyramid, that is, to the foreigners, was unaffected by the cyclical fluctuations in the wages of the other employees. Almost a century after the construction of the first blast furnace in Pracchia in 1543–44 under the supervision of a master from Gardone, Giovanni de' Tombonari,[31] data indicate that there was quite a gap between the pay of the upper layers and that at the base of the pyramid. In 1652 the furnace master earned seventeen *ducats* per month; his team, composed in this case of "an apprentice, a younger apprentice and two basket carriers," received a total of thirty-four ducats. People in prestigious and responsible positions, like Giovanni di Maria Stellini, steward and accountant of the furnace in Follonica, or Giovanni di Fabiano, in charge of repairs in the system of conduits in Follonica, were paid six and just over seven ducats per month, respectively.[32]

The wages of the other men working at the furnace were much lower. For a brief working season in 1577, Master Bettino d' Arti from Scalvo, a resident of the village of Zena, and the five members of his team earned 315 *lire* in coin, plus free board. In a period in which feeding one mouth was reckoned to cost one lira per day, the wages of a team of specialized workers was approximately three times normal subsistence wages. At the end of the century, the wages of a furnace master were more or less four times the wages of a specialized worker, and more than seven times the wages of an Elban iron miner.[33]

Economic considerations tended to maintain this chronic state of technological dependence, resulting in a fixed-wage configuration at

30. ASF, Magona, 2341, c. 13: "Le faccende si sono avviate benissimo e si lavora allegramente, facendosi roba buona e bella."

31. ASF, Magona, 1617, c. 27r.

32. Calculations were based on the analytic accounting contained in ASF, Principato di Piombina, 342.

33. Morelli, "Salari e Specializzazione," p. 15.

the tip of the pyramid, while increases in the prices of raw materials and fuel tended to lower wages at the bottom.[34] But the relative elasticity of the specialized labor supply ensured a constant flow of new foreign masters without having to resort to discretional wage hikes. The grand duke, agents, contractors, and lessees were all aware of the risks of a bottleneck. The convention signed by Major Capponi, the representative of the grand duke, and Roberto Odaldi, on October 7, 1594, admitted that "it will be difficult to smelt the ore and turn it into pig iron without the work of many foreigners like those from Brescia, Bergamo, Voltolino and other places from which the masters of the furnaces and ironworks come . . . if these men should not come as they usually do to perform those jobs, said Roberto will not be obliged to do more than is possible with the men available in the province."[35] The threat was more hypothetical than real. With the exception, as stated in many contracts, of "wars and impediments caused by the contagion of the plague" from which "God protect us," the flow of men "born of the mountains" did not diminish.[36]

Nevertheless, the factors linking enterprise and specialized labor slowly changed during the course of the century. The much-feared production competition from neighboring states—in particular, the Papal States—forced Tuscan entrepreneurs not only to try to secure an adequate supply of foreign masters, but also to start checking their expertise in loco. This was particularly necessary because contracting in the place of origin depended exclusively on the master's reputation or the personal trust he inspired in the grand duke's agent.

As requests for quality grew at the end of the century, especially in certain types of manufacture, such as weapons, more accurate controls were exerted on the work of the masters who had previously

34. On the trends at the time, see Giuseppe Parenti, "Prezzi e salari a Firenze dal 1520 al 1620," in *I prezzi in Europa dal XIII secolo ad oggi*, ed. Ruggerio Romano (Turin, 1967), p. 243.

35. ASF, Magona, 1620, c. 123: "Si rappresenta difficile il poter fare colare di dette vene e ridurre in ferri colati senza valersi del 'opera di molti forestieri come Breciani, Bergamaschi, Voltolini e d'altri luoghi che servono per maestri a' forni et alle ferriere . . . che non venendo di detti uomini come è solito di venire a lavorare di detti mestieri . . . detto Ruberto in tal caso venga scusato et no resti obligato a fare lavorare a' detti edifici più di quello che potrà con quelli uomini che potràhavere qua in provincia."

36. Quoted in Fernand Braudel, *Civiltà e imperi del Mediterraneo nell'età di Filippo II* (Turin, 1965), p. 39: "Guerre e impedimenti che succedano da contagioni pestilentiali."

been totally independent. Visits and inspections by the grand duke's agents became more frequent, and in some cases the masters were requested to give a demonstration of their ability.[37]

Frequent recourse was increasingly made to another instrument in order to ensure a constant level of output fashioned by demonstrably competent labor. Contracts were used to bind the masters in a closer and more personal way. The geographic mobility that had become a permanent feature of several generations in certain families like the Zeppini, the Gavazzeni, the Beronesi, the Graziotti, and the Tombonari, was now encouraged by a mixture of wages, bonuses, and *facoltà* (faculties) that gradually changed labor relations. Wages, previously conceived only in terms of time, were integrated at the end of the period into a system of production incentives and bonuses for special operations such as "working and reducing to pure iron the minute and rough iron . . . what one gets from slag." At the end of operations, masters were offered a share of the scraps.[38]

Incentives were no longer merely an extension of a highly attractive wage policy, but a real lever for increased production through the involvement of a small elite of employees in the success of the business. Second and third generation masters—the span of time under consideration here—did not come to Tuscany merely for economic advantage, but for the opportunity for social advancement probably denied them at home. A minor shift—from simple employee to small autonomous merchant—was already noticeable for many at midcentury. Master Niccolò Zeppini of Lavinone negotiated the sale of "some crates of steel" with agents of the Magona. While this would have been unthinkable only two decades earlier, when his father, Girolamo, worked for the grand duke, Niccolò signed a contract with GiovanMaria di Giovanni Comenzini in June 1640 entitling him to the possession (and perhaps sale) of half of the coal he was able to save during a smelting campaign.[39]

These were almost imperceptible manifestations of the extent of

37. This happened to Benedetto Giovanni de' Fumanti and Camillo Lorenzi de' Cappelli, who came to work in 1585 in the "bottega da arme di tutte quelle sorte che ricerce l'arte e il mestiere loro come corsetti, spade, pugnali" (shop that makes weapons of all sorts requiring a certain art and workmanship, such as Corsican spears, swords, and daggers). ASF, Magona, 1618, c. 51; ASF, Magona, 2251, c. 2, 35, 37, 53.

38. ASF, Magona, 1620, c. 18r: "Lavorare e ridurre in ferro sodo il ferrino minuto e grossello . . . quello che si è cavato dai loppi di ferro."

39. ASF, Magona, 2700, c. 25; ASF, Magona, 2693, c. 90.

the privileges already enjoyed by those at the top of the pyramid. By the end of the period examined here, the grand duke seemed to be willing to grant greater autonomy to one layer of employees as the price to be paid for keeping a technologically dependent production sector competitive.

The uncontrolled mobility of a master was the most evident feature distinguishing his position from that of other employees. In a closed working environment aggravated by social isolation, the right granted the master to "come and go" to his native town on a "bay horse"—the symbolic gift of the grand duke that emblematically replaced the *calze* (stockings) given to the first Bergamascan to arrive—was a freedom unknown to his subordinates.[40]

In this case, it is important to look beyond the figures. The long wage stagnation recorded from 1583 to 1613 and attested to by the trend in advances shown in Figure 2 does not reflect the real situation. The social ascent of the masters from the upper working class to the petty merchant class took place in a period of technological and productive adjustment and was masked by the stagnation in wages. In those years the options on slag and scrap iron and a certain share of coal offered the *fabbrichieri* (ironmasters) definitely improved (but to what extent is not known) their already comfortable salary.[41]

The dynamics of the history of the furnace masters are quite different from those of the parallel history of local labor, which are much more difficult to reconstruct. The cultural and economic distinction between foreign and native ironworkers had a technological base.

In Italy, as elsewhere in Europe, the blast furnace introduced by the Brescians was to coexist with the direct system used in the open-hearth furnaces. As Calegari has stated, "the blast furnace solution, later defined as 'progressive' or 'advanced', did not eliminate the other which was also defined *a posteriori* as 'backward' or 'obsolete'." The two systems complemented each other in production: the open-hearth furnace iron works added cast iron to the ore in the furnace, thus accelerating smelting.[42] The political scheme did no more than embrace the best technical solution—depending on the kind of min-

40. ASF, Magona, 1617, c. 27r.
41. ASF, Magona, 2693, c. 72.
42. Calegari, *Forni*, p. 93.

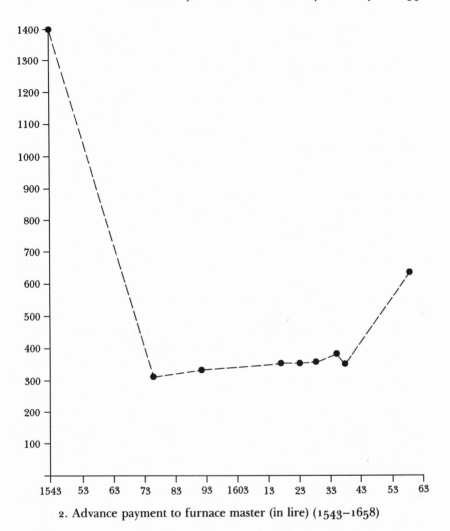

2. Advance payment to furnace master (in lire) (1543–1658)

eral to be smelted, as Maluquer de Motes has suggested—and combined, or rather juxtaposed, two culturally distinct production worlds.[43] The links between those worlds, that of the blast furnace and that of the open-hearth furnace, were generally limited to trade: one offered the other the raw material, cast iron, for production. There was no exchange of knowledge, labor, or expertise.

43. Maluquer de Motes, "Le techniche della siderurgia preindustriale nell'area mediterranea," p. 9.

This explains the absence of rejection phenomena. Social peace between foreign and local workers, between the world of the emerging technology and that of the traditional technology, was possible only because there were no conflicts of interest. Cosimo's plan was in a certain sense external to and uncontrollable by either the elite of educated and acculturated Brescian workers or the skilled, independent craftsmen such as local ironmasters.

The former saw the grand duke as a shrewd and generous entrepreneur who did not hesitate to have his agents use "all possible diligence in their travels to Brescia for the selection of experienced and expert men."[44] For the latter, he was a powerful merchant, capable of rendering more efficient a commercial system over which the provincial craftsmen had no control in the medium term.

The ironmasters were apparently totally free of any external pressure when carrying out their task. Writers of the time meticulously described the master's work as "to lift the incandescent iron from the center where it is the hottest with a shovel and to hammer it with a mallet . . . to attach one part to the other."[45]

The degree of specialization was great, but the ironmaster's responsibility for the entire production cycle was small and easily controlled. The more standardized operations could even be delegated to other workers.

The ironmasters also seemed to have more autonomy with respect to the rate of production. The pace of work at the furnace was dictated by eight or nine casts occurring in rapid succession for every charge, and was supervised directly and continuously by the master from his stand close to the stack; the daily rate at an ironworks was adapted to the much less urgent demands of the wrought-iron market.[46] In 1614 an agent of the Magona made a point of underlining, certainly not out of magnanimity, "that the iron workers are not required to produce a precise quantity of iron, but only as much as they can comfortably produce."[47]

This autonomy was, however, more formal than real. The range of action of the ironmasters was restricted by evident limits and by

44. ASF, Magona, 2693, c. 84: "Ogni possibile diligentia, in questo viaggio di Brescia di fare elezione di huomini pratichi ed esperti."
45. Della Fratta, *Pratica minerale*, p. 142: "Sollevare con un badile grosso il ferro infuocato nel mezzo dove appunto (la massa) è più calda e battendosi sopra con una mazza . . . attaccarne l'una parte all'altra."
46. Calegari, *Forni*, p. 90.
47. ASF, Magona, 1628, c. 15: "Che li fabbrichieri non habbino obbligo di fare una somma precisa di ferro ma solo quello che potranno comodamente fare."

subtle pressures linked to the evolution of Cosimo's plan from trade to production. The first limitation was represented by the kind of remuneration—by weight or by the piece: so much per *migliaro* (thousand pounds) of iron produced—which sometimes led to forced increases in productivity, such as during the downswing in prices at the beginning of the century, in an attempt to offset a falling income. This limit was intrinsic in a certain sense, yet it gave the master craftsmen the illusion of being able to decide on production and times and, thus, on their own economic status.[48]

Contracts between the Magona and the ironmasters soon became far more detailed. Besides the lengthening list of the kinds of iron to be worked—"verzella e verzellone, bastardo . . . modello tondo reggetta quadruccio" nales of 48, 36, 20, 15, and 11 inches—at so much per migliaro, the first unsettling mention was made of covert or overt checks on output, that is, the consumption of raw material and of coal.[49] No longer subjective, the ability of a good fabbrichiere (ironmaster) was now variable, judged and assessed by the requirements of a market and a production cycle no longer managed and directed in the ironworks.

No exact data are available on this phenomenon or on the intensity of the pressure put on a class of free craftsmen by the entrepreneurial world. But the references to the *difetti* (defects) or *mancamenti* (shortcomings) of some masters, the responsibility they must bear "should the works waste time and not work," and the fines imposed "if they waste time . . . they shall pay ten lire for each day and each furnace" are probably symptoms of the expansion of entrepreneurial power and the reduction of the freedom of the craftsman.[50]

A precise connection seems to be evident between technology, organization of production, and modes of controlling labor or, at least, the specialized labor that was more directly involved in the successful outcome of production. Control was strongest and most direct on the foreign masters called in to supervise the more compli-

48. Useful elements for analyzing the use of piecework plus the yield quotas imposed on the masters by the merchant-entrepreneurs can be found in C. Poni, "Misura contro misura: Come il filo di seta divenne sottile e rotondo," *Quaderni Storici* 47 (1981), 385–419, and M. Calegari, "Mercanti, imprenditori e maestri paperai nella manifattura genovese della carta," *Quaderni Storici* 69 (1985), 445–69.

49. ASF, Magona, 1625, c. 152.

50. ASF, Magona, 1622, c. 14: "Se le fabbriche perdessero tempo e non lavorassero; se perdendo tempo . . . debbono pagare per ogni giorno e per ogni fuoco di fabbrica lire 10."

cated phases of production. The means used were an explicit part of their remuneration. Rather than a debatable set of rules and regulations, checks and inspections, they took the form of a much more pressing and persuasive network of economic relations linking entrepreneur and wage earner. Wages allowed the entrepreneurs to take an active part in the dynamics of a labor market extending far beyond the political boundaries of their states. Even at times of crisis (1623–43), the grand duke maintained thorough control over job continuity and, as a result, over the productivity of the best paid, most specialized, and most mobile part of the employment pyramid by means of an incentive system that concretely enhanced income and social mobility.

But the link between technology, organization, and control was not always equally clear and linear. Simpler technology in the means of production, the diffusion of expertise, less investment by entrepreneurs, and the existence of a territorially consolidated organization of labor within a professional group were all factors that could radically change the bargaining basis between entrepreneurs and workers. These same factors undoubtedly affected the less productive spheres and could change the kind and intensity of control.

In the ironworking sector, wages were a direct manifestation of entrepreneurial intervention and—with reference to specialized labor—became typical of those phases of production in which technology produced an investment policy and a capitalistic, industrial-type evolution in production relations. On the other hand, piecework wages typical of all professional groups linked to the old manner of production were relegated to those production phases characterized by more backward technology and an organization of labor distinctive of artisanal production modes. In this context, the dual typology of wages and piecework was the direct outcome of a period of transition involving mixed solutions and unclear relations. Technological progress and/or the expansion of the market (or both) led to the slow intervention of merchant capital into the production sphere and simultaneously to the gradual transition from a world of independent producers to one of wage earners.

The process was neither rapid nor linear. Cosimo's plan called for the simultaneous, conciliatory use of old and new technical and productive forces; combined aspects of revolutionary originality with others that were apparently conservative; and used for the same production purpose the technically advanced blast furnace alongside the artisanal open-hearth furnace.

In this indistinct setting, in which the process of smelting and those who carried it out were apparently the primary concern of the entrepreneurs, the other workers seem to have been left unlimited organizational freedom. The relations established between Gelsino, Emilio da Empoli, Jacopo di Battista Mattei di Valico di Garfagnana—iron and nail masters—and the agents of the Magona seem to go beyond wage earning.[51] In fact former constraints were now left up to the workers' discretion; production modes and methods could be established by the experience and practice of the fabbrichiere; no bureaucratic supervision by the grand duke's inspectors was contemplated. In other words, the ironmasters were basically free producers in a single-client market. Their only obligation was to fulfill the commissions of the grand duke, in a manner that would be stipulated each time. Having set the price per weight of the goods—thus the price of the product and not of its production—the management of resources and labor, energy and raw materials, was borne by the masters. Theirs was the entrepreneurial task of working out the optimal combination of these production factors and, with them, the margin of profit.

Thus, relations continued to be strictly mercantile with the decisive variable being the quality of the product, not the quantitative measurement of the factors used to produce it. Even at the end of the century the contracts signed by the ironmasters with the Magona called for a relaxed pace of production, quite unlike the far more pressing rhythm of the blast furnace. A predetermined working season was dictated by the series of workdays lasting from morning until night and interrupted only by the holidays of obligation.

State entrepreneurs may have been willing to maintain the familial artisanal atmosphere of the ironworks so as to create an orderly productive environment. Such a regime was essential to achieve their goal of *colare il ferro* (smelting iron) in order to obtain the *ferraccio* (pig iron) that was the typical export of the Tuscan industry at the beginning of the seventeenth century.

This traditional work organization was not, however, destined to last long. Small, almost imperceptible additions to contracts that repeat the same price per migliaro and the same mode of payment suggest that the relationship between free producer and state merchant was shifting toward a more meticulous control of production. Symptomatic was the new definition of the ironmaster's ability. It

51. ASF, Magona, 2693, c. 96.

"must be recognized from his performance on the basis of the satisfaction of the agents of the Magona in terms not so much of the quality or quantity of iron produced, but of the consumption of coal, from which he is to make no profit." Furthermore, in a period in which the production of pig iron was certainly not standardized, it was equally emblematic that ironmasters were requested "to work pig iron to o/4" without this causing any change "or agreements with the charcoal makers . . . to make extra amounts." The present state of research does not provide quantitative information on the changes that resulted from the introduction of stricter controls. But sources from the 1620s, in which a reduction in costs had been observed, make more precise reference to a number of shortcomings of labor with respect to the unnaturally high levels of productivity expected by the ministers.[52]

The price per migliaro remained unchanged from 1589 to 1629, but the advances paid to the ironmaster—money for the purchase of production factors—tended to diminish, eroded by the rising debt load transmitted from generation to generation. In the case of Master Domenico di Jacopo Stefani di Valico di Garfagnana, advances were no more than figures on paper, as they were practically canceled by the "work debt to the rolling mill";[53] the debt of Francesco Odaldi, which grew from one work season to the next, was substantial enough to send him to the *delle Stinche* prison.[54]

Once again, a stable, if not stagnant situation, evidenced by the long succession of the same figures for advances and prices "according to custom," cast a shadow on the beginning of an important process of change in the labor world. The entrepreneurial risk, deliberately delegated to an apparently privileged class of specialized workers, squeezed profits, reduced the margins of technical and financial autonomy, and put formerly independent producers at the total mercy of merchants who, in this phase, had become the new entrepreneurs.

---

52. ASF, Magona, 2693, c. 72: "Deve essere riconosciuto delle sue operazioni secondo la satisfazione che gli si darà a' detti Magonieri non tanto della qualità o quantità di ferro quanto nel consumo del carbone sopra del quale non deve trovare utile alcuno"; ASF, Magona, 1693, c. 9: "O interesse con li carbonai . . . per conto di fare a migliaia."

53. ASF, Magona, 2433, c. 39: "Debito del lavorerio fatto al suo distendino."

54. ASF, Magona, 2470, unmarked.

Jaume Torras

8 From Craft to Class: The Changing Organization of Cloth Manufacturing in a Catalan Town

This essay describes the changes that undermined the traditional organization of cloth manufacturing during the first half of the eighteenth century in Igualada, a thriving textile center near Barcelona.[1] It is meant to contribute to a fuller understanding of the process through which the intricacies of the old corporate organization of work gave way to a greater polarization of functions between the clothiers' trade and the weavers', the latter being pushed into increasing subordination.

Several driving forces were effective well before any significant progress of mechanization. First, the reformist policies of Enlightened governments purposely tried to limit the capacity of the craft guilds and local governments to regulate the conditions in which industrial work could be performed—though in Spain such policies hardly encroached upon guild regulatory powers before the last decades of the eighteenth century.[2] Only in new industries, like cotton

---

1. This essay is based on a research project funded by the Dirección General de Investigación Científica y Técnica (project PS 89-0059).

2. Only during the 1780s were all textile entrepreneurs allowed to ignore guild regulations concerning the spatial setting of the production process (1787) and the characteristics of the fabrics they produced (1789). See J. C. La Force, *The Development of the Spanish Textile Industry, 1750–1850* (Berkeley, 1965), pp. 98–103. Earlier exemp-

textile manufacturing, did the state foster the integration of different work processes in single shops under a well-defined entrepreneurial hierarchy from the beginning of the century.[3] Second, and more effective, the move toward a different organizational framework for textile production was propelled during the eighteenth century by pressures stemming from the widening of markets and the emergence of new patterns of demand, both calling for more integrated entrepreneurial structures.[4]

Whereas all these forces operated more or less uniformly and simultaneously over a broad social space, the erosion of the old forms of work organization was extremely uneven from place to place and from trade to trade. Thus, additional explanations are needed to account for such differences. This case study suggests that, besides grand institutional or technical upheavals, attention must also be paid to social and political developments that can be observed only on a very small scale. Seemingly minor arrangements, coupled with the manifold effects of fast industrial expansion, brought about significant changes in the organization of cloth manufacturing, in particular in the basic relationship between clothiers and weavers.

The first part of the essay presents the organization of clothmaking in Igualada at the end of the seventeenth century; the second outlines the wider economic framework in which the industry expanded during the earlier decades of the eighteenth century; and the third focuses on the transformations in the relationship between the clothiers and the master weavers.

Clothmaking was a prominent sector of the Catalan economy in the fourteenth and fifteenth centuries when Barcelona, Perpignan, and other cities sold large quantities of middle-quality stuffs in dis-

---

tions from guild prescriptions had been granted as particular privileges to individual producers.

3. See J. K. J. Thomson, "State Intervention in the Catalan Calico-Printing Industry in the Eighteenth Century," in *Markets and Manufacture in Early Industrial Europe*, ed. Maxine Berg (London, 1991), pp. 57–89.

4. On the trend toward greater integration in the English wool industry, see Pat Hudson, *The Genesis of Industrial Capital: A Study of the West Riding Wool Textile Industry, c. 1750–1850* (Cambridge, Eng., 1986), esp. chap. 2. A discussion of this topic within a different analytical framework is S. R. H. Jones, "The Organization of Work: A Historical Dimension," *Journal of Economic Behavior and Organization* 3 (1982), 117–37; R. Millward, "The Emergence of Wage Labor in Early Modern England," *Explorations in Economic History* 13 (1981), 21–39.

tant (and, in some cases, politically subordinated) markets in the Levant, northern Africa, southern Italy, Sicily, and Sardinia.[5] This export-oriented, largely urban industry declined with the loss of the Mediterranean outlets for its goods in the sixteenth and early seventeenth centuries, when foreign competition increased in Iberian markets too. In the second half of the seventeenth century, the manufacturing of woolens was of some relevance only in small towns specializing in low-quality stuffs for the regional market.[6]

Igualada was one of these towns. About four hundred households made a living by working in service trades or in handicraft production to supply the needs of the surrounding countryside. The scope of production was larger in certain activities, especially the manufacturing of cheap cloth, a major source of employment in the town. This industry was well integrated into a wider network of specialization on a regional scale, indicated by the fact that the total sales of woolen stuffs in Igualada amounted to just one-sixth of local output.[7] Such integration still did not entail any significant degree of dependence upon the capital and the commercial skill of urban merchants.

In effect, the local master clothiers (*paraires*) were firmly in control of the cloth manufacturing process. Those clothiers for whom clothmaking was the main source of income were able to manage by themselves the purchase of raw materials as well as the marketing of the stuffs they produced. The first stages of the process (cleaning, sorting, carding, and preparing wool for spinning) were performed in their shops; then they put the fiber out in the town itself or in the nearby countryside to be spun by women and children at home. The main operation of the process, weaving, was carried out by independent master weavers following the specifications given by the ordering clothier, who owned the spun yarn. The finishing operations were again performed or supervised by the clothiers themselves, in

5. Eliayhu Ashtor, "Catalan Cloth on the Late Medieval Mediterranean Markets," *Journal of European Economic History* 17 (1988), 227–57; M. Riu, "The Woollen Industry in Catalonia in the Later Middle Ages," in *Cloth and Clothing in Medieval Europe*, ed. N. B. Harte and K. Ponting (London, 1983), pp. 205–29.

6. Valentín Vázquez de Prada and Pere Molas Ribalta, "La industria lanera en Barcelona (s. XVI–XVIII)," in *Produzione, commercio e consumo dei panni di lana (nei secoli XII–XVIII)*, ed. M. Spallanzani (Florence, 1976), pp. 553–65.

7. This is a rough estimate for the period July 1695 to December 1696 based on fiscal assessments of sales and output. Data in Arxiu de la Corona d'Aragó, Barcelona (hereafter ACA), "Generalitat," D-102, 2106–12.

their own shops or in the guild's facilities for common (and compulsory) use such as tentering grounds and a fulling mill.[8]

The customary regulation of clothmaking in Igualada set apart the clothiers' and weavers' trade, and weavers and clothiers were accordingly members of different guilds or confraternities.[9] The clothiers controlled the overall production process because they remained throughout the owners of the materials to be transformed. Nevertheless, the master weavers enjoyed a relatively strong position. The formal agreement of the assembly of masters of the craft ("la Comunitat y Parlament del offici") was needed before any request by the clothiers regarding the operation of weaving could be enforced in Igualada. For any technical or quality change required by the clothiers, the master weavers could renegotiate their share in the value created in the clothmaking process. The masters' power was limited, however, because the clothiers could (and often did) put out spun yarn to master weavers in other towns.

In the last decade of the seventeenth century, approximately 250 pieces of woolens (most of them cloths of sixteen hundred threads to warp) were produced every year in Igualada. The record books held by the farmers of a tax on the production and sale of wool cloth (the *dret de bolla i ploms de rams*) give a detailed picture of the workings of the industry in the town.[10] During a period of eighteen months (July 1695 to December 1696) for which comprehensive records are available, about forty clothiers were active in Igualada, although at widely different scales of operation. A small number of them dominated the trade; eleven masters accounted for two-thirds of the total production of the town. At the other end of the list, no fewer than twenty masters produced irrelevant quantities of cloth. In fact, many master clothiers in Igualada must have been engaged by the wealthier ones or must have had other sources of income.

Such a degree of differentiation is not surprising in an entrepreneurial activity in which the ability to gather and manage sizable cir-

---

8. G. Castellà Raich, *El Gremio de "Paraires" de Igualada y sus relaciones con la casa "Molí Nou"* (Sabadell, 1945); J. Riba i Ortínez, *La indústria tèxtil igualadina: Història d'un gremi* (Igualada, 1958).

9. The number of confraternities set up on a professional basis in Igualada hovered around six or seven during the seventeenth and eighteenth centuries. See Pere Molas i Ribalta, "Els gremis d'Igualada a la fi de l'Antic Règim," in *Miscellanea Aqualatensia/2* (Igualada, 1974), pp. 139–49.

10. ACA, "Generalitat," D-102, 2106–12.

culating capital, as well as commercial expertise, were more decisive assets than technical skill alone. The guild of the clothiers had clear economic functions, and it actually organized cooperation to achieve the most efficient use of facilities involving high fixed costs (the tentering grounds and a fulling mill). But it could not (and surely was not expected to) prevent economic differentiation from developing between masters. Activities related to the much more sizable circulating capital, like the purchase of raw materials or the marketing of finished cloth, were left unregulated and this allowed differentiation to take place.

The same record books throw a very different light on the group of the master weavers, whose activity depended more on good craftsmanship and required scarcely any capital. A small group of seven masters, together with a few journeymen weavers (not mentioned in the record books), wove almost all the woolens produced by the clothiers of Igualada.[11] Table 8-1 shows that differences in textile activity were considerable, but far from enormous. The differences could probably be explained, at least in part, by the family cycles (and the corresponding differences in the availability of labor force) of these artisan households. The customary regulation of the number of looms (two was the maximum) that a master was allowed to run set narrow limits to such differences anyway.[12] The weavers had to work on the ground floor of their shop (and home), close to the door, which favored collective control of work methods and times.

The record books also clarify the relationship between clothiers and weavers. Each master weaver seems to have worked for many clothiers during the eighteen months covered by the records. In this sense, none was the employee of any particular clothier. Instead, master weavers could regard each clothier as one customer among many, a customer with whom a separate agreement should be established for each operation. Special links could exist between particular masters. The same data show that every weaver had one or two clothiers who were dominant customers. In most cases, however, the

11. The clothiers put out 17 percent of the total to master weavers working outside Igualada at Capellades, a smaller neighboring town (from the source quoted in n. 10 above).

12. Written evidence of this limitation has been found only in a compilation of statutes from the middle of the eighteenth century. See Joan Segura, *Història d'Igualada*, fac. ed. (Igualada, 1958), vol. 2, p. 130.

Table 8-1. Cloth woven in Igualada from July 1695 to December 1696

Master weaver	Length in *canes*	Value in Catalan *rals*	%
Miquel Simorra	2,104	76,764	21.5
Jacinto Farrer	1,225	59,000	16.5
Benet Valls	1,724	58,406	16.4
Josep Llambert	1,464	51,804	14.5
Miquel Bas	1,330	49,667	13.9
Francesc Mestra	959	32,268	9.1
Pere Riba	848	28,765	8.1

Source: ACA, Generalitat, D-102, 2106–12.

cloth woven on behalf of the primary ordering clothier remained below 40 percent of the total output of a particular master weaver (see Table 8-2).

In sharp contrast with the clothiers, all master weavers seem to have been true specialists, whose main activity and source of income was weaving. With the exception of Francesc Mestra and Pere Riba, the masters should have been kept busy with their loom during at least thirty weeks in a year such as 1696.[13] The small confraternity of

Table 8-2. Weavers and clothiers in Igualada from July 1695 to December 1696

Master weaver	A	B
Miquel Simorra	20	26.8
Jacinto Farrer	11	41.0
Benet Valls	9	62.6
Josep Llambert	10	35.6
Miquel Bas	12	37.4
Francesc Mestra	11	29.0
Pere Riba	10	27.1

Source: ACA, Generalitat, D-102, 2106–12.

A: total number of clothiers for whom each weaver worked in the period July 1695 to December 1696.

B: share (in %) of the main ordering clothier in the total value of cloth woven by each weaver.

13. This is based on the realistic assumption that each master employed only one journeyman and acceptance of the data on the clothmaking process produced by a clothier of the same town in the middle of the eighteenth century. Ms. in Institut Municipal d'Història, Barcelona, "Junta de Comerç," vol. 81, fol. 43.

the Holy Trinity and St. Aloysius, of which the weavers were members, had succeeded in limiting the number of masters and the differences between them as well as preventing the development of strong bilateral relationships between their members and particular clothiers.

Besides the common membership in the same confraternity, other links existed between master weavers that surely enhanced the cohesion of this small group. Some basic biographical data about six of the seven masters listed in Table 8-1 have been gathered from the marriage acts in the parish registers of the church of Santa Maria in Igualada.[14] The resulting picture is most telling. Four masters were born in Igualada, and three of them were the children of local wool weavers (out of these three, two married the daughters of other local wool weavers). Only one of the six masters who appear in the records of the *bolla* was born in a different town (he was the son of a wool weaver there). The birthplace of the remaining one is not specified in the source.

This was not exceptional. If one looks at what is known about the background of these Igualada wool weavers it is clear that the same pattern holds for the whole period from 1615 to 1723 (see Table 8-3). During this period, thirty-three wool weavers married in Igualada. Many immigrants were arriving at this time,[15] but the wool weavers were recruited mostly among local families, especially weavers' families. Almost half (45 percent) of the grooms in the nearly two thousand marriages celebrated at Santa Maria in this period were born outside Igualada; this figure falls to just one-fourth (25 percent) in the case of the wool weavers. The data also show that a large majority of the same wool weavers were close relatives of fellow craftsmen; many of them were the sons or sons-in-law of local wool weavers.

What emerges from this short survey is that a small craft could succeed in preserving for its members the status of independent producers even in the context of a fairly developed specialization at a regional scale and in a town that was experiencing heavy immigration. An institutional framework that incorporated the weavers into

14. *Llibres de matrimonis* in the archives of the same church. In using this source I have benefited from the ongoing research of Assumpta Fabré on migration and occupational structure in Igualada in the seventeenth and eighteenth centuries.

15. J. M. Torras i Ribé, "Demografia i societat a Igualada durant els segles XVI i XVII," in *Miscellanea Aqualatensia/4* (Igualada, 1987), pp. 87–109.

Table 8-3. Birthplace and family background of Igualada wool weavers married between 1615 and 1723

Born	Number of cases	Profession of the father			
		unknown	clothier	weaver	other
Igualada	24	1	2*	13 +	6
comarca	6	1	2	2	1
outside	2	–	–	2	–
unknown	1	–	–	–	1
Total	33	2	4	17	8

Source: Llibres de matrimonis in the archives of the church of Santa Maria, Igualada.

*one married the daughter of a local wool weaver.

+ three married the daughters of local wool weavers.

Note: comarca refers to any birthplace within the small territorial administration of which Igualada is currently the center; "outside" excludes Igualada as well as *comarca.*

a recognized guild, separated from the clothiers, was crucial to this independence. But a strongly endogamous selection of its membership should also have been instrumental in reinforcing discipline and a sense of cohesion within this group.

During the first half of the eighteenth century this situation was radically altered. But, first, consideration should be given to the overall institutional and economic changes that occurred in this same period.

The Catalan economy was badly hurt by political and military events in the very last years of the seventeenth century and in the first two decades of the eighteenth century. Spain's War of Succession brought prolonged warfare to Catalan soil, which was most disruptive of activities based on extensive exchanges. Immediately after the war, Catalonia had to bear a vindictive fiscal burden, the costs of dramatic institutional changes, and a new arrangement of local power structures, all implying full political annexation of the region into Spain.[16]

At least until the mid-1720s, all available evidence tells of widespread economic hardship. In Igualada this conjuncture is well illus-

16. Henry Kamen, *The War of Succession in Spain, 1700–1715* (Bloomington, Ind., 1969); J. Mercader, *Felip V i Catalunya* (Barcelona, 1968).

trated by a sharp drop in the production of cloth. The average annual output of the 1690s steadily fell after 1702, and by 1710 it leveled out at nearly eighty pieces a year.[17] This lasting depression must have had deleterious effects on the textile community, and by 1723 there remained in Igualada only two master weavers. Recovery was very slow until the early 1730s, but then a considerable boom started. By 1742 an output of 500 pieces was reported; 1,750 pieces were reported in 1766, when Igualada had become a leading wool-textile center in Catalonia. The increase was all the more remarkable in that the average quality was then much higher than in the 1690s.[18]

This experience was not unique to Igualada, and the aggregate output of the Catalan wool-textile industry experienced a fourfold increase between the early 1720s and 1766, according to fiscal sources.[19] Such an increase cannot be explained only in terms of a growing regional demand for local textiles, and there is ample evidence that by the middle of the eighteenth century Catalan woolens (as well as other consumer goods) were becoming increasingly common in many regional markets throughout Spain. Catalan producers enjoyed easier access to these markets after 1717, when customs duties were abolished between Catalonia and the rest of Spain—an interesting outcome of the War of Succession. The resulting customs union, however imperfect, brought about a redirection of commercial flows that proved to be highly beneficial to Catalan industry. The regional economy became more oriented toward industrial production in particular when compared with that of other regions of Spain.

Shortly after the end of the War of Succession (in 1714), some clothiers in Igualada undertook to improve the quality of their goods in order to take advantage of the new situation, by trying to become suppliers of the state (providing cloth for the royal army)

17. Information is lacking for the next years until the end of the war in 1714. The estimate is based on the yearly account of *ploms* (pieces of lead attached to finished cloth after payment of the tax on production) needed by the master clothiers. Ms. in *Llibre de la Confraria y Offici de perayres de la villa de Igualada*, in Servei de Documentació, Museu Comarcal, Igualada.

18. Jaume Torras, "The Old and the New: Marketing Networks and Textile Growth in Eighteenth-century Spain," in *Markets and Manufacture*, ed. Maxine Berg (London, 1991), pp. 93–113. (Details on Igualada's cloth industry in this period on pp. 96–97.)

19. Jaume Torras, "Especialización agrícola e industria rural en Cataluña en el siglo XVIII," *Revista de Historia Económica* 2 (1984), 113–27.

and by looking for new customers in inland markets. Igualada enjoyed at least two advantages: (1) it lay on the main road connecting the Catalan capital, Barcelona, to interior Spain and (2) a small garrison was stationed in the town after the war.

Such an undertaking implied considerable changes in the type of product as well as in its marketing. The quality of the stuffs had to be upgraded from the common cloth of sixteen hundred threads to warp to the so-called fine cloths of twenty-two hundred to thirty-two hundred threads to warp. This change was necessary to meet the state's requirements; it was also the quality range in which Catalan cloth had a chance to succeed in Spanish markets. In the higher-quality range foreign competition was too strong and tariff protection almost nonexistent, while in the lower it was difficult to displace local rough stuffs.[20]

This was a highly successful choice. The population of Igualada increased from about 1,630 inhabitants in 1718 to 6,494 in 1797, under the influence of an expanding wool industry that was the main source of employment in the town.[21] Production was concentrated in the hands of a very few clothiers. More than two-thirds of the local output of cloth was produced in 1765 by only three clothiers (compared to eleven for the same proportion in 1695–96). Two of those three clothiers (Josep Torelló and Segimon Borrull, sons of rather modest paraires at the end of the seventeenth century) were brothers-in-law and in some matters had been operating as a single enterprise. In 1745 a royal decree had granted them, jointly, several tax exemptions and other advantages and distinctions, including the use of the trade mark "Fábrica Real de Paños de la villa de Igualada." Fine cloths of twenty-six hundred threads to warp were the main product of the firm that sold most of its cloth in central Spain, mainly in the capital city.[22]

20. A general outline of Spain's tariff policy in the eighteenth century is in E. Fernández de Pinedo, "Coyuntura y política económicas," in *Centralismo, ilustración y agonía del Antiguo Régimen (1715–1833)*, ed. E. Fernández de Pinedo, A. Gil Novales, and A. Derozier (Barcelona, 1980), pp. 125–30. On the favorable conditions enjoyed by British goods, J. O. McLachlan, *Trade and Peace with Old Spain 1667–1750*, repr. from the 1940 edition (New York, 1974).

21. On the economic history of eighteenth-century Igualada, see J. M. Torras i Ribé, "Trajectòria d'un procés d'industrialització frustrat," in *Miscellanea Aqualatensia/2* (Igualada, 1974), pp. 151–97.

22. Torras, "The Old and the New," pp. 93–113.

In Igualada economic distress in the first two decades of the eighteenth century led to a reduction in the number of master clothiers
as well as master weavers. In 1723 only two master weavers remained in the town, and about a dozen clothiers were more or less
active. Far-reaching changes can be traced in the proceedings of law-
suits brought by the weavers' guild against the clothiers in 1742 and
1758. Most of the following description, as well as the above esti-
mates of the number of masters, is based on the detailed inquiry that
ensued.[23]

In 1723 the two remaining master weavers of Igualada had one
loom each. But at least eight, perhaps as many as ten, looms for wool
cloth were in town. They were to be found in the shops of several
master clothiers who hired journeymen weavers to work directly for
them, instead of working with a master weaver as required by guild
statutes. These journeymen weavers "used to eat and to sleep in the
same houses [the clothiers'] and to work as journeymen weavers do."[24]
Apparently this was not an altogether new practice; the novelty lay
in its becoming the rule rather than the exception. Two of these
master clothiers not only had a journeyman weaving for them in
their own shops, but also had looms operated by journeymen in separate houses.[25] The implicit threat to the master weavers was that if
textile activity recovered they would be bypassed by the clothiers.

The first conflict arose in 1722–23, probably in connection with
some clothiers providing supplies for the army—and the consequent
sharp and short-lived rise in cloth production and change in the type
of fabrics produced. Several clothiers then proposed that master
weavers and master clothiers should be members of the same guild
and confraternity, that of the clothiers themselves—which would au-
tomatically have regularized the above situation. The suggestion was
dismissed by the provincial authorities, but the town council negotiated an agreement (*concòrdia*) between the concerned confraternities.
It explicitly declared that "any master clothier who wishes to be ad-

23. The answers of fifty witnesses were recorded, and both guilds had to produce
every sort of documentary evidence to assert their claims. Most materials are in ACA,
"Reial Audiència. Plets civils," no. 8297 (further quotations are abridged under the
form W v. C).

24. Declaration by the witness Jaume Bas, referring to the years 1717 and 1718
when he himself was an apprentice at the shop of Francisco Borrull, one of the five
clothiers who directly hired journeymen weavers, W v. C, fol. 57.

25. W v. C, fol. 60 (referring to the same Francisco Borrull) and fol. 79 (referring
to Segimon Borrull).

mitted to the mentioned confraternity of the Holy Trinity and St. Aloysius [of which the weavers were members, together with other crafts] may and shall be admitted therein as master weaver of wool fabrics without any examination, and he will be allowed to have as many looms and to employ as many journeymen weavers as he wishes" after payment of a substantial admittance fee.[26] One of the seven members of the town council was the clothier Josep Torelló. No less significant, the agreement was signed on behalf of the confraternity of the Holy Trinity and St. Aloysius by twenty-three masters who attended the assembly. Only one of them was a weaver.

Twenty years later, the master weavers in the confraternity of the Holy Trinity and St. Aloysius officially numbered twenty-six.[27] The weaving trade had prospered in those booming decades for the wool-textile industry. But the master weavers were irrevocably losing control over their segment of the clothmaking process. Actually they were only twenty-two in number; three of them had moved to other towns and a fourth was in the army. Of these twenty-two, four were master clothiers admitted without examination by virtue of the 1723 agreement; they could ignore the real master weavers when ordering a piece to be woven. Hardly surprising, among those four were the three biggest producers in town. They never attended the assemblies of the guild and, worse, they did not abide by its decisions.

At least five of the remaining eighteen master weavers were regularly employed by the three major clothiers—or *fabricants* as they liked to be called, instead of paraires.[28] The sources do not indicate how many journeymen and apprentices worked in the shops of the other thirteen masters, but doubtless they were outnumbered by those directly employed by the fabricants. Two fabricants alone, Josep Torelló and Segimon Borrull, gave work on a more or less regular basis to at least four masters and fourteen journeymen weavers.[29]

What were the consequences of these developments for the organization of work in the clothmaking industry? The clothiers who started hiring journeymen weavers did not consistently concentrate

---

26. ACA, "Notarial. Igualada," vol. 796 (B. Costa, "Manual," 1723), fols. 57–60.

27. Arxiu Històric, Igualada, notary Melcion, "Manual," 1743, fol. 268.

28. Four were employees of Torelló and Borrull (ibid., notary Matheu, "Manual," 1748, fol. 74); one was an employee of Lladó, the third of the biggest producers (ibid., notary Viladès, "Manual," 1748, fol. 14).

29. Ibid., notary Matheu, "Manual," 1748, fol. 74.

looms and workers in their own shops. The master weavers angrily complained in 1753 that in spite of statutes enjoining journeymen to work only in the shop of a master and under his supervision those who were employed by the fabricants wove "at their [the journeymen's] homes . . . paid at a piece rate, and in every respect like master weavers."[30] In fact, the clothiers assigned work to the journeymen weavers in the same way they had always done to the masters. These journeymen weavers, however, were far more dependable. They could not associate in the craft guild empowered to regulate weaving conditions in Igualada and control the number of people engaged in this operation. The bargaining power of the craft as a whole decreased. Conversely, the control of the production process by clothiers increased.

The implementation of the concòrdia of 1723 allowed the rise of a new type of entrepreneur, who enjoyed a command over the conditions of production that the clothiers had formerly shared with the master weavers. This was neither the result of any deliberate reformist policies nor the automatic outcome of an overall transformation of the economic or technical framework of the industry. For the wool weavers of Igualada, it was the outcome of a constellation of circumstances that were not present everywhere at the same time. Interestingly enough, an attempt in 1721 by the clothiers of Barcelona to gain a similar degree of control failed because of opposition from the municipal government.[31]

In Igualada the ability to influence local politics enabled some clothiers to take advantage of a critical conjuncture to modify the customary regulation of clothmaking and enhance their command over production. A relatively large community of weavers was reconstructed thereafter, but it lacked part of its former strength, that is, the cohesion that stems from a common background. The industry grew quickly, and skilled weavers were urgently needed. As the number of local weavers had drastically declined in the early decades of the century, few locals recruited into the craft had close relatives within it. Table 8-4 presents the geographical and professional origins of a significant sample of wool weavers in this period.

The resulting picture is quite different from that shown for the earlier period. After the 1723 agreement, native Igualada weavers

30. Ms. in the archives of the family Torelló, in Igualada, ref. no. B-659.
31. P. Molas Ribalta, *Los gremios barceloneses del siglo XVIII* (Madrid, 1970), p. 383.

Table 8-4. Birthplace and family background of Igualada wool weavers married between 1724 and 1747

Born	Number of cases	Profession of the father			
		unknown	clothier	weaver	other
Igualada	8	–	–	4	4
comarca	3	1	–	–	2
outside	22	3*	2	6	11
unknown	2	2	–	–	–
Total	35	6	2	10	17

Source: Llibres de matrimonis in the archives of the church of Santa Maria, Igualada.

*one married the daughter of a local wool weaver.

Note: comarca refers to any birthplace within the small territorial administration of which Igualada is currently the center; "outside" excludes Igualada as well as *comarca*.

were uncommon. And a weaver who was the son or son-in-law of a wool weaver of Igualada was rare indeed. This was especially so in the case of the weavers (masters as well as journeymen) regularly employed by the fabricants. The birthplace can be identified for thirteen (of a total of twenty) weavers who fall into this category: only three were born in Igualada, and only one of them was the son of a local wool weaver. (Curiously enough, his father was Benet Valls, the one who had agreed to the 1723 concòrdia). That local roots seem to have been somewhat stronger among masters who avoided direct subordination to the fabricants is hardly surprising.[32]

The main conclusion to be drawn from this case study refers to the forces at work in the series of changes that led to the demise of the corporate organization of work. This research suggests that close attention must be paid to developments at the local level, since they help explain the remarkable unevenness of the process from place to place or from trade to trade.

In Igualada the customary organization of clothmaking left the operation of weaving outside the direct command of clothiers, which had important consequences. On the one hand, this enhanced the bargaining power of the weavers' trade as a whole, because the as-

32. Birthplaces of the independent master weavers who were members of the confraternity in 1743 are known in ten cases (out of a total of thirteen). Six of the weavers were born in Igualada.

sembly of the masters controlled the local supply of this skill; on the other hand, it divided the craftsmen weavers into two categories, masters and journeymen, which scarcely had any objective basis. Such distinction was blurred by the changes described so far at the same time that full command over every phase of the production process fell into the hands of the fabricants, the main beneficiaries of the 1723 agreement. Spatial concentration of production under one roof was still in the future, but decisive progress had been made toward a sharper division of functions by concentrating in the hands of the emerging fabricants every decision-making capacity concerning the technical and organizational aspects of the work process.[33]

By the middle of the eighteenth century the customary regulation of work in clothmaking had ceased to be enforced in Igualada, not without reactions from the master weavers. In 1754 they left the confraternity of which they had been members for centuries and created an exclusive weavers' confraternity.[34] The new association was quite active in the following years, in response to the ongoing changes. The membership was enlarged by opening its doors to journeymen weavers, with a mere formality as examination to be admitted as masters. And in June 1757 a strike was declared by refusing to work for the fabricants who were requiring changes in the width of cloth without changes in the piece rate.[35] But this is part of a different story. The wool weavers of Igualada were no longer behaving as a craft; they were making their way toward what was to become a working class.

33. In other towns potential *fabricantes* had to wait until the 1769 "Reales ordenanzas para fabricantes de paños de todas clases y de bayetas finas del Principado" to gain a similar degree of control over the production process. The full text is in F. Torrella Niubó, *El moderno resurgir textil de Barcelona, siglos XVIII–XIX* (Barcelona, 1961), pp. 67–75.

34. In August 1754 the town council endorsed the statutes of this weavers' guild. Ms. in Institut Municipal d'Història, Barcelona, "Junta de Comerç," caixa 2, nos. 12, 16. See also J. Segura, *Història d'Igualada*, vol. 2, pp. 129–30.

35. The strike stopped weaving in Igualada for one month, until the clothiers recruited new weavers from outside. Ms. in Institut Municipal d'Història, caixa 2, no. 7.

Robert C. Davis

9 Arsenal and *Arsenalotti*: Workplace and Community in Seventeenth-Century Venice

The Venetian state shipyards, known as the Arsenal, ranked among the largest manufacturing centers of early modern Europe. By 1600 this complex, surrounded by its two and a half miles of towering brick walls, sprawled over sixty acres of docks, yards, storage sheds, and workshops. Here an average of at least four thousand shipbuilders, laborers, and allied craftsmen came to work daily, producing galleys, merchant ships, artillery, rope, and all manner of naval stores. The Arsenal was as renowned for its efficiency as for its size, with a remarkable ability to produce large numbers of fully equipped warships in a few months or even weeks.[1] Contemporary observers considered the shipyards one of the Republic's greatest wonders, and indeed, over the centuries the Arsenal of Venice has acquired its own small bibliography, as generations of later scholars sought to explain just how Venetian commercial genius gave rise to one of the greatest manufactories of the preindustrial world.[2]

Thanks to the extensive archival record that documents the Arsenal's operations, a great deal has been uncovered about the manag-

1. Frederick Lane, *Venetian Ships and Shipbuilders of the Renaissance* (Baltimore, 1934), pp. 139–45.
2. For a historiography of the Venetian Arsenal, along with a more detailed examination of the workforce itself, see R. C. Davis, *Shipbuilders of the Venetian Arsenal: Workers and Workplace in the Preindustrial City* (Baltimore, 1991), pp. 1–82, esp. n. 204.

erial structures that kept this state enterprise well supplied and operating smoothly. Yet much less has come to light on the social dynamics behind the running of this production center. Such essentially administrative sources speak only obliquely about hierarchies within the workforce, the presence or importance of a surrounding worker community, or indeed even about the practical relationships between the shipyards' managers and the mass of artisans. In particular, little is to be found about the workings of power in the Arsenal—except, of course, in so far as the state's documentary record presupposed the one-way flow of force wielded by its agents within the shipyards' management over its subjects in the workplace. Considering the Arsenal's essentially Old Regime character, the secular product of slow growth and overlaying traditions, such a lapse is hardly surprising. The ties that bound shipbuilders and the state were not only complex but also well hidden. Lines of power ran well below the surface, and the resulting quid pro quo was almost buried from sight by centuries-long encrustations of custom, deference, and privilege.

Yet the formal outlines of power within the Arsenal are fairly easy to trace, following the shipyards' management hierarchy. By 1600 a small army of administrators had evolved to run the shipyards: besides a score or more of clerks and bookkeepers, nearly one hundred technical, supervisory, and disciplinary managers oversaw the process of production down to the smallest details. Over them all were the noble representatives of the Republic's governing elite, a clear reminder that this immense source of military power was firmly in the control of Venice's aristocracy. Representing the Senate were the six *Patroni e Provveditori all'Arsenale*, who directly ran the establishment. Three *Savii agli ordini*, who reported to the doge's *Collegio*, and a host of specially designated magistrates, *capi*, and *Inquisitori* provided still further levels of aristocratic oversight.[3]

This elaborate bureaucracy, which came into its own in the two centuries following 1450, flowered, it might be said, at the expense of the independent shipbuilding sector of the city. The evolving concept of manufacturing efficiency within the Arsenal was largely based on the triumph of a system of centralized and bureaucratically

---

3. M. Forsellini, "L'organizzazione economica dell'Arsenale di Venezia nella prima metà del seicento" *Archivio veneto* 5th ser., 7 (1930), 55–59; Lane, *Ships and Shipbuilders*, pp. 147–54.

controlled production at the expense of the traditions of corporate self-governance and independent craftsmanship. By the mid-seventeenth century, shipbuilding in the Arsenal no longer followed the *bottega* practices of the private yards, in which a team of masters working under loose leadership collectively carried a ship or galley through all the successive steps of construction, from laying the keel, to caulking the seams, to applying the final decorative carvings. Instead, state-planned shipbuilding developed a line system of production, based on standardization of design and interchangeable component parts that were crafted by specialists at designated locations within the state shipyards and assembled by work gangs.[4]

In several senses, this bureaucratic, centralizing style of management gave the shipbuilding workforce at the Arsenal its special character. As the overall construction process was streamlined and integrated, the duties of individual craftsmen became simpler and more repetitive: the result was lowered levels of skill among shipbuilders, as the required apprenticeship training was successively reduced. Step by step, guildsmen in the Arsenal surrendered their claims to fix craft standards, working conditions, and apprenticeship examinations or even to have any say in wage rates. No longer establishing their own pace and tasks, these new-style shipbuilders worked under the strict control of gang bosses and disciplinary officers— agents of the state, with the authority to fine, fire, or even arrest any master who dared to disobey orders. By the mid-1600s, many Arsenal administrators had stopped even referring to these artisans as *maestri*, calling them instead simply *operai*, or workers.[5]

Yet if these shipbuilders lost much of their traditional identification with their particular guilds, the state supplied them instead with a larger corporate identity. To tame and gain the allegiance of the city's independent shipbuilders, a prize that was greater than the status of free guildsmen was offered to those willing to enroll as Arsenal workers: the guaranteed right to keep on earning the state's wages for life. In this era before pensions, when an aging artisan's ability to earn declined with his ability to work, the possibility for a shipbuilder to keep on receiving his pay long after he could no longer carry out the strenuous demands of his craft was a powerful

4. Frederick Lane, *Venice: A Maritime Republic* (Baltimore, 1973), pp. 362–64.

5. Archivio di Stato di Venezia (hereafter ASV):Senato Mar, filza 340, July 6, 1641; filza 511, August 28, 1660; ASV:Collegio V (Segreta) bu. 57, *relazioni* of Bertucci Trivisan and Sebastian Foscarini.

incentive for enrollment. Masters kept on dragging themselves to the Arsenal until the very day of their death, in order to keep receiving their daily *soldo*. More significantly, this right to state employment was inheritable; most shipbuilders enrolled their sons as apprentices with the state in their turn. By the mid-seventeenth century, these craftsmen had become a virtual caste in the city's social hierarchy, so closely bound with the institution where generations had worked that they even took its name for their own, calling themselves the *arsenalotti*.[6]

The Arsenal's embracing paternalism was inextricably bound up with the power its agents exercised over workers' lives. Such power was especially centered in the Patroni, who ran the state shipyards both as government magistrates and as factory administrators. Overall directors of the primary military resource of an absolutist regime, the Patroni theoretically enjoyed complete power over the workplace during their thirty-two-month terms of office. How they disciplined their workforce was left almost completely to their discretion. The Patroni could be sure their will would be backed up within the Arsenal through the services of special disciplinary officers, who circulated through the shipyards armed with pistol and knives, keeping the workforce under continual surveillance. Masters who shirked or disobeyed were usually disciplined by having their pay docked, the punishment for those who broke factory regulations. For graver infractions such as fraud, theft, or fighting, the Patroni acted less as administrators than as magistrates. As such, they could hold formal trials and had the power to condemn the guilty to punishment ranging from temporary confinement in the Arsenal's own small prisons (*camerotti*), to banishment from the Republic, or even death—public hangings were carried out in the *Campo dell'Arsenale*. A serious miscreant was likely to find himself involved in criminal proceedings rather than simply being fired. Perhaps the Patroni were reluctant to expel arsenalotti permanently from the shipyards because such a move would effectively bar the sons of these workers as well. In any event, after serving their sentences, many offenders seem to have been taken back into the Arsenal workforce without too many difficulties.[7]

6. Cf. M. Aymard, "L'Arsenale e le conoscenze tecnico-marinaresche. Le arti," *Storia della cultura veneta* 3 (1980), 289–315; Lane, *Ships and Shipbuilders*, pp. 186–87.

7. On the criminal activities of Venetian shipbuilders, see Davis, *Shipbuilders*, pp. 53, 78–79, 118–35.

This double role of magistrate and administrator allowed the Patroni to mete out their law with a paternalistic hand designed both to chastise the guilty and provide a public lesson to the workforce, which made a virtue out of punishments involving humiliation before a worker's assembled peers. In the sixteenth century (less so in the seventeenth), a petty thief's punishment might well be a whipping around the Arsenal, while wearing a sign on his head proclaiming his crime and with the object of his theft (if it were small enough) hanging from his neck.[8]

State power not only controlled the arsenalotti in their workplace, but also reached into their lives in the surrounding community as well. Growing with the state shipyards over the centuries, the worker neighborhoods surrounding the Arsenal were almost entirely dependent on the government for survival. The Arsenal loomed, then (as indeed it still does), less like a factory than a medieval castle, in the heart of what was in part a company town, but also a kind of government fief. Those who ran the shipyards were far from indifferent to what their workers might do in the privacy of their homes. Like all medieval lords, the noble Patroni of the Arsenal constantly meddled in neighborhood life, no doubt with the idea that the 150,000 or more ducats that the state poured annually into the district in the form of wages and salaries gave them ample justification for doing so.[9]

At first sight, the walled and fortified Arsenal might well appear to have had only the slightest contact with the surrounding cityscape. The state shipyards were one of the most protected areas of Venice, isolated at the eastern tip of the city and surrounded by thirty-foot-high brick walls studded at intervals with watchtowers. To those who ran it, the Arsenal represented both Venice's repository of the technical secrets of nautical craftsmanship and design and its storehouse for an immense wealth of raw materials, weaponry, and naval stores. Entry into the shipyards had to be rigidly controlled, limited to just two heavily guarded points: a land gate for the passage of workers and a water gate for the transit of ships and raw materials. In the

8. ASV:Collegio V (Segreta) relazioni, bu. 57, 1633, fol. 5v; ASV:Arsenale, reg. 133, July 23, 27, 1501; March 14, July 15, 1505; Lane, *Ships and Shipbuilders*, pp. 194–95.

9. Average for the first half of the 1600s: Forsellini, "L'organizzazione economica," pp. 115–17.

1620s an encircling canal was dug outside the walls, completing the process of isolation.[10]

The Venetian state had physically cut the Arsenal off from free public access, but this did not mean that its agents were in any way constrained from intruding in the affairs of the surrounding community. Indeed, the state's involvement in workers' lives gave the arsenalotti neighborhoods a character all their own, quite unlike other popolani districts in Venice. That the parishes around the shipyards lacked Venice's typical jumble of neighborhood food merchants and shopkeepers was simply because there was less need for them than elsewhere. Instead, the Patroni themselves handled much of the provisioning of the Arsenal's workers and their families. They licensed several of their subordinates to run bread, cheese, and dried fish (*salumi*) concessions just outside the shipyards' gates and employed another officer especially to distribute free wine to masters when they were at work. The district was also one of the least cosmopolitan in Venice, since the state, with its persistent fears of espionage in the Arsenal, made a point of discouraging foreigners from joining the shipbuilding guilds or from setting up homes in the area.

In the arsenalotti community, all rhythms of local life were controlled by the enormous manufacturing institution at its center. Such was the state's power locally that it even distorted the neighborhood demographic profile, leaving the district with a striking shortage of men. The Arsenal was a widow maker, for state policy required that every shipbuilder serve a tour of duty at sea with the fleet, usually as ship's carpenter or petty officer. As a result of this naturally hazardous duty, so many masters were killed or ended up enslaved that in the seventeenth century the local community had an imbalance of as many as 135 adult women for every 100 men.[11]

The demographic effects of state policy on the arsenalotti community was still more starkly demonstrated when plague broke out in the city. In some ways the shipbuilders enjoyed a favored status among the city's workers during times of plague, since the government at least made sure they had enough to eat. Venice, like many other early modern states, relied on containment, isolation, and the

---

10. Lane, *Venice, A Maritime Republic*, p. 362. E. Concina, *L'Arsenale della Repubblica di Venezia* (Milan, 1984), p. 180.

11. For more on the unique community of the *arsenalotti*, see Davis, *Shipbuilders*, pp. 83–117.

blockade of trade to keep the plague from spreading. But if the state-imposed quarantines slowed the pestilence, they also left many ordinary artisans out of work, faced with the dismal prospect of death by starvation.[12] As prized government workers, the arsenalotti usually continued to receive at least half their daily wage, even if they were quarantined in their houses or carried off by ship to one of the pest houses (*lazaretti*) located on outlying islands. For ship-builders who were still healthy and wanted to work, but who lived some distance from the Arsenal, the state was willing to bend the strict rules banning ordinary citizens from leaving their parish while plague raged. These arsenalotti assembled every morning near Venice's customs house, on the opposite side of town; a boat would ferry them back and forth to work. For each day they came to work, they received their full soldo.[13]

Nevertheless the state left little doubt that its favoritism toward the arsenalotti was inspired more by the desire to maintain a steady output of galleys than by humanitarian motives. This was particularly clear in 1630–31, during Venice's last (and arguably one of its worst) outbreak of plague. After four months of pestilence had killed off nearly 300 masters and apprentices and quarantined another 160, the Senate began to worry about preserving its Arsenal workforce. The Patroni of the Arsenal were ordered to turn the shipyards themselves into a haven for a certain number of workers, converting covered yards into dormitories and setting up a chapel for religious services; sufficient clean bedding was to be collected and contracts issued for supplying those inside with food.[14]

The Arsenal was never more literally a castle, garrisoned within by its workers and besieged from without by the invisible force of the plague. But not all masters were invited into the relative security of the walled compound. The Senators decided that it would be worth the expenditure to bring in only the two hundred or so most skilled arsenalotti, that is, "the bosses and the chief masters . . . those that would be the most appropriate for the work that presently so needs

12. See Carlo Cipolla, *Faith, Reason, and the Plague in Seventeenth-Century Tuscany* (New York, 1979); G. Calvi, *Histories of a Plague Year: The Social and the Imaginary in Baroque Florence* (Berkeley, 1989), esp. pp. 155–96.

13. ASV:Arsenale, bu. 17, June 29, October 6, 1576.

14. ASV:Senato Mar, filza 274, December 7, 1630; ASV:Arsenale, reg. 139, December 21, 1630; Museo Correr di Venezia (hereafter MC):Gradenigo 193 II, fol. 162r.

to be done." The rest of the workforce, "consisting of the old men, the boys, and such like," would be left to take their chances on the outside. At first it was thought that those locked out of the Arsenal—since they would have no chance to work at all—should be given their full wages as compensation. After a few weeks, however, it was noticed that too many of these continued to brave the infested streets every Saturday to come in and collect their pay. One Patron then suggested opening up just a part of the shipyards for them, a nonquarantined area where these unfortunates could be put to work so that the state might "receive the benefit of the wages it is paying."

The Senate's rather cynical offer to protect only those shipbuilders whose skills made their survival profitable to the state eventually foundered on its own shortsightedness: those invited to enjoy the comparative safety of the shipyards were told they would have to leave their wives and children behind. The Patroni thought they could convince these managers and principal masters to desert their families by offering them some additional pay, a bonus that would encourage them to go "with a more tranquil soul." This failed to satisfy these privileged few, however, and after nearly fifty days of quarantine, they petitioned to be let out to "see their homes again."[15] The state's experiment in applied demographics was rather short-lived, but it had a decided impact on the community, coming as it did at the height of the pestilence. Whereas 922, or nearly 50 percent, of all master and apprentice shipbuilders would die before the plague waned in late 1631, the Arsenal's managers weathered the epidemic much better, for less than 15 percent of all bosses and foremen perished.[16] What this meant to the arsenalotti community would become evident in later years as certain management families emerged from the pestilence largely intact and with a higher profile locally than in previous decades. In the generation after the plague, fathers, brothers, and sons of such families suddenly monopolized lists of Arsenal bosses and those of private shipyard owners, raised to their superior status, in effect, by the calculated policies of state.[17]

The Arsenal's paternalistic powers were felt in many corners of its

15. ASV:SM, reg. 88, December 3, 1630 and February 20, 1630 m.v.; filza 274, December 7, 1630; January 16, 1630 m.v.

16. ASV:Arsenale, reg. 139, September 3, 1630–February 12, 1632 m.v.; ASV:Collegio V (Segreta), *relazione* of 1633, fols. 10r-v.

17. ASV:SM, filza 294, December 9, 1634; ASV:Collegio V (Segreta), *relazioni* of 1645 and 1660.

dependent community. The Patroni took care to see to the upkeep and maintenance of local public works, making sure that wooden bridge pilings were replaced, that local canals were kept cleared, and that neighborhood squares—especially the Campo dell'Arsenale, just outside the shipyard gates—remained tidy. These duties were specifically reserved to the Patroni by the Senate, just as they alone had the authority to inspect and license Venice's private shipyards, or *squeri*. Such powers weighed significantly on the arsenalotti community because these private yards provided the only significant source of employment outside of the Arsenal itself. These local squeri cannot really be said to have operated independently at all; their business was, by law, carried out under the watchful eye of their state-run competitor.[18]

The Arsenal even provided for the spiritual needs of its workers and local residents, although this may have been more by chance than clear calculation. An image of the Virgin, originally painted in the late fifteenth century, turned up within the shipyards in the 1530s. Thanks to its reputation for miraculous cures, the image soon began attracting local worshipers, drawn originally by tales of its powers and eventually by the promise of a plenary indulgence. In time the Senate ordered that a shrine be established for the image, placing it under the care of the Arsenal magistrates. This small chapel, dedicated to the *Beatissima Madonna all'Arsenale*, would be constructed just in front of the imposing towers that flanked the water gate of the shipyards. Here, almost literally nestled under the wings of the Lion of St. Mark, the Virgin linked workplace and community, acting as an advocate for both. The Patroni had masses for the safety of the Arsenal (especially from fire) and the ships it produced said before her altar; arsenalotti on their way to work stopped off in the mornings to ask her blessing. When masters were sent off to serve with the fleet, their wives would pray to her image for their protection; when they returned, they made sure that the ships on which they crewed fired a salute as they sailed past her chapel on the Rio dell'Arsenale.[19]

The Patroni also took on the responsibility of keeping an eye on the forty or so state-owned houses that the Arsenal maintained in

18. ASV:Arsenale, reg. 139, March 9, 1624; reg. 142, January 10, 1679 m.v.; June 14, 1688; July 4, 1689.

19. ASV:Avogaria di Comun, *civile*, bu. 164/23; MC:Gradenigo, 193 II, fols. 150–152v; ASV:Senato Mar, reg. 101, March 28, 1643.

the community for the accommodation of the shipyards' top managers and administrators. Charged by the Senate to see that these buildings were in good repair, the Patroni would further serve as arbitrators on the frequent occasions when their tenants got caught up in community disputes regarding boundary walls, garden trees, and even peeping toms.[20] Essentially a management enclave within the company town, the houses clustered near the Campo dell'Arsenale and neighboring *fondamenta* and established the Arsenal's official presence outside the barrier of its walls. The houses were mostly large and conferred some of the state's considerable prestige on their occupants, allowing these officers to maintain impressive households of family, guests, and servants. Often serving as the sites for celebrating baptisms or weddings of friends and relations, managers' houses allowed the Arsenal's presence to manifest itself even in the community's sacred celebrations.[21]

The transmission of the Arsenal's power and influence to its managerial class was not confined to this enclave alone. Local residents could quickly identify the Arsenal's foremen, subforemen, and overseers, for many went about in the town splendidly dressed in their formal long robes of office. The authority these bosses wielded over shipbuilders in the workplace was inevitably translated into personal status throughout the arsenalotti community. Not surprisingly their powers were reflected in day-to-day local affairs—preserved in particular in the notarial records, where managers are repeatedly to be found serving their neighbors as character witnesses, settling local disputes, or standing as godfathers.[22]

Nowhere was the controlling force of the Arsenal over its dependent community more thoroughly tested than in cases of theft and pilferage from the shipyards; such crimes almost inevitably ended up involving Arsenal magistrates with local neighborhood life. Convinced, along with the rest of the Venetian patriciate, that the natural "greed of the plebeian soul" would invariably lead workers to steal from the rich Arsenal storehouses, the Patroni and their depu-

20. ASV:Arsenale, reg. 138, January 2, 1618 m.v., May 29, 1619; reg. 139, June 1, 1620; reg. 140, April 14, 1644; reg. 142, July 4, 1686; ASV:Collegio, *risposte di dentro*, filza 66, March 16, 1666.

21. On the social role of these houses in the *arsenalotti* community, see Davis, *Shipbuilders*, pp. 57–58, 85–87.

22. Davis, *Shipbuilders*, pp. 60–61, 147–48; ASV:Arsenale, reg. 139, May 17, 1621.

ties waged an endless war against arsenalotti thieves. Considering Venetian mercantile sensibilities, many thought that the shipyard's best line of defense lay in ever more efficient bookkeeping. Generations of administrators devised increasingly sophisticated invoicing systems to ensure that all Arsenal materials, down to the last nail and wood scrap, were accounted for. Ideally, such careful bookkeeping would trace the progress of goods throughout the shipyards, establishing the responsibility of whoever handled them from the first moment materials arrived or were produced, to their storage by the appropriate warehouse officers, until they were issued to foremen and gang bosses for final doling out to individual workers at the construction site.[23]

Yet while such bookkeeping safeguards were ever more effective on paper, they tended to founder in practice. This was due in part to the quantity of materials required—just one frigate could consume more than thirty-six hundred pounds of nails—but difficulties also arose from the virtual blizzard of chits (polizze) that had to be carefully filled out and preserved. Inevitably, many managers and bosses found little time or appetite for such paperwork and did their best to avoid it or pass it on to underlings. When the Patroni or Inquisitori actually tried to use the bookkeeping records to establish an officer's accountability for missing goods, they often discovered that many of the records had been lost by the accountants charged with keeping them.[24]

The unreliability of the Arsenal's record keeping system meant that the state depended to a great extent on actually catching thieves in the act. The shipyard's police captain and four gatekeepers (portoneri) were responsible for maintaining a line of defense at the Arsenal's main gates, where they were supposed to search carefully any worker suspected of stealing goods and to arrest anyone who was caught or who resisted inspection. In practice, this system too was of only limited use. The masters rarely left the yards in an orderly fashion, but instead charged through the gates at quitting time—a chaotic mob numbering in the thousands that pushed and shoved in a way that made any systematic search practically impossible. Using their overcoats or the ample pockets of their work aprons as cover,

23. Lane, Ships and Shipbuilders, pp. 154–60; Forsellini, "L'organizzazione economica," pp. 65–70.
24. ASV:Collegio V (Segreta), bu. 57, relazione of 1633, fol. 6r; ASV:Avogaria di Comun, penale, bu. 4/4, fols. 88r-v.

masters were especially adroit at making off with ship's hardware: anything from a handful of nails to the no less than 140 pounds of iron once said to have been smuggled out by "the best and cleverest of them all."[25]

One inevitable result of such weaknesses in the Arsenal's security system was that a good deal of the work of tracking down thieves had to be pursued beyond the shipyard walls, out in the arsenalotti community itself. Once stolen goods had left the shipyards, finding them was much more difficult, for not only were shipbuilding products such as timber, rope, rough and finished metals, or sailcloth easily resold, but they could also be quickly put to use by the many arsenalotti who ran their own private shops or shipyards in the district. Mixed in with the otherwise perfectly legitimate supplies of a local shipwright, blacksmith, or rag dealer, stolen goods were not easy to identify. As early as the fifteenth century, the Patroni tried to thwart those who dealt in contraband Arsenal products by marking the more valuable goods in a way to make them recognizable.[26] Finished metalwork turned out by the Arsenal's smiths—axes, cleats, and especially nails, which could sell for forty to eighty soldi for a "card" of one hundred—was to be stamped with a special mark (*bollo*) to identify it. Likewise, much of the rope and hawser line originating in the Arsenal's ropeworks (the *Tana*) was to have specially colored strands woven in to mark it as the production of the state. Different colors could further indicate if the length of rope was of a type restricted for the specific use of the fleet or if the Arsenal had produced it for legitimate sale to private merchant captains. Inevitably, not all finished metalwork or rope was so marked, either because of haste or laziness on the part of those who produced it. Nevertheless, the Patroni apparently took such lapses in stride. When suspect but unmarked materials turned up, it was still believed possible to distinguish them from private goods by their high quality and particular form; to do so the Patroni were always prepared to convoke a panel of expert witnesses from among the Arsenal foremen and bosses.[27]

For the job of actually going out into the local community and

25. ASV:Arsenale, reg. 137, March 23, 1601, reg. 141, May 6, 1664, reg. 142, March 22, 1687; ASV:Avogaria di Comun, *penale*, bu. 74/2, 141/8, 214/2; ASV:Collegio, *risposte di dentro*, filza 34, October 9, 1643.

26. Davis, *Shipbuilders*, pp. 121–23.

27. ASV:Avogaria di Comun, *penale*, bu. 4/4, 141/8, 243/16, 272/6, 333/10.

hunting down stolen Arsenal property, the Patroni could call on special state agents, including the *fanti* of the Arsenal itself and the *capitani* of the Council of Ten. These officers were empowered to carry out raids in any part of the crowded city, but since most Arsenal theft was committed by workers of the shipyards, they were most likely to descend on the houses and workshops of residents of the arsenalotti community. Those who fell under suspicion enjoyed few protective rights, for state agents took it for granted that without warning (and preferably at night) they could smash down the doors of any home or shop, impound and carry off any suspicious goods, and detain anyone found on the premises. Should the pursuit of their duties require it, they were also within the law to requisition the boat of any local resident.[28]

For tips on who was stealing or stockpiling Arsenal goods, state agents maintained their own networks of spies, active in this company town much as their counterparts flourished elsewhere in Venice. Some informers, the ubiquitous *sbirri*, worked for the authorities in a full-time, professional capacity forever on the lookout for anything suspicious. Others acted on impulse, and might betray their neighbors for reasons of personal spite or for the generous rewards that were promised, rewards that would be taken from the thief's personal belongings after his conviction. To encourage these occasional spies to come forth, the Patroni installed a special slot in the shipyard wall near the Chapel of the Madonna to receive denunciations—not unlike the more famous Lion's Mouth in the Ducal Palace. Those who informed against their neighbors were above all promised anonymity, an essential guarantee against possible reprisals by friends or relations of the accused.[29]

Judging by surviving criminal *processi*, the Arsenal's heavy reliance on informants and spies to denounce pilferers, thieves, and shirkers had a marked effect on the general atmosphere of local society.[30]

28. ASV:Avogaria di Comun, *penale*, bu. 141/8, 272/6, 333/10.

29. P. Skippon, *An Account of a Journey Made thro' Part of the Low-Countries, Germany, Italy, and France* as cited in A. Churchill and J. Churchill, *Voyages*, vol. 6, p. 509; ASV:Avogaria di Comun, *penale*, bu. 243/16.

30. How strong an effect may be judged by an anonymous plea in crude block letters found in ASV:Avogaria di Comun, *penale*, bu. 189/5:

> A lying accuser has falsely denounced me
> I was arrested and fired from my job

Having no idea who their accusers were, those arrested often tried to clear themselves by attacking the personal motives of everyone they could think of who might conceivably bear them a grudge. Some Arsenal inquiries degenerated into forums for airing neighborhood grievances, as lines of witnesses were called by the accused to describe long-standing rivalries and vendettas that may in fact have had nothing whatever to do with the original charges.[31] The general climate of suspicion fostered by the use of spies, along with a pervasive worker solidarity, made most arsenalotti extremely reluctant to volunteer any information to the authorities. Workers called in as witnesses often came up with the most extraordinarily vague and evasive replies, even when they themselves were apparently not at risk. They failed to remember the names of coworkers they had spoken to or events they had observed just the day before, excusing their inattention on the grounds of haste or even nearsightedness. One elderly witness seemed to think that everyone would be better off if they minded their own business, telling the Inquisitors, "being only a poor, old man, I have other things to do than worry about these matters."[32] Just as truculent was a young shipwright named Nico, who when summoned to testify against a neighbor, refused to admit having seen anything. "I am never in the street," he bluntly responded. "When I come out of the Arsenal, I stay at home working."[33]

Faced with such unhelpful and evasive witnesses, the Patroni were not above using local women and children for information in criminal matters, thus further involving the community in the shipyards' affairs. Young boys may have been fairly forthcoming with their testimony because until reaching the age of sixteen they were considered immune from prosecution. Some local women, on the other hand, appear to have talked freely simply because they enjoyed the attention they received as witnesses. Venetian females generally, and

---

Oh God, what a disgrace
I will defend myself and my innocence will come out
But I am ruined

Envy is great in the Arsenal
God bless all the innocent ones
And punish the guilty

31. ASV:Avogaria di Comun, *penale*, bu. 74/2; 214/2; 333/10., fols. 24r-31v.
32. ASV:Avogaria di Comun, *penale*, bu. 214/2, fols. 12v and 14v.
33. ASV:Sant'Uffizio, bu. 86, contra Camilla Padoana.

especially girls and unmarried women, were expected to remain indoors. Spending most of their time confined to their houses, arsenalotti wives and daughters were curious about the doings in their local street, looking frequently from their windows and balconies. In contrast to their male neighbors, many women appear to have been extremely sharp-eyed, noting any irregularities or strangers in their immediate vicinity and reporting on them quite willingly to the authorities.[34]

Combining as they did wide-ranging economic and judicial authority with unofficial but equally imposing social powers, the Patroni and their agents in the Arsenal might well seem to have enjoyed a complete dominance over the arsenalotti, both in the workplace and in the neighboring community. This picture, of a manufacturing complex holding in thrall its dependent company town, does indeed largely fit the way in which the absolutist regime of baroque Venice would have seen itself. But did the arsenalotti themselves experience their relationship with their state-employer in these same terms? Much evidence suggests quite the opposite: that the community of Venetian shipbuilders, having in many ways grown along with the Arsenal over the centuries, had developed individual and communal means of protection against the state's paternalistic meddling in their affairs. Arsenalotti clearly never imagined that they could or even should directly challenge the overwhelming power of the state. Throughout the entire seventeenth century, they never mounted any significant group protest, despite the steady decrease in the value of their wages and the ever more stringent control of their workplace. Coming to see themselves as part of the institution, rather than in opposition to it, shipbuilders generally seem to have been well aware that infiltration and subversion were more effective than confrontation against their absolutist masters.

The powers of Arsenal administrators over shipyard and local affairs were in fact undermined from several different directions, reflecting the difficulties that Old Regime magistrates could experience in trying actually to implement their theoretically extensive powers. Within the shipyards themselves the authority of the Patroni

34. ASV:Avogaria di Comun, *penale*, bu. 214/2, fols. 17–19; 333/10, fols. 31r-v; on women and neighborhood life in this community, see R. T. Rapp, *Industry and Economic Decline in Seventeenth-Century Venice* (Cambridge, Mass., 1976), pp. 78–81; Peter Burke, *The Historical Anthropology of Early Modern Italy* (New York, 1987), pp. 31–33, 45.

was initially weakened by the chain of command through which they were forced to operate. Coming and going in their thirty-two-month terms, the Patroni had no choice but to depend for much of their understanding of actual affairs in the shipyards on the eighty or so technical and supervisory officers of the Arsenal.

The management hierarchy placed an administrative screen between the Patroni and the workplace itself, a situation still further confused by the venal nature of many supervisory posts.[35] Sold to investors who never intended to carry out the duties personally, management offices were customarily rented out to substitutes. The rent that such an office might command varied, but it could easily exceed what the position itself paid, leaving its "tenant" to seek his profit from whatever extras the post might offer. For some supervisors or watchmen, this might consist of relatively innocuous actions, such as providing guide services to foreign visitors in exchange for a tip; others sought to profit by forcing workers to pay them a fee (*tarriffa*) in exchange for what should have been the normal services of their office. Tenants might also look for greater, if more risky profits—some accepted bribes to look the other way while thieves came and went from the shipyards; others actually organized their own criminal rings to make off with Arsenal goods.[36] Patroni wishing to keep firm control over the workforce could do little with such untrustworthy assistants. They could fire or prosecute a substitute for corruption, but they were unable to take an office away from its actual owner, who was perfectly free to rent it out to another tenant just as corrupt as the first.

Venality of office essentially institutionalized corruption in the Arsenal, a situation made still worse because most substitutes were recruited from among the arsenalotti themselves, the very workers such officers were charged with controlling. In reality the Patroni could not hope to accomplish much, either in the Arsenal or out in its company town, without working through the agency of their own employees. The job of maintaining the local infrastructure naturally fell to the shipbuilders. They were, after all, something of the handymen of the Republic, relied upon for building fortifications out in the Empire, plus everything from raising sunken ships to repairing drawbridges. It seems to have made perfect sense to the Sen-

35. See E. G. Spencer, "Between Capital and Labor: Supervisory Personnel in Ruhr Heavy Industry before 1914," *Journal of Social History* 9 (1975), 180–81.

36. ASV:Arsenale, reg. 137, November 6, 1607; ASV:Avogaria di Comun, *penale*, bu. 141/8; 333/10, fol. 3r.

ate and Patroni to turn to the arsenalotti for taking care of local public works, as well as for carrying out the Arsenal's inspection duties. Masters became so accustomed to exercising these responsibilities that by the seventeenth century it was generally understood that outsiders would not bid against them for the contracts. While the Arsenal's authority in such matters gave it the legal right to interfere in local worker affairs, in practice the inverse was actually the result: by taking over the daily implementation of these powers the arsenalotti who rented offices or won public works contracts ended up running much of their community on their own.[37]

The contrast between the official powers of the Patroni and their actual application of those powers becomes even clearer in the matter of local policing. The fanti of the Arsenal and the capitani of the Council of Ten were, indeed, outside appointments, but most of the regular guard work in and around the shipyards was firmly in the hands of the arsenalotti, who patrolled in squads under their own officers. The somewhat novel practice of workers policing both their workplace and their own community on behalf of their employer was born of the state's search for a more reliable force of watchmen combined with the intense localism of the arsenalotti. Until the 1560s the office of guarding the Arsenal from fire, theft, or espionage had been venal: forty or so posts for night watchmen were sold to investors, who then hired substitutes to carry out the actual duties. As elsewhere, farming out these offices provoked complaints, in particular that owners were renting their positions to "old and useless men . . . [persons who were] not even natives of this city." In 1562 the Patroni abolished the system and turned the task over to the shipbuilders, choosing eighty masters by lot every six months. Approximately fifty of these manned the watchtowers along the Arsenal walls, while the remainder were divided into two groups—one to watch the shipyards' main gate from their guardhouse on the opposite side of the Campo dell'Arsenale, the other to patrol the Campo della Tana around to the east. In times of war or potential disorder, the Senate could create a third squad to patrol by boat along the canals that encircled the shipyard walls.[38]

Arsenalotti patrols circulated freely, not only about the Arsenal

37. For more on the duties of the *arsenalotti* as city contractors, guards, handymen, and firefighters, see Davis, *Shipbuilders*, pp. 150–74.

38. ASV:Avogaria di Comun, *civile*, bu. 169/7; AVS:Senato Mar, filza 323, April 2, 1639; filza 572, February 1, 1669 m.v.

but also along any of the dozens of streets and small campi adjoining the shipyards. Their jurisdiction covered two of the four local parishes and a good part of a third, effectively making them the masters of the entire community. The Patroni justified this abdication of their authority on the grounds of charity and practicality: guard duties allowed shipbuilders a chance to increase their meager wages and simultaneously provided policing services at a good price. Whether the state really had much choice in the matter, however, is not altogether clear, for arsenalotti were quite unwilling to be policed by anyone other than themselves. On more than one occasion they violently resisted outside interference in their community, and when the capitano of the Ten and his boatloads of sbirri came to the district to make an arrest, the shipbuilders were quite ready to attack these state officers with knives, swords, muskets, and even small cannon.[39]

The Patroni may have felt compelled to accept this partnership with the arsenalotti as the price of civic tranquility, but other magistrates warned against the dangers of trusting the Arsenal to worker guardsmen whose amateur status made them difficult to control. The authorities produced a long litany of complaints against the shipbuilders: that they abandoned their posts or would not show up at all, that they fell asleep on duty, that they lit fires in their watchtowers to keep warm and cook meals. The Patroni and special Inquisitori were forever discovering suspicious holes in the Arsenal walls or finding watchtowers with unbarred windows, which offered easy opportunity for guards to pass stolen goods out to confederates waiting below in the dark in their silent boats. So little did the Arsenal administrators trust their own guards that they considered it necessary to have a special officer on hand to search the masters every morning as they went off duty.[40]

Controlling the considerable entrepreneurial spirits of arsenalotti was further complicated for the state by the webs of patronage networks and kin relationships in which even the meanest shipbuilders routinely moved and found protection. The social glue that kept the

---

39. ASV:Consiglio dei Dieci, *proclami*, bu 13, March 23, 1611; bu. 25, December 15, 1649; bu. 26, July 24 and September 5, 1651; *parti criminali*, reg. 55, February 22, 1638 m.v.

40. ASV:Avogaria di Comun, *civile*, bu. 169/7; ASV:Arsenale, reg. 137, February 19, 1613 m.v., January 23, 1614 m.v.

arsenalotti community together, such networks reflected the stability and continuity of the Arsenal's company town. But patronage and kin ties were also a form of power—perhaps the only kind of power readily available to those such as the Arsenal shipbuilders whose traditional protective guild and community structures had been subverted by the state in the name of efficiency and control. Kin solidarity was a particularly important counterweight to the absolutist pretensions of the state; among arsenalotti the sense of family obligation effectively undermined the managerial structures through which the Arsenal was theoretically run. Rather than consider themselves a caste apart, whose loyalties belonged solely to the Arsenal, officers of the shipyards actively promoted the fortunes of their relatives and did their best to cover up for kin that got into trouble. As a result, few rules or workplace regulations existed that some boss was not willing to bend in the name of family, whether it was a supervisor turning over his Arsenal house for a poor relation to occupy, or a boss blacksmith arranging for his wife to take over the job of running his department when he was busy elsewhere.[41]

The tendencies of managers to protect their own and close ranks against the police made investigations into Arsenal theft especially difficult. As one boss put it, keeping a pilfering relative out of the clutches of the Arsenal police was no more than an act of "charity."[42] On the other hand, when those in power in the shipyards hatched their own illegal schemes, naturally they turned to their kin as the safest confederates for defrauding the Arsenal. A paymaster was accused of using relatives as runners in a loan-sharking ring among the masters; a blacksmith had his wife and young apprentices hide hardware inside their clothes, on the evident assumption that the gatekeepers would not search women or children as they left. Kin also provided the best of all contacts with the outside world when loot had to be unloaded. So a gang boss found when he arranged for his apprentice sons to smuggle nails out of the Arsenal, then turned the loot over to his boatman brother-in-law to hawk from ship to ship in the harbor.[43]

The subversive force of kin networks around the Arsenal was all

41. ASV:Avogaria di Comun, *civile*, bu. 94/7, fol. 11r; *penale*, bu. 214/2, fol. 16r.

42. Sometimes even at the risk of losing their own jobs: ASV:Avogaria di Comun, *penale*, bu. 214/4, fols. 20r-22v.

43. ASV:Collegio V (Segreta), *relazione* of 1670, fol. 4r; ASV:Avogaria di Comun, *penale*, bu. 4/4 and 159/7.

the stronger for not being restricted simply to the worker population of the arsenalotti community. Kinship also linked workers with the patrician elite, thanks to the artificial family bonds formed by godparenting. The arsenalotti actively sought out Venetian nobles and *cittadini* to serve at their children's baptisms, and the ties between *compari* had the effect of bringing a shipbuilder into the vertical linkage chains that dominated the early-modern Venetian world of clientage and service. If a worker had the good fortune for his aristocratic *compare* to be chosen as Patron of the shipyards, he had indeed won the patronage lottery. Such a master could look forward to thirty-two months of profitable connections with the highest levels of Arsenal administration. One ordinary shipwright named Menego was said "to have earned more than 500 ducats and filled his house with a mountain of [walnut] chests" during his compare's stint as Patron.[44]

Patronage and the reciprocal sense of obligation that it engendered helped bridge the social gulfs that yawned in baroque Venice, and may have played an important role in the Republic's centuries of social tranquility. The fact that the Patroni were themselves often found at the apex of local networks and patronage chains only serves to underscore that Venetian patricians were very much at home in this social world, a world in which both noble magistrates and ordinary artisans were protected and made their way through favors given and received.[45] Upon taking over administration of the Arsenal, many a new Patron soon enrolled his own retinue of servants, *bravi*, and flunkies from among his worker compari or other arsenalotti—much in the same way that nobles in the city routinely enlisted personal retainers for protection and prestige. Such a practice made sense especially in the shipyards, where an entrenched management bureaucracy might otherwise prove uncooperative to the wishes of a newly arriving Patron. With a small army of robust shipbuilders at his disposal, any Patron could expect to impose his will on the shipyards, threatening and sometimes actually thrashing workers or even guild foremen who might think to oppose him. The powers of such networks, however, were easily open to other abuses. One Patron was not above using his retainers to smuggle women

44. ASV:Avogaria di Comun, *penale*, bu. 234/6, fol. 8r (2d filza); Davis, *Shipbuilders*, p. 71.

45. Lane, *Venice: A Maritime Republic*, pp. 427–31.

into the locked shipyards to help him pass his nights on guard duty; others found that with the assistance of such worker-confederates they could easily make off with whole boatloads of valuable and bulky materials such as walnut planks. Only with persistent efforts could outside Inquisitors hope to uncover such abuses: inside the Arsenal few workers or managers would denounce a Patron at the risk of a beating from his personal band of arsenalotti thugs.[46]

When combined with the corrupting effects of venality of office, clientage chains could effectively break down the state's most elaborate security systems and open the walled Arsenal to the infiltration of outsiders. None of the Senate's firm injunctions seem to have been totally effective in keeping nonshipbuilders from entering the shipyards; once inside they soon set about getting free drinks from the Arsenal's wine cellars or carrying out some profitable (and completely illegal) business of their own. Arsenal gatekeepers were consistently sloppy about checking those coming in, willing to look the other way either for personal friendship or a bribe. Many outsiders managed to get in with the excuse of being related to someone working inside; others entered on the heels of arsenalotti friends or "persons of quality" who would vouch for them.[47]

The Patroni were particularly concerned about those who smuggled food and drink into the shipyards to sell to the masters on the job, perhaps annoyed by the threat such hawkers posed to their own food monopoly in the Arsenal. Some of those who smuggled food and drink into the Arsenal were bakers or sausage dealers with their own shops in the community; others were evidently relatives of masters or even shipbuilders themselves. Together they appear to have been sufficiently well organized actually to set up whole rows of stalls (*banchetti*), causing the Patroni to lament that they made the Arsenal look "as if it were a lunch counter (*furatola*) . . . with little respect for that which should be honored."[48] Despite orders for the Captain of the Arsenal to break up the stalls, confiscate all food and wine, and arrest these transgressors, he rarely seems to have done so, either because he was too well bribed or too intimidated to make the effort. For those with something to sell, the Arsenal was clearly an attractive

46. ASV:Avogaria di Comun, *civile*, bu. 210/6; *penale*, bu. 234/6, fols. 4v and 8v (1st filza).

47. ASV:Arsenale, reg. 137, April 24, 1609; reg. 140, June 15, 1649.

48. ASV:Arsenale, reg. 136, August 12, 1562, August 11, 1572; reg. 140, May 15, 1645; ASV:Senato Mar, reg. 111, January 21, 1650 m.v.; ASV:Avogaria di Comun, *civile*, bu. 210/6, fols. 26r, 39r.

marketplace, and its protective walls must not have been particularly daunting. The Patroni once exclaimed with some bitterness: "This morning in the Arsenal we have seen with our own eyes many men and women that were not of the workforce, who should not have entered [the shipyards] without permission of the Patron of the Guard; of these we only managed to put four in prison, many of the rest having run off and hidden themselves in the Arsenal."[49]

Such complaints make it clear that part of the Patroni's difficulty in keeping the Arsenal inviolate lay in its very size: so much space was encompassed by its walls that the state sometimes risked losing control of it altogether. Those caught at the gate while smuggling out Arsenal goods could run back into the shipyards and conceal themselves within the vast expanse of warehouses and vaults. Faced with so many hiding places, the authorities showed scant willingness to hunt out such fugitives.[50] The problem was complicated by the little sheds (*camerelle*) that foremen and gang bosses were forever building between the vaults of the shipyards. Supposedly built for storing personal equipment and plans, these sheds also provided excellent hideouts for managers' relatives or clients who might have sudden need of concealment. Some of them even had mattresses inside. As with food sellers in the Arsenal, the camerelle seemed to the Senate an intolerable privatization of what was intended to be state-owned, factory space, the more so since the keys to the sheds remained firmly in the hands of their builders. The authorities waged a two-century long, largely unsuccessful campaign to destroy these camerelle, along with the similar open-air shed/kitchens (*fogoni*) that were magnets for masters who wished to cook food or keep warm rather than work. Repeated attempts to have the structures knocked down were frustrated, and not only by the sloth of disciplinary officers responsible for the job. When it came to holding on to their own private space within the shipyards, the owners of camerelle were themselves quite capable of appealing for help higher up the Arsenal's patronage chain.[51]

So completely did residents of the arsenalotti community manage to penetrate the Arsenal in their midst that some even took the logical next step of taking up residence there full time. Outlaws in particular favored the walled shipyards as a hiding place: a 1640 investi-

49. ASV:Arsenale, reg. 137, June 9, 1608; reg. 571, fols. 29–32.
50. ASV:Avogaria di Comun, *penale*, bu. 214/2, fols. 2v-6v.
51. ASV:Arsenale, reg. 136, December 20, 1568; reg. 140, September 23, 1644; ASV:Avogaria di Comun, *civile*, bu. 210/6.

gation uncovered ten or more such *banditi* in the Arsenal. They were men who had been banished for crimes ranging from burglary to giving false testimony to murder (their most common offense), but who had sneaked back into Venice to hide out in the Arsenal. Some of them were arsenalotti and actually went to work in the daytime, apparently profiting from the collusion of their guild timekeepers to remain on the state's paybooks; others evidently remained un-molested because they enjoyed the protection of different authori-ties in the shipyards. Not the least of these might be the Patroni themselves, who could for reasons of their own see to it that such fortunate banditi were given food, blankets, and the keys of their own camerella. Some of these outlaws managed to stay in the ship-yards this way for two years or more, living off the Arsenal's wine and whatever food their wives managed to sneak in for them.[52]

The banditi who made the Arsenal their home were not a passing phenomenon; they turn up in reports of guards' captains in the shipyards throughout the seventeenth century. The persistence of these outlaws testifies to the high levels of tolerance, not to say indo-lence, that could endure in a preindustrial manufactory such as the Arsenal, despite the cloak of military security with which the state institution was tightly wrapped. Indeed, no one seems to have seri-ously tried to roust these outlaws from their lairs. Ordinary masters apparently sympathized with them; foremen and gang bosses were aware that they might well enjoy the protection of figures higher up in the Arsenal administration; and the guards' captains themselves were evidently too frightened to confront armed, desperate men in the dark shipyards—several were in fact attacked when they tried to do so, and once a nightguard was killed.[53]

On the whole, it would not seem that the Venetian Arsenal, de-spite the economic, judicial, and social powers it wielded, ever com-pletely dominated either shipbuilders on the worksite or local resi-dents in its surrounding company town. Instead, the state was often hard put just to keep at bay a plebeian invasion that continually sought to turn the Arsenal's fortified factory space to private ends. In their administration of the Arsenal the Patroni were forever find-ing that business had to be accomplished in and around the ship-

52. ASV:Avogaria di Comun, *penale*, bu. 80: "banditi in Arsenale."

53. ASV:Collegio, *risposte di dentro*, filza 40, February 3, 1649 m.v.; filza 51, Febru-ary 6, 1658 m.v.

yards less through any rationalized process of work rules or community regulations than through an appeal to custom, to the private interests of a venal bureaucracy, and to the claims of family and clientage ties.

The dynamics of power in the Arsenal tended, then, more toward the establishment of balance—whether between employer and workers or between workplace and community—than wholesale domination by any one element in the social equation. This is hardly surprising, for having grown up together over the centuries, the Arsenal, its workforce, and its dependent company town were in a sense all different sides of the same imperial institution. Apparently both those who ran the state shipyards and those who labored there recognized the workings and limitations of each others' power, tacitly agreeing to seek what profit they could and to avoid those challenges that might threaten the delicate equilibrium of the relationship.

Questions of power dynamics in such a workplace can assume implications for the larger power relationships between states. Quite possibly the strength of Venetian shipbuilders relative to their state-employer played a role in Venice's losing its innovative edge over competing foreign states in the fast-changing world of seventeenth-century shipbuilding. Such an equilibrium is less evident in other large, national shipyards of the early-modern era. The arsenals at Chatham, Marseille, and Livorno sprang up so quickly that their workforces never established for themselves the kinds of prerequisites and patronage chains that were enjoyed by the arsenalotti and that could interfere with the state's quest for technological innovation or its drive toward centralization.[54] But in baroque Venice, civic and social values had their own claims against the strictly diplomatic needs of the state. The Arsenal could certainly boast that particularly Venetian virtue, stability. An institution as much as a manufactory, the shipyards could be termed a genuine public patrimony, one that was shared—although at times somewhat grudgingly—by state and workers alike.

54. *Arsenali e città nell'Occidente europeo*, ed. E. Concina (Rome, 1987); P. W. Bamford, *Fighting Ships and Prisons: The Mediterranean Galleys of France in the Age of Louis XIV* (Minneapolis, 1973); A. Riege, "The Development of a Small Village to an Important Naval Town in England: Chatham, 1550–1697," paper given at the Istituto Internazionale di Storia Economica "Francesco Datini," XIX Settimana di Studi di Prato, 1987.

Jan Materné

10 Social Emancipation in
    European Printing Workshops
    before the Industrial Revolution

In many respects the world of books and printing before the factory is a world we have lost. It is not so much the book itself but the working experience behind it that really set apart the preindustrial era of printing.[1] Any understanding of the social, economic, and cultural components of early modern printing work must include the forces of technology and labor organization. This essay uses the rich business archives of the Plantinian printing house in Antwerp to define more precisely the position and characteristics of the labor force in that workshop and in European printing houses generally during the early modern period.[2] It suggests that the Officina Plantiniana, with its large volume of business, enjoyed remarkably regular productivity—regular productivity that was the handiwork of a stable labor force—despite the limitations imposed on compositors and pressmen by the hand-powered screw press. Accordingly, this essay offers a rather different image of craft labor from the autobiography of the glazier Ménétra or the archives of the Société Typographique de Neuchâtel.

Recent research on how workers in the book and printing indus-

1. Robert Darnton, "Arbeiders komen in opstand: De grote kattenslachting in de Rue Saint-Séverin," in *De grote kattenslachting & andere episoden uit de culturele geschiedenis van Frankrijk* (Amsterdam, 1986), p. 91.
2. Jan Denucé, *Inventaris op het Plantijnsch Archief* (Antwerp, 1926).

tries reacted to technological innovations addresses itself almost exclusively to the last 150 years.[3] But the outcome of technical changes in the earlier preindustrial world of printing, though less studied, is no less important.

Technology played an important role in preindustrial letterpress printing. The work of a printing house required complicated equipment for compositors as well as pressmen, to mention only the two main categories of craftsmen.[4] The former made use of type-cases, composing sticks, galleys, and chases. The presswork of the latter demanded even more equipment: the printing presses and their accessories; balls for inking and lye-troughs for washing the forms; basins for wetting the paper; the miscellany of furniture and other small items essential for a smooth flow of work.[5] In the sixteenth century printing technology, the printing press, the most sophisticated piece of equipment in the printing shop, had already reached an advanced level. Further developments in the seventeenth and eighteenth centuries were neither considerable nor mechanically important.

For more than three centuries the hand-powered screw press, built of wood for the most part, was the principal instrument of letterpress printing in Europe. The mechanism consisted of a fixed wooden frame containing two moving parts: the first assembly carried the type and the paper in a horizontal movement in and out of the press; the second, the impression assembly, pressed each paper down separately onto the regularly inked type. Although little is known about its real shape and construction in the late fifteenth and early sixteenth centuries, the wooden printing press was presumably built and used in ways that varied only slightly from country to

3. Madeleine Rebérioux, "Les ouvriers du livre devant l'innovation technologique: Esquisse d'une réflection," *Histoire, Economie et Société* 2 (1986), 223–31.

4. This essay does not include the work of bookshop-assistants, proofreaders, collators, type founders and cutters, (copper)plate printers, engravers, bookbinders, or ink- and papermakers. For an overview of the different jobs in the world of books in Antwerp and in general, see Jan Materné, "L'édition et l'imprimerie à Anvers vers 1550–1650," in *La ville en Flandre: Culture et société 1477–1787*, ed. Jan Van der Stock (Brussels, 1991), pp. 279–90; Hendrik D. L. Vervliet, "Concentration vs. Specialization in the Technical Printing Professions from the Fifteenth to the Nineteenth Centuries," paper presented at the Istituto Internazionale di Storia Economica "Francesco Datini," XXIII Settimana di Studi di Prato, 1991.

5. *'Vande druckerije': Dialoog over het boekdrukken, toegeschreven aan Christoffel Plantijn, in een anonieme bewerking uit het laatste decennium van de zestiende eeuw*, ed. Bert Van Selm (Leiden, 1983).

country and from century to century. A closer examination of old illustrations, contemporary descriptions, business records, and the printing presses still preserved, however, reveals many variations and uncertainties.[6] Two of these peculiarities deserve particular attention.

First, some unclear sixteenth-century woodcuts, used as printers' devices, suggest a difference between the wooden hand-presses with a wooden screw and those with a metal screw. Because of greater frictional losses, among other reasons, the wooden screw press could produce little more than half the power developed by the metal one from an equal pull on the bar of the impression assembly. However, wooden press screws were not necessarily made obsolete by metal ones; their use was determined by the state of metal technology in the place of origin.

The only real turning point in the hand press period seems to have been the construction of a new wooden printing press by the famous Dutch cartographer and printer Willem Janszoon Blaeu (1571–1638), whose press refinements were described and illustrated in greater detail by Joseph Moxon in his *Mechanick Exercices on the Whole Art of Printing* (London, 1683–84).[7] In this authoritative manual for craftsmen as well as laymen, Moxon was very enthusiastic about the "new fashion." "If possible," he wrote, "I would for Publick benefit introduce it."[8] The advantages of the Blaeu press, favored particularly in the Low Countries, apparently were of considerable importance.[9] However, the only real difference to emerge from Moxon's illustration and description was the construction of the so-called Blaeu-hose. The function of the hose was to produce a perfectly perpendicular movement of the platen by means of a flat-bottomed block in iron or copper that helped push down the paper onto the inked type. Oscillation or tilting of the platen would have adversely affected the printed page. The Blaeu-hose must, for that reason, have caused less friction and oscillation.

6. Frans A. Janssen, *Over houten drukpersen: Een studie van het bronnenmateriaal met het oog op de reconstructie van een houten drukpers te Amsterdam* (Amsterdam, 1977).

7. Frans A. Janssen, "Eine Notiz über die sogenannte Blaeu-Presse," *Gutenberg-Jahrbuch* (1977), 155–59.

8. Joseph Moxon, *Mechanick Exercices on the Whole Art of Printing (1683–1684)*, ed. Herbert Davis and Harry Carter, 2d ed. (London, 1962), p. 45.

9. Moxon, *Mechanick Exercices*, p. 45: "The new-fashion'd presses are used generally throughout all the Low-Countries." Some critical remarks, however, will be found in Janssen, *Over houten drukpersen*, pp. 35, 44.

The new hose, as well as other minor differences, clearly fails to explain the high esteem which the Blaeu presses enjoyed in English eyes. The case becomes even more complicated because of the rapid demise of the "new fashion" in England.[10] This raises forcefully the problems of availability of complex equipment and materials, transmission of technical information, and construction of machines in preindustrial times. Unlike the English experience with the very restrictive guild policy of the Stationers' Company,[11] in the Low Countries personal instruction and oral transmission of experience with the help of models were safeguarded by a relatively free and dense network of printers and constructors. According to Moxon, the general spread of the old-fashioned presses in England was due to the fact that "many Press-men have scarce reason enough to distinguish between an excellently improved Invention and a make-shift."[12]

Presses were most commonly built one at a time and it was important that subsequent craftsmen were able to observe and understand the unusual characteristics of their model, either as an actual press or in the form of drawings with comments. Not only eye-catching features but even smaller details concerning the material chosen and the proper dimensions, which influenced the final strength and accuracy of the presses, all had to be taken into account. Looking at the sheets coming off the presses, experts such as Moxon—who himself stayed for several years in Holland—were aware of the fact that apparently small differences in the quality of the construction could visibly affect the final product. Moreover, wooden printing presses had to be repaired or refurbished from time to time. Plantin clearly provided regular replacements and made special arrangements to ensure that equipment breakdowns did not interrupt production and idle journeymen.[13] The sixteenth-century accounts of the Plantinian workshop in Antwerp show that by the end of its working life

10. Lawrence C. Wroth, *The Colonial Printer*, 2d ed. (Portland, 1938), p. 73: a quotation from the Scottish printer Watson (1713), "Our presses are now generally of the old English Fashion, which they were not formerly."

11. Donald F. McKenzie, "The Economies of Print, 1550–1750: Scales of Production and Conditions of Constraint," paper presented at the Istituto Internazionale di Storia Economica "Francesco Datini," XXIII Settimana di Studi di Prato, 1991.

12. Moxon, *Mechanick Exercices*, p. 45.

13. Maurits Sabbe, "De Plantijnsche werkstede: Arbeidsregeling, tucht en maatschappelijke voorzorg in de oude Antwerpsche drukkerij," *Verslagen en mededeelingen van de Koninklijke Vlaamsche Academie voor Taal- en Letterkunde* (July 1935), 618.

there was often little left of the original press.[14] Thus, in the Low Countries there was a better chance of less obvious improvements being introduced in the process of repair and renewal. Differences of this kind might be the most intriguing in a period characterized by a so-called stability in terms of equipment and techniques.

Careful investigation of the accounts submitted by carpenters and smiths working for the Officina Plantiniana might help us to date more exactly the invention of the Blaeu press. For now it may be said that two of the printing presses preserved, probably the oldest in the world, give evidence that after the death of Christopher Plantin in 1589 the Moretuses adopted all kinds of small improvements.

Only by the end of the eighteenth century had the disadvantages, economic as well as typographic, of the wooden hand-press become obvious. The wooden printing press was relatively slow, weak, and very tiring to operate. The material and manner of its construction prevented the press from producing sufficient pressure in order to get the clear and sharp impressions that were required. Printing a form in its entirety exceeded the means of man and machine. As a result one-half of each form was printed at a time on the wooden hand-press, after which the remaining half was done. Attempts to meet more sophisticated requirements resulted in the construction of iron hand-presses in England, Germany, and the United States in the beginning of the nineteenth century.[15] The iron presses, such as the Stanhope and Columbia, were superior in almost every respect: they printed larger sheets better with less effort. The first true cylinder machine, a sort of press in which print was no longer achieved by means of a flat surface being pressed on to the printing form but by a cylinder rolling across the form, was built in 1812 and based on the ideas of Friedrich Koenig. It brought about a radical change in printing methods by tripling the speed of production compared to the wooden press, from 200–250 sides per hour to 700 sides per hour. In 1816 the new presses could already print both sides of the sheet one after the other, thus achieving an output per hour of 900–

14. Léon Voet, *The Golden Compasses: A History and Evaluation of the Printing and Publishing Activities of the Officina Plantiniana at Antwerp*, vol. 2 (Amsterdam, 1972), pp. 136–39.

15. Frans A. Janssen, "A Note on the Dingler Handpresses," *Quaerendo* 6 (1976), 154–65.

1100 sheets printed on both sides, or about nine times the output of the hand-press.[16]

The impressive production figures achieved by new printing technology and work organization in the early nineteenth century indicate even more clearly that early modern printers everywhere handled comparable tools and materials in similar ways. But did they also make the same sort of arrangements for fitting the individual processes of hand press printing into complete patterns of work? Given the present state of research, generally based on detailed analyses of old books, printers' manuals, business records, and all kinds of legal prescriptions and contracts, there is good reason to believe that the identical nature of the printers' equipment did not necessarily entail identical working arrangements. Although intermediate models of work organization might show up, a major distinction has been made between continuous production on the one hand and concurrent production on the other.[17] Did compositors and pressmen continuously work as a team on a single job or did they follow independent rhythms for the sake of a higher level of productivity?

Because of the huge differences in forms and size of printing work, from labels and bills to books both short and long, a real balance between composition and presswork could not have been kept easily in the workshop if books and minor jobbing had been printed continuously. If each printing job had been done in turn—the craftsmen not taking up a new work before the old one had been finished completely—either compositors or pressmen would regularly have been waiting for their colleagues to complete their respective stages in the process of production. No matter how detailed the daily timetables of setting, correcting, and printing in the workplace were—from about six o'clock in the morning until about eight o'clock in the evening[18]—the least technical fault or social problem

16. James Moran, *Printing Presses: History and Development from the Fifteenth Century to Modern Times* (London, 1973); Hans J. Wolf, *Geschichte der Druckpressen* (Frankfurt, 1974).

17. Donald F. McKenzie, "Printers of the Mind: Some Notes on Bibliographical Theories and Printing-House Practices," *Studies in Bibliography* 22 (1969), 1–75.

18. Jean-François Gilmont, "Printers by the Rules," *The Library*, 6th ser., 2 (1980), 129–55; Lotte Hellinga and Wytze Hellinga, "Regulations Relating to the Planning and Organization of Work by the Master Printer in the Ordinances of Christopher

could have caused delay. Printers, therefore, preferred the method of concurrent production, whereby several jobs were worked simultaneously, irrespective of the productive capacity of the printing shop. It follows that a book was not necessarily set by a particular compositor or printed at a particular press. Working this way an individual book took longer to print than it might have done by serial production, but in the concurrent system a whole series of books could be printed in less time altogether and the gaps filled up with ephemeral work. By utilizing plant and labor more intensively, all kinds of work could be printed at lower cost. The gains to masters and men, at least those involved in a piecework system, increased accordingly.

However, the universal application of concurrent printing from the sixteenth to the eighteenth century is not an established fact.[19] Documents from the Plantinian business archives raise the possibility that only from the last third of the sixteenth century was a single job no longer entrusted to several compositors at a time.[20] The timetables of the compositors disappeared, suggesting that a balance between composition and presswork at each press no longer had to be ensured.[21] Whereas in the beginning all attention was paid to implementing better timetables to suit continuous production and whereas a system was established among workers involving compensations for accidental losses, after some time it must have become clear that establishing a less rigid relationship between the printing tasks opened new possibilities. It nevertheless remains an open question as to whether prevailing printing practices could be abandoned at a stroke in a period that was often characterized by the forces of tradition.

In this context we should not forget that the new printing industry in the Low Countries was not really subjected to the very restrictive guild policies that prevailed in other crafts. On the contrary, the printing workshop was very much a world of its own with its own rules.[22] Christopher Plantin was able to adopt an organizational

---

Plantin," *The Library*, 5th ser., 29 (1974), 52–60; Sabbe, "De Plantijnsche werkstede," pp. 619–20, 660.

19. Gilmont, "Printers by the Rules," p. 130.
20. Voet, *Golden Compasses*, vol. 2, pp. 303, 312–13.
21. Gilmont, "Printers by the Rules," p. 154.
22. Jan Craeybeckx, "De handarbeiders: De 17de en de 18de eeuw," in *Flandria*

model that derived from his greater concern for efficiency. According to printing regulations in France, Switzerland, and Germany, the distrust among journeymen of the novel concurrent production system apparently had much to do with the fear of being left suddenly without work.[23] The reputation of the master printer for maintaining a regular and abundant supply of work, therefore, seems to have been of greater importance. No doubt Plantin earned the confidence of the workers in this regard, which enabled him to introduce more flexible working models.

The shifting patterns of concurrent production resulted in a complex work organization even in the smaller workplaces. Production patterns in larger shops with more than two presses and several craftsmen at work, though essentially alike, were even more complicated. The fluctuating productive capacity of printing shops, which depended on the size of the plant, the number of craftsmen, and the amount of work, made it all look even more so. Concurrent production thrived on multiple orders, but if the flow of orders suddenly changed, the printer would try to alter the number of craftsmen and the terms of their piecework contracts. Indeed, fixed-capital investment was limited, since the cost of presses amounted to no more than 15 percent of total investment. The price of a printing press varied from 33 to 50 percent of the annual earnings of one journeyman and equalled about 10 percent of the price of a type stock able to keep the press occupied regularly. It follows that more than 50 percent of the printer's investment in plant was spent on type. In fact, it was the extent of the type stock that limited production.[24]

The Plantinian workshop, owning a type stock that was noticeably larger than that of its contemporaries, was among the first European printing houses to make a conscious break from the constraints of continuous production.[25] Beyond considerations of quantity, the quality of type depended not only on the type founders and cutters

Nostra: Ons land en ons volk zijn standen en beroepen door de tijden heen, vol. 1, ed. J. L. Broeckx et al. (Antwerp, 1957), pp. 281–328; Robert Darnton, "Work and Culture in an Eighteenth-Century Printing Shop," *Quarterly Journal of the Library of Congress* 39 (1982), 34–47.

23. Gilmont, "Printers by the Rules," p. 142; Jacques Rychner, "Running a Printing House in Eighteenth-Century Switzerland: The Workshop of the Société Typographique de Neuchâtel," *The Library*, 6th ser., 1 (1979), 16.

24. Philip Gaskell, *A New Introduction to Bibliography*, 2d repr. (Oxford, 1979), pp. 38, 163.

25. Voet, *Golden Compasses*, vol. 2, pp. 51–126.

but also on the compositors: they were asked explicitly not to leave it lying around in order to avoid losses and damage.[26] Forced to work within his stock of type, the printer could vary his output by altering the amount of piecework offered to his craftsmen and by varying his labor force. Jobs may have been shared occasionally between several shops in order to suit the productive capacities of the individual houses, to share work equitably among partners, or to speed completion of a job. Very rarely, a journeyman, unable to earn a full week's piecework in one workshop, could take a job elsewhere. This would have stimulated the spread of information about the internal affairs of the printing shop.[27]

The cost of equipping a small printing shop was not in itself enormous, but more than half as much again was needed to cover the wages and overhead, before the sale of books could bring in a return. Moreover, the cost of paper, normally bought in advance by the printer, could even exceed the cost of printing on it. Paper expenses amounted to 50 to 75 percent of the direct costs of book production. Wages counted for nearly all the rest.[28] For short press runs, the compositors' wages made up the larger part of labor costs. For larger runs, the pressmen's wages—always directly proportional to the number of copies printed—grew in significance. So long as printing presses were powered by hand, it was almost impossible regardless how large the run to reduce substantially the real unit cost of a single book.

Printing businesses were owned by the master printer, possibly in partnership with other printers and financial backers.[29] For the most part, the master, usually a well-trained printer, directed the whole business personally, taking its profits as his own. In larger printing shops the master employed an overseer as his deputy and several educated men as proofreaders. They were paid, respectively, a regu-

26. Sabbe, "De Plantijnsche werkstede," pp. 624–25, 639, 654; Christian Coppens, "Un règlement de l'imprimerie de Jean-Louis de Boubers en 1781," *Quaerendo* 19 (1989), 96–97.

27. Sabbe, "Plantijnsche werkstede," 627–28, 631, 640, 686; Coppens, "Un règlement de l'imprimerie," p. 99.

28. These costs could vary depending upon the number of illustrations. See Florence Edler, "Cost Accounting in the Sixteenth Century: The Books of Account of Christopher Plantin, Antwerp Printer and Publisher," *The Accounting Review* 12 (1937), 226–37; Voet, *Golden Compasses*, vol. 2, pp. 379–86.

29. Robert M. Kingdon, "Christopher Plantin and His Backers, 1575–1590: A Study in the Problems of Financing Business During War," in *Mélanges d'histoire économique et sociale en hommage au professeur Antony Babel*, ed. Anna-Maria Piuz and Jean-François Bergier (Geneva, 1963), pp. 303–16.

lar wage and time wages or piecework rates. Journeymen and apprentices—not to be confused with collators and bookshop assistants—made up the greater part of the labor force on which book production and minor jobbing were based. The total number of printing craftsmen per working press usually fluctuated between three and four, but it could be as few as two or as many as six depending upon the efficiency of organization, the type of work, and the edition quantity. In the later sixteenth century the Officina Plantiniana reduced the average number of craftsmen per press to well below four, demonstrating the efficient organization of that workshop.[30]

Each press was usually worked by a crew of two pressmen, who alternately did the actual printing by pulling the bar and made simultaneous preparations, that is, preparing and distributing the ink. In some cases, the pressman worked alone or together with helpers to speed up his work. The ratio of compositors to pressmen changed according to the extent to which production was concentrated on ordinary presswork. The rate of printing being reduced by more than half in the case of service books, a single compositor could feed a press operated by a printing crew.[31] In general, journeymen printers specialized as compositors or pressmen and most of them were paid for piecework. Compositor's piece-rates were very often calculated by sheet, form, and even by page or book; pressmen were paid for the number of sheets or tokens that they pulled.[32] Employed journeymen, though entitled to bind apprentices of their own, usually contracted work out to other journeymen instead.

In the Plantinian workshop the masters employed only one journeyman per press, called the *premier*, making him responsible for taking a second hand and paying him from his own double wage. Press teams continued to receive wages when one of the two partners was sick, meaning that some arrangements had to be made for replacements.[33] Along with ordinary piece-rates, some journeymen might deal with odd jobs at time rates or be contracted by the master for a fixed wage to set so many pages or pull so many sheets in a

30. Raymond De Roover, "The Business Organization of the Plantin Press in the Setting of Sixteenth-Century Antwerp," *Gedenkboek der Plantin-dagen 1555–1955* (Antwerp, 1956), pp. 230–46.

31. Voet, *Golden Compasses*, vol. 2, pp. 325–26, 333–36.

32. Gaskell, *New Introduction*, p. 173; Voet, *Golden Compasses*, vol. 2, pp. 325–26.

33. James C. Riley, "Sickness in an Early Modern Workplace," *Continuity and Change* 2 (1987), 384.

day. The latter system whereby the craftsmen contracted to produce so much in a day essentially came down to a form of piecework. The contracted wage fluctuated with the amount or the difficulty of work the journeymen would or could do. In contrast with setting wages, conditioned rather by the size or variety of type, printing wages depended upon the use of colors or the run, that is the number of copies of a particular work. Journeymen finally had some bonuses for urgent work and other perquisites, for example, a free copy of each book produced with their help, besides occasional gratuities from authors and visitors.[34]

Printing technology remained fairly stable and patterns of production varied along set lines in European printing workshops in the seventeenth and eighteenth centuries. So it follows that variations in productivity in shops of similar size depended upon the goodwill of the skilled craftsmen and the successful implementation of labor organization. If the workshop was well supplied by the master, it was not the printing presses, and therefore the pressmen, that dictated the rate of work, but rather the purely manual labor of the compositors that assembled the available type stock into lines, pages, and forms, corrected them after proofreading and distributed the text back in the appropriate compartments of the type-cases. With the forms ready on time, the quality and the pace of actual printing were subject not only to the accuracy and strength of the hand-powered presses, but especially to the ability and steadfastness of the pressmen themselves. The crews of pressmen had to work together efficiently at each press. If the printing personnel was to achieve the desired piece-rates, and the master his profits, there had to be a general interdependence and understanding. Social behavior therefore was as important as skill. Not only frictions between employer and employee, but also tensions and irregularities among the workers themselves had to be avoided for the sake of all parties.

The social structure regulating labor conditions and relations of masters, journeymen, and apprentices was the guild. In Germany this medieval institution and its mores were assumed by printing artisans and broadened by their new industry. Elsewhere, as in Venice (1542), London (1557), and Antwerp (1557), the guilds were federations of masters imposed on the industry by the authorities for the

34. Voet, *Golden Compasses*, vol. 2, pp. 309–28.

purpose of better government supervision of book production.[35] In Antwerp, for example, the Guild of St. Luke, which included printers and practitioners of other artistic professions, excluded journeymen. Having no say in the affairs of the guild, the journeymen organized their own association, or chapel. Their jurisdiction was the shop rather than the town, and their organization lacked any legal right of existence. The origins of these chapels are somewhat obscure, but the existence of a well-established *compagnie des imprimeurs* in the Plantinian workshop from its very beginning in the mid-sixteenth century clearly indicates that they had earlier roots and may have originated elsewhere.[36] As a rule the masters, including Plantin and the Moretuses, tolerated these chapels. Not that the masters approved of these autonomous institutions, but they grew more and more convinced of the social and economic advantages of an organization to which all free journeymen of a certain business necessarily belonged. By regulating good social behavior and mutual help among interdependent journeymen and by settling their disputes, the chapel contributed to the implementation of a labor organization that was essential to efficient work. Maladjusted journeymen were prevented, by sanctions if necessary, from causing their masters and colleagues to lose profits and earnings. By way of exacting fines and contributions for drinks and parties, the printers' chapel enforced social stability and had a stimulating effect on sociability within the walls of the workplace, particularly at the cost of quarrelsome and negligent journeymen.

The chapel might have encouraged persistence and stability among journeymen in an age when incentives for such behavior were rare. If a craftsman was able to make ends meet, he might well upset the complex course of production by bothering his fellows, interrupting his work, or simply staying away (for example, Saint Monday).[37]

There was little uniformity in the journeyman's rate of productivity as a result of different abilities and attitudes toward work. Despite the greater flexibility of concurrent production, which relaxed the relationship between composition and presswork, aberrant be-

35. Voet, *Golden Compasses*, vol. 2, pp. 357–75.

36. Léon Voet, "The Printers' Chapel in the Plantinian House," *The Library*, 5th ser., 16 (1961), 1–14.

37. See Douglas A. Reid, "The Decline of Saint Monday: 1766–1876," *Past and Present* 71 (1976), 76–102.

havior could go too far even in the eyes of the journeymen themselves. Work and socializing necessarily went together in preindustrial printing shops with their long working days, but preserving order lay in the hands of the community, not in those of individual workers. No doubt the master printers preferred the journeymen to apply the penalty system themselves in order to maintain discipline in the workshop. The sanctions and penalties of the chapel served to discipline work as well as foster sociability. For his part the master printer could concentrate on supplying work, marketing products, and improving printing standards. If some printing houses, like the Plantinian workshop, regularly produced work of a high technical standard, it was because the masters insisted on it, not because the journeymen really chose to do so. Nearly all pieceworkers in one way or another, the craftsmen worked no more conscientiously than the master or his overseer made them. The degree to which the chapel was used by the journeymen to combine against the master and his overseer could not outweigh the advantages of social peace, mutual help (for example, in the case of sickness), and a minimum standard of regularity within the workplace.

This is not to say that the workshop functioned as some kind of happy extended family; on the contrary, internal organization and discipline only occasionally succeeded in regulating its internal tensions. Masters and men shared common assumptions about how work had to be done in order to satisfy all parties. In the Plantinian office, the chapel, after having come into conflict with the master in the early 1570s, reemerged with more rights and privileges than ever before. At least from the beginning of the seventeenth century, it grew into a strong, self-governing institution of free pressmen and compositors, in which the master rarely interfered, except to pay his dues and, so, to encourage the system.[38] This kind of open solidarity in this large printing workshop not only gave rise to a more dynamic management and entrepreneurship, but also stimulated a visible, autonomous workers' culture, the harmony of both being substantial to a new equilibrium. Limited social emancipation within the walls of the workplace was therefore a key to social stability and economic progress.

An understanding of living and working in a printing shop must include an understanding of prefactory workers' consciousness in its

38. Sabbe, "De Plantijnsche werkstede," p. 608.

own terms. As an unusually literate group, printers offer direct contact with the artisan mentality and behavior. Historians such as Robert Darnton and Jacques Rychner have used a variety of evidence, such as wage accounts, workshop ordinances, letters, family papers, printer's manuals, and memoirs to shed more light on the basic character of work as it was experienced and understood by the journeymen themselves.[39] I would like to take account of complementary sources that originated from the heart of the printing workshop: the complaint, breach, sick-fund, and journeymen books (*clacht boeck, breuckenboec, journael vande rekeninghe der busse, vry-gesel boeck*) of the Plantinian working people.[40]

Thanks to the unique records kept by the Plantinian house in the seventeenth and eighteenth centuries, very detailed information is available about the internal structure and operation of the printers' chapel.[41] Except for apprentices and newly recruited journeymen who had worked in the office for less than one year and six weeks— the period after which they had to be declared free in an expensive baptismal ceremony—the chapel consisted of all compositors and pressmen of the workshop. Having been baptized in another workshop was not enough to retain one's status when entering the Plantinian printing shop. As free members of the chapel, the journeymen had nothing further to pay—except for some gratuities in the case of weddings, births, and deaths—and they could draw their portions from entry fees, bonuses, and fines in the form of cash, beer, and bread.

The chapel was ruled by a representative committee, called the law (*de wet*), elected every year and comprising roughly 33 percent of all journeymen. Its leading figures were the prince, or captain; seven aldermen; one or two treasurers; one secretary; and two proctors to keep order. The law had legislative, judicial, and police power. It prepared or amended the workshop regulations in cooperation with the master and judged all complaints or offenses, usually at regular quarterly meetings. It was the duty of the secretary to write these

39. Darnton, "Work and Culture," pp. 34–47; Jacques Rychner, "A l'ombre des Lumières: Coup d'oeil sur la main-d'oeuvre de quelques imprimeries du XVIIIe siècle," *Studies on Voltaire and the Eighteenth Century* 155 (1976), 1925–55.

40. Museum Plantin-Moretus Antwerp, Plantinian Archives (hereafter PA), nos. 264, 334, 340, 432–33, 666, 697, 772, 1168. Some scattered data are given in Sabbe, "De Plantijnsche werkstede," pp. 598–600; Léon Voet, "Arbeidsvoorwaarden en sociale voorzorg in de Plantijnse drukkerij (16de-17de eeuw)," *Fonds Informatief* 2 (1989), 8–9.

41. Sabbe, "De Plantijnsche werkstede," p. 595.

offenses down in the complaint books and to announce in the middle of the workshop the judgments and the punishments. The fines were deducted from the offenders' share of the general fund, if necessary even from his weekly wage. If the case of the plaintiff were rejected, in particular in an emergency meeting that could be asked for, then he would have to pay for the jug of beer and the cake the committee was entitled to consume each sitting. Complaints about internal affairs and problems had to be solved between the men themselves, without consulting outsiders. The journeymen did not want the master to get mixed up with their arrangements.

The law was a representative body. Apart from the captain, who retained power from his election to office until the end of his career in the workshop, all journeymen regularly changed positions at the yearly elections. In the years between 1671 and 1707 the majority of all journeymen held office at least once.[42] Newly recruited and free journeymen could hold an office rather easily. Positions were almost equally divided between compositors and pressmen, taking into account the greater number of the latter category. One of the two proctors and three out of seven aldermen were always compositors; only in the offices of secretary and treasurer did the pressmen count twice as many incumbents. Looking at the replacements of craftsmen in these two offices, however, it becomes clear that they were not favored positions.

The Plantinian workshop ceased to function as a large-scale enterprise in about 1765, after which it did little more than stagnate with a much reduced staff.[43] The absence of documentary evidence for these later years suggests that the economic decline probably meant the end of the chapel and the sick fund as well. The last complaint book preserved concerns particularly the period between the Wars of the Spanish and Austrian Succession of the early and mid-eighteenth century.[44] Complaints and offenses registered in the period 1741–69 cover only 4.6 percent of all cases. The extant accounts of the regular sick fund of the Plantinian office also came to an end in the late eighteenth century.[45] My research, therefore, concentrates on the interwar period.

42. PA, no. 1168.
43. Léon Voet, "Boeken en drukkers," in *Antwerpen in de XVIIIde eeuw: Instellingen, economie, cultuur* (Antwerp, 1952), pp. 314–47, esp. p. 324.
44. PA, no. 264.
45. Voet, *Golden Compasses*, vol. 2, p. 375; Riley, "Sickness," p. 363.

The Plantinian office was still an international printing house during the first half of the eighteenth century, and it is worth studying in detail the main characteristics of the labor force at work. In addition to the complaint, breach, and journeymen books, evidence is offered by the *Livres des Compagnons* and the *Semaines des Compagnons*, in which is noted how much work each man did during the preceding week and how much pay he received for it.[46] I present some straightforward statistical information on the kind of craftsmen that were engaged, on their careers, and on the intensity of work, all in order to provide a basis for better understanding the social behavior and relationships within the workshop.[47]

I have carefully reconstructed the careers of all pressmen and compositors who worked in the Officina Plantiniana from 1713 until 1740. In this interwar period of twenty-eight years, only seventy-six names appear in the wage books.[48] This is not to say that the Plantinian workshop had lost much of its grandeur by that time. On the contrary, the printing house usually employed five to ten compositors and operated between seven and twelve presses, each handled by a first pressman (premier) and a second (*compagnon*). The workshop usually consisted of about twenty-seven craftsmen involved in letterpress printing. It follows that an average journeyman in the Plantinian printing shop worked for a period of twenty-one and a half years. This is remarkable stability, especially when compared to the famous Swiss printing consortium, the Société Typographique de Neuchâtel. Whereas the personnel in this printing shop turned over every half year,[49] the work force of the Plantinian office turned over every ten years. A first pressman had an average career of twenty-seven years, a compositor eighteen years, and a second pressman fourteen years. In the Swiss shop, craftsmen were already called regulars if they stayed for more than one year.[50] The Plantinian journeymen almost all worked fifty and one-half weeks a year in the interwar period. The average compositor never worked less than thirty-eight weeks a year (1715), and the average pressman no fewer

46. PA, nos. 782, 793, 817.

47. McKenzie, "Printers of the Mind," pp. 1–75.

48. Three cases are not yet identified and some anomalies still have to be investigated.

49. Robert Darnton, *The Business of Enlightenment: A Publishing History of the "Encyclopédie" 1775–1800* (Cambridge, Mass., 1979), chap. 5.

50. Rychner, "Running a Printing House," p. 13.

than forty-nine weeks (1719). During the period in question, only 5 percent of the labor force—that is, first printers and compositors—stayed away or temporarily left the company for more than one year but less than two years. Even diseases and injuries only subtracted a small part of working time.[51]

Nor did the mean income of piecework per head of the work force fluctuate spectacularly in those years. Compositors, first pressmen, and their partners earned about six *guilders* weekly. Supposing that first pressmen divided their wages equally between themselves and their companions—as seems to have been the case in the first half of the eighteenth century[52]—the mean weekly income of a compositor was slightly higher than that of a pressman (6.4 guilders versus 6 guilders).[53] The lowest average wage of a pressman and compositor amounted to 5.1 (1729) and 5.5 (1724) guilders a week; the highest weekly averages came to 6.9 (1721) and 7.4 (1729) guilders. However, individual journeymen worked at their own pace and performed to their own capacities and liking. Average weekly earnings of individual craftsmen who worked in the Plantinian house during the interwar period show remarkable differences from worker to worker. Among compositors, about 66 percent had an average income between five and seven guilders a week; about 20 percent earned less than five guilders or more than eight guilders a week. Among first pressmen—receiving double wage for themselves and their partners—about 75 percent had an average weekly income during their career between 10 and 13 guilders—that is, between 5 and 6.5 guilders per head. Approximately 20 percent of the press teams earned fewer than ten guilders, and about 10 percent came to more than thirteen guilders weekly. Tracing the income of individual workers, the pattern again shows some variation in the weekly earnings and, therefore, output of the same worker.[54] In many cases, however, the average individual weekly wage remained fairly stable

51. Riley, "Sickness," p. 380.
52. G. Impens, "Lonen in de Plantijnse drukkerij (16e-18e eeuw)," in *Dokumenten voor de geschiedenis van prijzen en lonen in Vlaanderen en Brabant (XVe-XVIIIe eeuw)*, ed. Charles Verlinden et al., vol. 2 (Bruges, 1965), pp. 1057–1235.
53. When a compositor was absent, he was not paid. But if one of the two pressmen was absent, the other could have kept the press running, taking all the earnings. The income of an individual pressman, therefore, may have been higher than indicated here.
54. I assume here that the terms of piecework remained more or less the same; I did not take monetary factors into account.

over subsequent years, suggesting that the division of labor, according to the supply of work, depended particularly on personal abilities. Whatever might have been the reason for occasional absences, when a Plantinian journeyman was at work, he apparently achieved a stable personal level of production in absolute or in relative terms.[55] His average weekly income on a yearly basis did not fluctuate much. In fact, once at work, a journeyman could not afford to be very irregular. His colleagues depended upon him to work in conjunction with other hands. The pattern of work followed no daily routine, so there might have been some interruptions or ups and downs within one week.

Pretending that these skilled craftsmen, who made twice as much money as most common laborers, earned far less than they could have because they chose to do less work is rather misleading.[56] The main conclusion that I can draw from those preliminary statistics is that, though preindustrial work in European printing industries tended to be irregular in some sense, in the large Plantinian workshop it was surprisingly stable.[57] The patterns suggest industrial artisans rather than labor aristocrats. The masters of the Plantinian printing house, the Moretuses, may have become investors in trade and finance and not depended solely on the expansion of their printing and publishing business to make their fortune.[58]

Book production in the Plantinian workshop during the first half of the eighteenth century was fully concentrated on liturgical publications.[59] High-quality and well-illustrated missals, breviaries, and books of hours found their outlet on the important home market and were among the principal finished export articles. Although large consignments of Roman Catholic service books were sent all over Europe, the Plantinian house had vested interests in the very traditional Spanish book market. Until the 1760s the Spanish printers were not able to compete with the Plantinian workshop es-

55. This is an impression that I hope to demonstrate more exactly in the future.

56. Darnton, "Work and Culture," p. 42.

57. Interpreting the yearly differences in income is very difficult without knowing the evolution of the supply of work (e.g., the special demands from booksellers for delivering new editions as quickly as possible), the age and physical abilities of individual workers, etc.

58. Karel Degryse, "De Antwerpse fortuinen. Kapitaalaccumulatie, -investering en -rendement te Antwerpen in de 18de eeuw" (Ph.D. diss., State University of Ghent, 1985).

59. PA, nos. 782, 793, 817.

pecially for lack of sufficiently well-equipped type foundries and experienced printing houses.[60] On the other hand, the Société Typographique de Neuchâtel, near France and Germany, was engaged in cutthroat competition with other printing houses to get a greater share in the partly clandestine and very competitive market of more popular new books. This market was characterized by a coming and going of printing workers according to particular projects, as in the printing of the famous *Encyclopédie* of Diderot and D'Alembert. The only one to stay for a longer period was the overseer or foreman, who managed the international labor force.[61] The international composition of the printing personnel was also true of the Plantinian workshop, but in the latter, the printing craftsmen were employed on a long-term basis. In this context it becomes clear why the chapel, and not the foreman, grew in significance. Because the Plantinian workers were not hired just for one printing job, there was need of an institution that could ensure stable relations among workers and a minimum level of regularity over a longer period of time.

Printing was highly task-oriented, with minimal mobility between roles. Among the seventy-six workers of the Plantinian office, about 25 percent started and stayed working as compositors; about 20 percent worked constantly as companion-pressmen during their career; and about 10 percent did nothing else but operate the printing press as first pressmen. Thirty-three craftsmen, or about 40 percent of all seventy-six printing workers, combined two or three activities during their stay at the Plantinian shop: twenty-five became companion as well as first printer; only three craftsmen were companion and compositor; another five did all three jobs. Thus, the majority of workers never changed jobs, and if they did, they were pressmen and not compositors. There was no great mobility between pressmen and compositors: about 10 percent of the labor force in the Plantinian shop worked at the type-case as well as at the printing press. Only about 33 percent of all printing craftsmen ever did the work of a compositor; most of them were specialists in this job. And of those being pressman and compositor during their career, the time spent

60. Diane M. Thomas, *The Royal Company of Printers and Booksellers of Spain, 1763–1794* (New York, 1984).

61. Jacques Rychner, "Fonctions et tribulations d'un prote au XVIIIe siècle: Jacques-Barthélemy Spineux, 1738–1806," in *Aspects du livre neuchâtelois: Études réunies à l'occasion du 450e anniversaire de l'imprimerie neuchâteloise*, ed. Jacques Rychner and Michel Schlup (Neuchâtel, 1986), pp. 187–269.

effectively on composing work usually amounted to less than 20 percent or more than 80 percent respectively.

Of those who combined several jobs in the workshop, the greatest part—about 80 percent—started their career as compagnons-pressmen. Only one of them started his career as a compositor; six began as premiers-pressmen. It took a long time for those who started as companions to become first pressmen or—in a few cases—to become compositors. More than half of them had to wait between five and fifteen years. And after having become first pressmen, they could once again have been asked to work as companions. The average part of a career spent on leading presswork did not really depend upon starting in the workshop as a compagnon or premier. Among those who combined first pressmanship with companionship, the ones having started as first pressmen spent 70 percent of their time in that function; the others who started as companions spent 56 percent of their time as first pressmen. This greater mobility between premiers and their partners makes us believe that the premier had nothing more than the advantage of being the most responsible pressman. This hypothesis is confirmed not only by the fact that they alternately did the same kind of work or seem to have been paid equally, but also by the way newcomers were integrated into the workshop. In 1713 four running presses were added to the plant and seven new pressmen were employed. One old companion became a new premier; the three other premiers were newcomers. Two of them also had new partners. Only one new companion took the place of another old companion, who himself became the partner of a new premier. In 1722 the five new presses were staffed by three old companions and two newcomers as premiers; among the five companions of the new presses were four newcomers and one old companion. In 1732 three new running presses were added and staffed by two newcomers and one old companion as first printers; all of the three companions of these new presses were again newcomers. Thus, the old printing press teams were not easily changed because of the arrival of new craftsmen. Nor did the two members of a press team directly change positions between themselves. In most cases it was a compagnon who went from one premier to another. The compagnon, belonging to that group that never reached the position of premier, changed presses on average every seven years. Very rarely did a compagnon who had left his premier ever go back to him. Abraham Goossens worked under the leadership of seven different premiers within a period of eighteen years. Christian de Coninck was the companion of Zacharias de Coninck for a period of twenty-one years. No doubt family relations, friendship as well as antagonism, played a role in these stories of internal mobility within the workshop.

In the knowledge that pressmen depended heavily on a group of compositors with whom they generally did not change positions, it is very interesting to make use of the complaint books to analyze their internal relations. Among the craftsmen working exclusively at the type-case between 1713 and 1740, all were involved in at least one offense. The average compositor was as much an offender as he was a plaintiff, totally irrespective of the function of the person with whom he had difficulties. In 53 percent of the compositors' cases registered and identified, compositors and first pressmen were involved; in 33 percent of the disputes, compositors and companion-pressmen had problems with each other; only in 13 percent did compositors have troubles among themselves. Reading several hundreds of these little stories, it is not always clear what was the particular cause or the real background of a quarrel or of a formal charge.[62] In many cases journeymen complained of having been objects of ridicule, of having swallowed insults, or of having lost a fight.

The figures of conflict visibly reflect task-oriented tensions and problems that were closely related to the prevailing working organization in the shop. These findings are confirmed by the contemporary statements of Nicolas Contat, a Parisian compositor, who made mention in his memoirs of the existence of two estates within the printing houses of the French capital: the *casse* and the *presse*.[63]

---

62. My social database has not been finished.

63. *Nicolas Contat dit Le Brun, Anecdotes typographiques où l'on voit la description des coutumes, moeurs et usages singuliers des compagnons imprimeurs*, ed. Giles Barber (Oxford, 1980), part 2, chap. 2.

Leonard N. Rosenband

11 Hiring and Firing at the Montgolfier Paper Mill

In 1781 the veteran hands at the Montgolfier paper mill quit en masse. The Montgolfiers had recently engaged a flock of apprentices for their expanding shops and then prevented these young men from sharing in the journeymen's rituals. In protest the veterans moved on. The Montgolfiers responded with an elaborate set of hiring arrangements designed to banish the workers' rights and customs from their mill.

This essay examines the nature and purposes of hiring and firing practices at the Montgolfier mill, Vidalon-le-Haut, during the 1780s.[1] Labor discipline in early industry is generally portrayed as a vector of technological advance. The Montgolfiers, however, believed their new disciplinary regime rested on the authority of reason and science as well as the proper powers of the master within his craft and mill. And generations of turbulent relations between France's papermakers and paperworkers contributed much to the distinctive shape of the Montgolfiers' *nouvel ordre*. Accordingly, Vidalon-le-Haut becomes an intriguing locus for an important question: What did a novel approach to the recruitment and management of labor entail

1. Much of the material in this essay will appear in revised and expanded form in my book, *Managing to Rule: The Montgolfier Paper Mill, 1761–1805*. I thank the University of Illinois Press for permission to use the material here.

during the twilight of the Enlightenment? At Vidalon-le-Haut it centered on the Montgolfiers' efforts to replace proud men, opposed to
change and consumed by Rabelaisian appetites, with persistent, doc-
ile hands.

The principal limits to the Montgolfiers' plans were the high degree of skill and large number of skilled men required to produce
fine paper. Increasingly, historians recognize that the transition to
modern industrial capitalism was "a process that fostered a *variety* of
possible forms of industrial organization."[2] Seemingly contradictory
phrases, such as "factory artisan," reflect our sharpened, yet unset-
tled, perception of the complex process of early industrial development. Papermaking shared this category-defying quality. During the
eighteenth century it still consisted of a series of centuries-old artisanal procedures performed in a mill. Even at Vidalon-le-Haut, a
large enterprise, the appearance and quality of the product reflected
the skill of individual craftsmen. Consequently, the Montgolfiers
promised one customer that only workers with particularly steady
hands would fashion her paper.[3]

Yet papermaking by hand was also capital-intensive. Never a cottage industry, it took place in substantial shops with capital equipment, an extensive division of labor, and close supervision of work.
Many essential manufacturing processes, from glassmaking to soap-
boiling, shared these basic features. Nevertheless, current students
of early industrialization, preoccupied with the place of dispersed
production in the lineage of the mechanized factory, have given
scant attention to concentrated manufacture.[4] This neglect is especially surprising since the culture and organization of work is now
joining mechanical innovation at center stage in the study of industrialization. With its complex division of labor, the manufactory provides a splendid setting for the study of nascent attempts to manage
skilled labor. Equally, these skilled workers, whose numbers would
swell alongside the ranks of machine-tenders in the nineteenth century, deserve attention, for they endured the first efforts to obtain
regular attendance, application, and output.

2. Sean Wilentz, *Chants Democratic: New York City and the Rise of the American Working Class, 1788–1850* (New York, 1984), p. 12.

3. Archives Nationales (hereafter AN), 131 MI 53 AQ 25, January 20, 1780.

4. On the absence of attention to centralized rural production in the discussion of
protoindustrialization, see D. C. Coleman, "Proto-Industrialization: A Concept Too
Many," *Economic History Review*, 2d ser., 36 (1983), 443.

In the eighteenth century, declared Lalande in his *Art of Papermaking*, paper was "an everyday merchandise."[5] It was the handiwork of artisans who labored in mills at tasks that had changed little since European papermaking blossomed in thirteenth-century Italy. Essentially, papermaking consisted of three stages: the rotting and mechanical reduction of old linen into pulp; the creation of the sheet; and the preparation of the paper for ink and for shipment. At Vidalon-le-Haut veteran hands known as *les gouverneurs* (beatermen) supervised the labor of rows of women as they removed knots and caked dirt from old linen and then sorted the rags according to their qualities. The beatermen watched over the stamping mallets as they separated the linen, already weakened from a period of fermentation, into filaments. Lalande marveled that these old hands slept through the routine crash of the mallets, yet rose at the sound of storm-quickened blows in time to prevent the muddied water from soiling the pulp.[6]

The vatman transformed the pulp into a sheet of paper. First, he dipped his mold, a rectangular, wire mesh bounded by a wooden frame, into a vat of warm, watery pulp. Then he lifted the mold and shook it according to custom so that the fibers of the infant sheet "shut." Next he passed his mold, with the fresh sheet clinging to it, to the coucher.

The coucher's main tool was a stack of hairy felts, which he rested on a small easel. He needed steady hands and good timing, because he had to "flip" six or seven sheets of paper per minute from wire to felt. Once his pile of felts and paper reached a customary height, it was pressed heavily. The layman then separated the paper from the felts, a delicate task with great potential for damage. Lalande considered this job "suitable only for people who have practised it from an early age and not for uneducated, inexperienced country-folk."[7] The wives and daughters of the vat crew hung the paper on rows of horsehair cords in packs of three to eight sheets. (Even the most skillful women wrinkled and tore many sheets.) The sizerman gathered this paper and immersed it in an emulsion made of hides, hoofs, tripe, and alum. Generally reserved for writing paper, this

5. J.-J. Lefrançois de Lalande, *The Art of Papermaking*, trans. Richard Atkinson (Kilmurry, Ireland, 1976), p. 56. Lalande originally published his *Art de faire le papier* in 1761.

6. Ibid., p. 18.

7. Ibid., p. 41.

process filled the paper's pores, thereby preventing ink blots. Finally, female hands sorted the paper by size, weight, and appearance, removed blemishes, and assisted the loftsman in wrapping the reams.

Described this abruptly, papermaking by hand may appear uncomplicated, but in fact it was a precise art that demanded quick movements and sure hands, as well as a practiced eye to coordinate a production process that required weeks to turn discarded rags into paper. Indeed, the product itself was so easily marred that the journeymen shared a slang for their most frequent errors: Wrinkles were *pieds-de-chèvre* (goat's feet); awkwardly distributed pulp produced *andouilles* (sausages); and splashes of pulp left *châtaignes* (chestnuts).

For the journeymen, papermaking was a web of family and friends, skills and slang, festivities and memories, and long hours on the road and in the mills. As they moved from mill to mill, lasting no longer than a pile of fermented rags or the seasonal flow of a mountain stream, they jealously guarded the skills and customs that separated them from the rest of the floating poor. Considering themselves "of another essence, different from and more distinguished" than other craftsmen, French paperworkers let only their sons, nephews, and brothers enter the trade.[8] Across Europe the paperworkers' defense of the familiar had taken on proverbial trappings. It was said they allowed "nothing new to be introduced or anything traditional to be discontinued."[9]

The journeymen paperworkers of France fashioned festive customs to celebrate their passage through the routine experiences of their trade. Thus a tramping paperworker's knock at the mill gate became something special if he also requested his *rente*. Work came to a halt as wine was brought out to welcome the newcomer. This practice introduced the journeyman around the shop without the permission of the boss—and often despite his wishes. As the Montgolfiers knew, it sometimes set off drinking sprees that lasted for days. They therefore warned one of their foremen to make sure that

8. Quoted in C.-M. Briquet, "Associations et grèves des ouvriers papetiers en France aux XVIIe et XVIIIe siècles," *Revue internationale de sociologie* 5 (1897), 186.

9. Quoted in G. Schaefer and A. Latour, "The Paper Trade before the Invention of the Paper-Machine," *Ciba Review* 72 (1949), 2654.

none of their hands abandoned Vidalon-le-Haut for some horseplay, "especially by means of les rentes."[10]

The apprentice learned the paperworkers' raucous ways along with his trade. When he completed his formal apprenticeship with the Montgolfiers, the fledgling layman or coucher still had to pay his fellow journeymen for the right to join them at meals.[11] In fact, the paperworkers never missed a chance to bestow their approval and accord status. Inevitably this recognition had a price. A tramping journeyman treated his new mates when he found work; so did an old hand when he moved from the coucher's easel to the vatman's mold.[12] Unable to ban such customs, the mill owners and directors of Angoumois reached formal agreement with their workers to limit these levies.[13]

A hostile observer concluded that the paperworkers formed "a sort of little republican state in the midst of the monarchy."[14] Whether he was drawing a comparison with the solidarity or the aggressiveness of the ancient republics, this metaphor was apt, for it caught the assertive, cohesive, and independent turn of the paper-workers. Moreover, in times of trouble, the paperworkers could count on their association, which was national in scope but regional in effect. It made use of arson, fines, threats, walkouts, warnings, and circular letters to bring recalcitrant masters into line and, to con-vince wayward brothers, resorted to beatings as well. This association closed the circle formed by the workers' efforts to control access to the craft, maintain familiar skills, and preserve their joyful noise. The proper order of papermaking was inverted, wrote one contempo-rary: "The masters are like slaves of the journeymen and workers."[15]

Old Pierre Montgolfier, the patriarch of Vidalon-le-Haut, also railed at the disorder in his craft.[16] Formal and precise, he favored technological improvement and stiff-necked dealings with workers.

10. AN, 131 MI 53 AQ 23, document 17.

11. AN, 131 MI 53 AQ 23, document 5.

12. Henri Lacombe, "Les 'vins' des papetiers d'Angoumois," in Contribution à l'his-toire de la papeterie en France, vol. 2 (Grenoble, 1935), pp. 125–29.

13. Ibid., passim.

14. Quoted in Alexandre Nicolaï, Histoire des moulins à papier du Sud-Ouest de la France, 1300–1800, vol. 1 (Bordeaux, 1935), p. 64.

15. Quoted in Nicolaï, Histoire des moulins à papier, p. 60.

16. On the Montgolfier family, see Rosenband, Managing to Rule and Charles C. Gillispie, The Montgolfier Brothers and the Invention of Aviation, 1783–1784 (Princeton, NJ., 1983), pp. 7–15.

Under his direction Vidalon-le-Haut became one of France's largest paper mills, with a reputation for innovation and quality wares. As he aged, Pierre surrendered daily management of the mill to his rough-and-ready son Jean-Pierre, while reserving the making of general policy for his calculating son Etienne. They shared Pierre's enthusiasm for improvement in technique and rigid relations with workers. "Nothing is more revolting," Pierre fumed, "than the tyrannical power that the worker exercises with respect to his master, nothing more debauched and insolent than this wretched bunch of rascals."[17] He vented this anger thirty years before the invention of the papermaking machine.

Apparently yet another of his sons intended to do more than shout. A nineteenth-century source claimed that "an ingenious artist (Monsieur Montgolfier) [probably Joseph, the original mind behind the invention of the hot-air balloon] contrived three figures in wood to do the work of the [vat crew]; but, after persevering for six months, and incurring considerable expense, he was at length compelled to abandon his scheme."[18] Like the wooden workers depicted in the plates of the *Encyclopédie*, Monsieur Montgolfier's automatons, if they existed, represented an idealized—and lifeless—world of work.[19] To comprehend this vision of shops drained of the workers' ceremonies, disputes, and humor, we must turn our attention to the scientific thought of the eighteenth century.

Science as a method, not as a source of technique, matters here. According to William Sewell, the scientific thought of Diderot and his contemporaries was "profoundly analytical."[20] In practical terms the scientific scrutiny of a process of production began with its dissection. Once he had separated this process into its constituent parts, the philosopher (or entrepreneur) could measure and experiment and, then, expunge those elements based on artisanal intransigence

17. Quoted in Germain Martin, *Les papeteries d'Annonay (1634–1790)* (Besançon, 1897), p. 3.

18. Richard Herring, *Paper & Paper Making, Ancient and Modern*, 3d ed. (London, 1863), p. 53.

19. On the representation of work in the plates of the *Encyclopédie*, see W. H. Sewell, Jr., "Visions of Labor: Illustrations of the Mechanical Arts before, in, and after Diderot's *Encyclopédie*," in *Work in France: Representations, Meaning, Organization, and Practice*, ed. Steven Kaplan and Cynthia Koepp (Ithaca, N.Y., 1986), pp. 268–79. Also note the comments of Robert Darnton, *The Business of Enlightenment: A Publishing History of the "Encyclopédie," 1775–1800* (Cambridge, Mass., 1979), p. 242 n. 98.

20. Sewell, "Visions of Labor," pp. 276–77.

or the rule of thumb. Freed of these burdens, the manufacturer could produce a more rational technology and more orderly shops.

In 1780 the Montgolfiers won a government subsidy to remodel their shops along Dutch lines. The smooth grain and handsome blue surface of Dutch writing paper had captured a substantial share of the French market. The Dutch advantage lay primarily in a device known as the Hollander beater. Working like a mechanized mortar and pestle, this machine ground unfermented linen between a rotating drum armed with steel bars and a bedplate fitted with blades. Nicolas Desmarest, an informed French observer, reported that two of these devices did the work of more than eighty stamping hammers.[21] The Dutch technique also altered work around the vat, but failed to change the crew's basic tasks. Still, Vidalon's journeymen grumbled, especially as the Montgolfiers reached beyond their ranks to enlarge the mill's labor force. In the autumn of 1781 the journeymen walked out several times, consulted with workers from nearby mills, and finally abandoned Vidalon-le-Haut. But the threat posed by these journeymen and their association had not ended. They lingered in town and on a March night in 1782 evidently battered three of their replacements.

Vidalon-le-Haut was a mill village, housing a labor force in 1784 of about 120 men and women and 40 of their children.[22] Approximately 50 of these hands were male paperworkers. For the most part, these young men were the sons of day workers and vineyarddressers, trained in their new craft by the Montgolfiers. They were the raw clay of an experiment that cut across assumptions Old Regime employers in general held about their workers. When a mason in Renaissance Florence or, as Robert Darnton has argued, a compositor in eighteenth-century Neuchâtel signed on with a new master, he had "no notion of joining a firm."[23] He finished a particular building or book and then moved on or was fired. The petty producers who owned or leased most paper mills, masters of a production process subject to frequent disruption, were equally uninter-

21. Nicolas Desmarest, "Papier (art de fabriquer le)," in *Encyclopédie méthodique: Arts et métiers mécaniques*, vol. 5 (Paris, 1788), p. 495.
22. M.-H. Reynaud, *Les moulins à papier d'Annonay à l'ère pré-industrielle, les Montgolfier et Vidalon* (Annonay, 1981), pp. 137–38.
23. Darnton, *Business of Enlightenment*, p. 203. See, also, the discussion of labor turnover in Richard Goldthwaite, *The Building of Renaissance Florence: An Economic and Social History* (Baltimore, 1980), pp. 298–301.

ested in maintaining permanent workforces; neither did they believe that the workers, those feckless and contentious "gadabouts," would remain. But the Montgolfiers' passion for scientifically precise, technologically innovative shops led them to dream of a new sort of worker. In a mill ruled by law rather than lore, they would train a stable company of men with a tractable personality.

The Montgolfiers treated hiring as the first step in their effort to produce this new kind of workforce. Obtaining an adequate supply of youths for apprenticeships never troubled them. (Indeed, Olwen Hufton maintained that the crowded Vivarais, in which Vidalon-le-Haut was located, was one of eighteenth-century France's "reservoirs of men").[24] When a candidate arrived at the mill, the Montgolfiers carefully evaluated his appearance, much as they examined a heap of rags. They found Antoine Voulouzan "of good size for his age [and] sufficiently well built." Vidalon's bosses looked for a solid constitution and ample energy, perhaps uncommon features among the poor of the Vivarais. They observed that one youth was "tall [and] vigorous" and a second "big enough and perky." Baugi, "small but well made," would do. A "rather handsome face" had surely enhanced his prospects, since the Montgolfiers read much from a young man's physiognomy. A youth with a "comely physiognomy" was doubtless promising, but what of poor Escomel, burdened with a "somewhat affected appearance"? Lucky André Force offered both a "pleasant face" and a "good body." And strong Jean Barjon, with his determined countenance, might be able to stand up to the journeymen of the paperworkers' association.[25]

Although the Montgolfiers discerned diligence and aptitude in a youth's face or build, they did not trust appearance alone. They also looked into each greenhorn's family background. Did the candidate come from a papermaking family? Jean Texier, who landed an apprenticeship, was the son of a stonecutter. His father's innocence of papermaking and the journeymen's ways no doubt boosted Texier's chances. Was the prospect's family intact? That is, could the Montgolfiers turn to the boy's family for aid in disciplining him? Géry's mother was dead, but his father, a day laborer, lived in a nearby village. Finally, was the aspirant an orphan? If so, did he have the

24. Olwen Hufton, *The Poor of Eighteenth-Century France, 1750–1789* (Oxford, 1974), p. 15.
25. AN, 131 MI 53 AQ 23, document 12; ibid.; AN, 131 MI 53 AQ 24, April 20, 1789; AN, 131 MI 53 AQ 23, document 12; ibid.; ibid.

blessing of someone trusted by Vidalon's masters? The word of one of the Montgolfiers' cousins secured a spot in the mill for the orphan Mayol.

While the Montgolfiers continued to replenish their workforce throughout the 1780s with home-grown apprentices, they also netted veterans from the stream of journeymen that flowed around their mill. The Montgolfiers dealt warily with these men. Even when an itinerant came to their mill from a manufacturer they knew intimately, the Montgolfiers asked for his *certificat de congé* (record of previous employment and conduct). In 1739 the French government prohibited master papermakers from hiring any tramping worker unless he could produce this document.[26] A decade later *lettres patentes* extended this ban to all craft communities.[27] These measures emerged from the lawmakers' belief that workers were inherently turbulent and that men on the move were particularly troublesome. As one official put it, the ease with which "seditious" paperworkers quit their bosses and found employment in other mills was "the abuse whose reform would contribute infinitely to suppress the other abuses."[28]

Certainly, paperworkers could still obtain work without written references, but the journeyman who had not taken proper leave of his former master soon learned that he had little chance of employment at Vidalon-le-Haut. Of the fifty-eight journeymen paperworkers and beatermen secured by the Montgolfiers from April 1784 through December 1789, at least forty-six (79.3 percent) carried a certificat de congé.[29] Perhaps these tramping workers simply outwitted the Montgolfiers, for one contemporary reported that paperworkers were "always bearers of several congés."[30] However, the Montgolfiers knew the rules of the game too. Ever alert to tainted or inflated references, they demanded that one-third of the journey-

26. The edict of 1739, the French government's most comprehensive effort to regulate hand papermaking, is reproduced in Lalande, *Art of Papermaking*. On written discharge, see article 48, pp. 72–73, and article 53, p. 73.

27. For an exhaustive discussion of the police of tramping in various trades, see S. L. Kaplan, "La lutte pour le contrôle du marché du travail à Paris au XVIIIe siècle," *Revue d'histoire moderne et contemporaine* 36 (1989), passim.

28. Quoted in Briquet, "Associations et grèves," p. 173.

29. This figure was compiled from AN, 131 MI 53 AQ 24, "Journal concernant les ouvriers et ouvrieres servants et valets commencé le 4 avril 1784." The last entry is dated January 22, 1790.

30. Quoted in Kaplan, "La lutte," p. 385.

men they hired from April 1784 through December 1789 endure a probationary period of two weeks or more.[31]

While papermakers commonly poached hands from each other, Jean-Pierre Montgolfier sacked a skilled man and his wife because they had duped the son of their former boss into granting their congés.[32] "You will find me anxious," he informed their rightful master, "to maintain proper conduct among workers and concord between manufacturers."[33] As Vidalon's bosses fashioned their new order, they savored opportunities to demonstrate their authority, as well as that of their fellow *fabricants.* The certificat de congé was a legal mandate to do so. When Augustin Valençon, a skilled apprentice, slipped away from Vidalon-le-Haut with a few livres in advances, he became a dangerous man. If Valençon agreed to repay the debt, the Montgolfiers would not trouble his stay with his new master, Thollet of Saint-Didier. But if Valençon reneged, Jean-Pierre Montgolfier reminded Thollet that "it is advantageous for you, for me, and for our *confrères* to make an example. Please fire [Valençon] for having come sans certificat without having satisfied his debt to his first master."[34] Such aggressive attention to proper leave-taking infuriated the journeymen of Dauphiné. They retaliated with a ten-livre levy on any man who had toiled for the Montgolfiers.[35]

Every journeyman and most apprentices received a number in the Montgolfiers' account books, a practice Vidalon's bosses had followed long before 1781. The Montgolfiers also issued a small record book to every journeyman and apprentice. His little log reminded each Vidalon hand every payday of the mill ordinances he had to obey if he wanted to remain on the Montgolfiers' payroll. On several occasions the Montgolfiers even expected newcomers to affirm this particular set of regulations, "les usages de la maison" (house rules). One journeyman "promised to observe" these ordinances in October 1786; four days later a second pledged "to abide by" them.[36]

Reflecting the Montgolfiers' determination to gain unfettered con-

31. This figure was compiled from AN, 131 MI 53 AQ 24.
32. Ibid., May 7, 1787.
33. AN, 131 MI 53 AQ 28, May 7, 1787.
34. Ibid., November 4, 1786.
35. H. Gazel, *Les anciens ouvriers papetiers d'Auvergne* (Clermont-Ferrand, 1910), p. 203 esp. n. 1.
36. AN, 131 MI 53 AQ 24, October 19, 23, 1786.

trol over Vidalon's shops, the house rules prohibited interference by journeymen in the affairs of their fellows, fines imposed by workers, and all of the journeymen's customs, especially the festive rentes. These regulations expressed the Montgolfiers' recipe for harmonious shops: do what the bosses want, when they want it, with the attitude they demand. Elsewhere, paperworkers claimed the right to choose their tasks.[37] But Joseph Buisson began his stint at Vidalon-le-Haut under the obligation to work at the job assigned to him and beside the men chosen by his new masters. (He was also never to drink in Vidalon's shops.) The carpenter Gagneres agreed to work from four in the morning until a quarter after seven in the evening. The paperworker Violet and his two sons found out that on Sundays and holidays they would retire "at eight o'clock at the latest."[38] Before the journeyman Tissier even received a day's pay, he learned that he would lose forty *sous* if he abandoned his work without permission. He also discovered that he must behave "with decency."[39] And Russet, who came to Vidalon-le-Haut from Savoy, where the journeymen exercised their powers and celebrated their customs with little or no limit, found out that his new masters expected him to be "submissive and obedient."[40]

When a worker left Vidalon-le-Haut, he was caught up in a new round of paperwork. To the Montgolfiers, dismissal and departure were the last moments in a disciplinary process that began even before they engaged a worker. They updated the worker's certificat de congé, drew up his account, assessed penalties for sick days and drinking bouts, appraised his attitudes and skills, and indicated if and under what circumstances he should be rehired.

In 1787 Louis Pichat lost his job when the Montgolfiers caught him making a fire with their wood. Cashiering Pichat ended his apprenticeship, so Vidalon's bosses subtracted sixteen livres from his outstanding wages. With that settled, the Montgolfiers noted that they would not block any manufacturer who chose to provide Pichat with work. Pichat might have considered himself fortunate; at least he was not blacklisted.

Blacklisting usually followed the sudden end of a turbulent career. The certificat de congé provided a vexed master with the means to

37. Kaplan, "La lutte," p. 368.
38. AN, 131 MI 53 AQ 24, June 22, 1784.
39. Ibid., October 30, 1785.
40. Ibid., January 16, 1786.

malign a journeyman's talents.[41] Or a master could thwart a skilled man's prospects by giving him papers marked "incorrigible drunkard," as a journeyman sacked by the Montgolfiers discovered.[42] And how helpful was François Millot's discharge? While affirming his skill around the vat, his certificat de congé warned that he was unable "to submit to the rules of the house" and had struck a fellow worker.[43]

Whether the finish was stormy or silent, workers and masters alike rarely offered the six weeks' notice mandated by the government. Both the Montgolfiers and their workers found a variety of reasons for these quick endings. After two days with the Montgolfiers, one woman quit to sell wine in town. Angered by the frailty he detected in Vidalon's apprentices, a journeyman stalked out of the mill in October 1786 with some pay and his credentials still in the Montgolfiers' hands. (One wonders if the debility he detected was backbones bent to the master's will.) For their part, the Montgolfiers "let Le Bon's wife out of the six weeks [notice] out of consideration for her, [a] good worker, [a] mild and quiet woman." At the same time, they released Duranton's wife from her obligation to give six weeks' notice "in order ᴛo be rid of her." She was neither clean nor orderly, spent her time taking care of her children, and produced little work.[44]

Of course the Montgolfiers also took advantage of the disciplinary potential of hasty leave-taking. Jeanne Brialon fled in 1785 without her discharge papers and without offering proper notice. If her new boss, a widow named Palhion, failed to return her, Etienne Montgolfier threatened to seek the stiff penalties he found in royal ordinances, a fine of one hundred livres against Brialon and a levy of three hundred livres against her mistress. (The edict of 1739 and later decrees targeted the journeymen's power, which the mill women did not share; nevertheless, the Montgolfiers and other papermakers expanded the codes to include their female hands.) He justified his resolve by pointing to "the sacrifices I made to establish order and the subordination of the workers in my mill."[45] Every master papermaker could profit from his daring. None would be allowed to stand in the way of his success: "Madame Palhion must

41. Kaplan, "La lutte," p. 376.
42. AN, 131 MI 53 AQ 24, August 21, 1785.
43. Ibid., October 4, 1787.
44. Ibid., August 16, 1786.
45. AN, 131 MI 53 AQ 27, August 18, 1785.

appreciate that I will not allow the [workers'] abuses to be rein-troduced [at Vidalon-le-Haut]."[46] He vowed to pursue Brialon, if she took flight again, until he lost her trail. He would then obtain a judg-ment preventing her from toiling in the "*pays* or the environs."[47]

Brialon soon returned to Vidalon-le-Haut. The Montgolfiers waived her obligation to remain for six weeks, granted her a certificat de congé, and sent her back to Madame Palhion. At the outset of this affair, Vidalon's bosses noted that "this case will serve as an example for the others."[48] At its close, the Montgolfiers explained that they hounded Brialon "to prove to the workers that they will be punished for improper conduct."[49] So would the Montgolfiers' fellow paper-makers.

Since the Montgolfiers expected many of their workers to come and go, they carefully readied their accounts for the return of famil-iar faces. Jelbi, a "well-behaved lad, not debauched, understanding reason but a bit fickle" should be rehired in an instant.[50] Millot was worth taking back after he had knocked around and "learned man-ners."[51] However, the Montgolfiers were not always this sure. About Fagot, they wrote: "young; one doesn't know what this one can be-come."[52]

What became of Fagot and the other men hired under the Mont-golfiers' new regime? First, it is important to note that Vidalon's bosses relied on disciplinary resources beyond pledges, probation, and a paper trail of their own and the government's making. The Montgolfiers favored long contracts, offered good wages and annual bonuses, and provided housing, meals, and holiday feasts. Whereas journeymen in other mills labored under customary workloads or until the pulp ran out, Vidalon's hands toiled within precisely timed workdays and relatively lengthy work-years.

It is possible to identify forty-three paperworkers and foremen at work at Vidalon-le-Haut in April 1784. Thirty-four of these men were trained by the Montgolfiers from 1780 through 1784. During the 1780s, 55.9 percent (nineteen of thirty-four) of these hands

46. Ibid.
47. Ibid.
48. Ibid., June 27, 1785.
49. Ibid., August 27, 1785.
50. AN, 131 MI 53 AQ 24, October 17, 1789.
51. Ibid., October 4, 1787.
52. Ibid., January 24, 1785.

spent five years or more at Vidalon-le-Haut.[53] At the end of the decade, ten of them still labored there. Such persistence was not unheard of during the close of the Old Regime and the Revolutionary era. Of eighty male hands who toiled at Oberkampf's calico printing works at Essonnes from 1760 to 1820, almost half lasted six years or more.[54] Nevertheless, the stability of the workers at Vidalon-le-Haut was unusual. More typical was the unpredictable glazier Ménétra, who switched bosses in Paris six times in less that two years, or the equally flighty paperworkers of Thiers who, said one official, "decamp on the first whim that comes to them."[55]

Such wanderlust also characterized the experienced paperworkers engaged by the Montgolfiers from April 1784 through December 1789. Only one in five of these veteran hands lasted more than a year at Vidalon-le-Haut.[56] To be sure, even this cadre of comparatively stable *compagnons papetiers* was remarkable. After all, the printing journeymen who toiled for as many months in one shop in Paris were known as *les anciens*.[57] Substantial labor turnover was the rule at Vidalon-le-Haut and in the skilled crafts of Old Regime France in general. In the midst of this instability, Vidalon's masters secured a stable core of home-grown paperworkers and even a few persistent journeymen.

Emotions often ran hot when workers quit Vidalon-le-Haut or were sacked. Yet the Montgolfiers found more mild-mannered men to applaud than contentious hands to condemn among both the journeymen and the apprentices who left the mill from April 1784 through December 1789.[58] In an industry of proud, ungovernable

53. This figure was compiled from AN, 131 MI 53 AQ 24. This figure depicts total, rather than consecutive, years of employment at Vidalon-le-Haut. Few of these lengthy careers at the mill were interrupted more than once or twice; and a trip home was more likely to prompt a break in service than a stint with another master.

54. Serge Chassagne, *Oberkampf: Un entrepreneur capitaliste au siècle des Lumières* (Paris, 1980), p. 245, table 15.

55. For Ménétra, see Daniel Roche, "Commentary: Jacques-Louis Ménétra: An Eighteenth-Century Way of Life," in J.-L. Ménétra, *Journal of My Life*, with an introduction and commentary by D. Roche, trans. Arthur Goldhammer (New York, 1986), p. 285. For the paperworkers of Thiers, see Pierre Léon, "Morcellement et émergence du monde ouvrier," in *Histoire économique et sociale de la France, 1660–1789*, vol. 2, ed. Fernand Braudel and Ernest Labrousse (Paris, 1970), p. 660.

56. This figure was compiled from AN, 131 MI 53 AQ 24.

57. Robert Darnton, *The Great Cat Massacre and Other Episodes in French Cultural History* (New York, 1984), p. 81.

58. This conclusion is based on data drawn from AN, 131 MI 53 AQ 24.

men, the Montgolfiers ruled a labor force that, taken as a whole, was more tractable. But Vidalon's masters, who envisioned their mill as a masterpiece of rational design, wanted more. They shared Josiah Wedgwood's dream of workers so disciplined, so mechanical that they responded to the bosses' will like a single pair of hands.[59] Instead, pranks and truculence persisted under their new regime, as did confrontations with workers in groups of three and four. Nevertheless, the workers' shouts after 1781 were random noise, not the challenge of a collective voice.

What did an innovative program of hiring and labor management entail during the twilight of the Enlightenment? The experience of the Montgolfiers and their workers suggests that this question cannot be explored by focusing on the bosses alone. Old Regime papermaking was fractured by two distinct visions of its proper order. The Montgolfiers linked a craftsman's sense of mastery and hierarchy with an Enlightened improver's desire for independence from all restraints, whether they involved the work process or the ideal recruit. For their part, the workers sought to maintain *their* independence by preserving familiar techniques, controlling access to the craft, and celebrating their festive customs. Accordingly, technological change itself did not give the Montgolfiers' new regime its distinctive character. Rather it was the conflict between two visions of the *bon ordre* of papermaking that set the Montgolfiers' nouvel ordre apart.

This conflict brings us to the question of proletarianization and its connection to the work process. Paperworkers were by definition proletarian, since they labored for wages in sheds and mills with rags and tools provided by their employers. Yet the coercion embedded in these arrangements was muted by the workers' powers, powers that emanated from their skills above all, but also from the synchronized nature of their work, their customs, their combination, and their collective actions. Thus proletarianization, as experienced by Vidalon's new workers, consisted of more than immersion in capitalist relations of production. It encompassed the loss of contested ground to the bosses, especially the workers' capacity to express and

59. Wedgwood's vision is from John Merriman, "Introduction," in *Consciousness and Class Experience in Nineteenth-Century Europe*, ed. John Merriman (New York, 1979), p. 5.

enforce their version of the proper order of the craft.[60] It is apparent in the Montgolfiers' boastful claim, "We have shaken off the yoke and trained new workers without refusing veteran *bons sujets* who wish to follow *la règle de la fabrique*."[61]

Still, it is important to consider how fragile all of this was, for Vidalon-le-Haut was not all of French papermaking, and the Montgolfiers worried in 1789, eight years after their old hands had left en masse, that a newcomer had "secretly" tried to renew the workers' old ways in their mill.[62] If Vidalon's bosses sought to fashion workers as wooden as Joseph Montgolfier's automatons, they were surely disappointed. Others chose a different route. Perhaps it is only fitting that the papermaking machine, patented in 1798 by a man "impatient with the irascibility and ill temper of the workers," was a mechanical mimic of the skilled men it displaced.[63]

Sidney Pollard once described the accommodations demanded of England's first generations of industrial workers as the "adaptation of the labour force."[64] At Vidalon-le-Haut this process began before the labor did. Across the Channel entrepreneurs were designing equally complex systems to school their new hands in the standards and procedures of mill work. The Montgolfiers' regime, as sophisticated as the disciplinary regimes of Boulton and Wedgwood, suggests that the genesis of modern labor management was not uniquely British.[65]

60. My thinking about proletarianization was influenced by Christopher H. Johnson, "Patterns of Proletarianization: Parisian Tailors and Lodève Woolens Workers," in *Consciousness and Class Experience*, ed. John Merriman; Richard Price, *Labour in British Society: An Interpretative History* (London, 1986); and, Charles Tilly, *The Contentious French: Four Centuries of Popular Struggle* (Cambridge, Mass., 1986).

61. AN, 131 MI 53 AQ 27, June 27, 1785.

62. AN, 131 MI 53 AQ 24, February 20, 1789.

63. Dard Hunter, *Papermaking: The History and Technique of an Ancient Craft*, rev. 2d ed. (New York, 1978), p. 343.

64. The quoted phrase is the title of chapter five, Sidney Pollard, *The Genesis of Modern Management: A Study of the Industrial Revolution in Great Britain* (Cambridge, Mass., 1965), p. 160.

65. This sentence is a play on Pollard's title cited in the preceding note.

NOTES ON CONTRIBUTORS

HAIM BURSTIN is Associate Professor of Modern History at the University of Siena, Italy. In addition to many articles on the French Revolution, he is the author of *Le faubourg Saint-Marcel à l'époque révolutionnaire: Structure économique et composition sociale* (1983) and *La politica alla prova: Appunti sulla Rivoluzione francese* (1989). He is currently completing work on political life in the Parisian Faubourg St-Marcel from 1789 to 1795.

CHRISTOPHER CLARK is Professor of American social history at the University of York, England. Among his several publications on aspects of work in early modern America is *The Roots of Rural Capitalism: Western Massachusetts, 1780–1860* (1990).

ROBERT C. DAVIS is Assistant Professor of History at Ohio State University. The author of *Shipbuilders of the Venetian Arsenal: Workers and Workplace in the Preindustrial City* (1991), he has recently completed a study of fist fights.

CHRISTOPHER H. JOHNSON is Professor of History at Wayne State University. As well as many articles on aspects of French social and economic history in the early modern and modern periods, he is the author of *Utopian Communism in France: Cabet and the Icarians, 1839–1851* (1974). He is currently completing a book on the rise and fall of industrial Languedoc.

SUSAN C. KARANT-NUNN is Professor of History at Portland State University. She is the author of numerous works on aspects of the history of the Reformation and of early modern Germany. These include *Luther's Pastors: The Reformation in the Ernestine Countryside* (1979) and *Zwickau in Transition, 1500–1547: The Reformation as an Agent of Change* (1987). She is currently completing a book on the social and cultural history of former silver-mining cities in the Saxon Erzgebirge.

JAN MATERNÉ is a research assistant at the National Foundation for Scientific Research of Belgium and a doctoral candidate at the Catholic University of Leuven. The author of several articles on economic history, he is currently completing a study of early modern work and business at the Plantin-Moretus printing house in Antwerp.

ROBERTA MORELLI is Professor of Economic History at the University of Rome, II. An expert on late medieval and early modern Italian economic and business history, she is the author of several articles and *La seta firentina nel Cinquecento* (1976). Her current research interest is technology and labor in the tobacco industry of the eighteenth and nineteenth centuries.

LEONARD N. ROSENBAND is Associate Professor of History at Utah State University. In addition to articles on papermaking and work in early modern France, he is completing a book, *Managing to Rule: The Montgolfier Paper Mill, 1761–1805* (University of Illinois Press, forthcoming), and beginning a new study of Nicolas Desmarest and capitalism at the close of the Old Regime.

THOMAS MAX SAFLEY is Assistant Professor of History at the University of Pennsylvania. He has written extensively on the legal, social, and economic history of the early modern family including *Let No Man Put Asunder: The Control of Marriage in the German Southwest, 1550–1600* (1984). At present he is working on various aspects of early modern economic history, including the orphanages of Augsburg; poverty, family, and charity in Augsburg; a political economy of early modern urban families; and regional industrial development in the Allgäu of southern Germany.

JAUME TORRAS is Professor of Economic History at the Pompeu Fabra University of Barcelona, Spain, where he studies the economic and political history of Spanish rural society in the early modern and modern periods. His works include *La guerra de los Agraviados* (1967) and *Liberalismo y rebeldía campesina: 1820–1823* (1976).

CHRISTINA VANJA is Head of the Archives of the Landeswohlfahrts-
verband Hessen Germany. In addition to articles on the history of
women and work, she has written *Besitz- und Sozialgeschichte des
Zisterzienserinnenklöster Caldern und Georgenberg und des Prämonstraten-
serinnenstiftes Hachborn in Hessen im späten Mittelalter* (1984) and *Das
Zisterzienserinnenkloster St. Georgenberg in Frankenberg an der Eder*
(1989). She is currently at work on aspects of women's charity work
in the late medieval and early modern periods.

INDEX

Library of Congress Cataloging-in-Publication Data

The Workplace before the factory : artisans and proletarians, 1500–1800 / edited by
  Thomas Max Safley, Leonard N. Rosenband.
    p. cm.
  "The proceedings of a colloquium held at the University of Pennsylvania on
October 11 and 12, 1990"—Pref.
  Includes bibliographical references and index.
  ISBN 0-8014-2847-5. — ISBN 0-8014-8092-2 (pbk.)
  1. Work—History—Congresses. 2. Work environment—History—
Congresses. 3. Artisans—History—Congresses. 4. Proletariat—History—
Congresses. 5. Industry—History—Congresses. I. Safley, Thomas
Max. II. Rosenband, Leonard N.
HD4847.W67 1993
306.3'6'09—dc20   93-1479